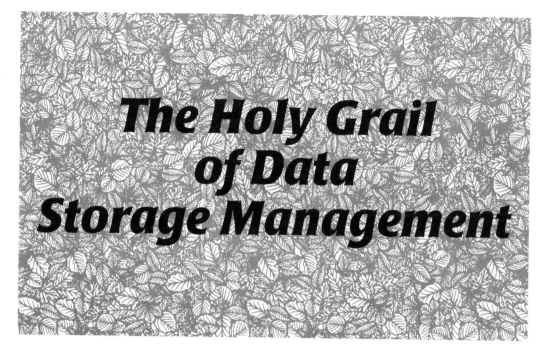

The Holy Grail of Data Storage Management

Jon William Toigo

with illustrations by
Margaret Romao Toigo

Prentice Hall PTR
Upper Saddle River, New Jersey 07458
http://www.phptr.com

ISBN 0-13-013055-9

90000

9 780130 130556

Library of Congress Cataloging-in-Publication Data

The Holy grail of data storage management/ by Jon William Toigo;
    with illustrations by Margaret Romao Toigo.
      p. cm.
    ISBN 0–13–013055–9
    1. Database management. 2. Computer storage devices. I. Toigo,
Jon William
    QA76.9.D3 H652 1999
    005.74--dc21   99–31710
                                          CIP

Acquisitions editor: *Tim Moore*
Cover designer: *Anthony Gemmellaro*
Cover design director: *Jerry Votta*
Manufacturing manager: *Alexis R. Heydt*
Marketing manager: *Bryan Gambrel*
Project coordinator: *Anne Trowbridge*
Compositor/Production services: *Pine Tree Composition, Inc.*

ISBN: 0–13–013055–9

Prentice-Hall International (UK) Limited, *London*
Prentice-Hall of Australia Pty. Limited, *Sydney*
Prentice-Hall Canada Inc., *Toronto*
Prentice-Hall Hispanoamericana, S.A., *Mexico*
Prentice-Hall of India Private Limited, *New Delhi*
Prentice-Hall of Japan, Inc., *Tokyo*
Prentice-Hall (Singapore) Pte. Ltd., *Singapore*
Editora Prentice-Hall do Brasil, Ltda., *Rio de Janeiro*

CONTENTS

Glossary   265

Index   313

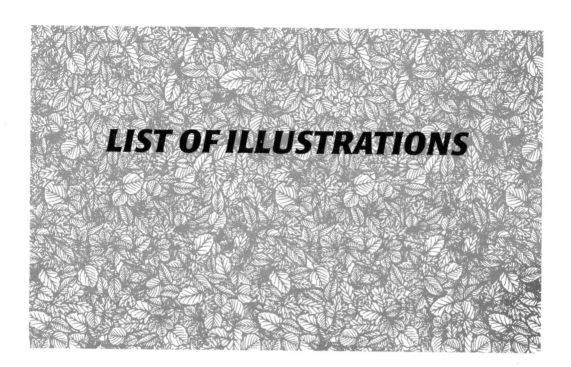

LIST OF ILLUSTRATIONS

LIST OF TABLES

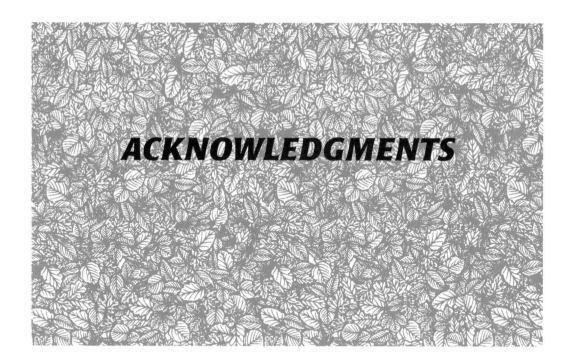

ACKNOWLEDGMENTS

A technology magazine editor once cautioned a young writer that his articles contained too many quotations from employees of technology product vendors. Concerned that such commentary would be so filled with marketing hyperbole that nothing of value would be contributed to the reader, he suggested that the writer steer clear of vendor interviews in the future.

The writer was aghast at the editor's directive. Like Willie Sutton, who robbed banks because that was where the money was, it seemed an obvious bit of *a priori* wisdom that technology companies, whose futures were determined by the technical excellence and innovation of their products, would provide a fount of technological expertise.

The view of the writer was confirmed over time. The publication for which the editor worked soon found itself without advertisers and closed its doors. The editor, a principled fellow, tried to ply his skills and point of view at other publications, which also failed. At last report, the editor had taken a position in an academic institution, where he found support for his purist view of vendor-free technology journalism.

His cautionary remarks, while not without merit, were short-sighted. To be sure, a technology writer must develop an "ear" to filter the "market speak" from kernels of valuable information contained in vendor interviews. Like political journalists, technology writers who have cultivated such a capability are able to determine the worth of an interview within the first few minutes of conducting one.

Graciously handled, the writer can usually parlay even the most marketing-oriented interview into a successful request for follow-up discussions with more technically oriented persons within the organization. Eventually, the tenacious writer develops a network of personal contacts within that layer of vendor personnel who actually know the objectives, the practical value, and the limitations of their particular hardware or software.

The content of this book has been greatly expanded and enriched through interviews with many of the industry's brightest minds. The author wishes to thank the many industry experts from companies such as Quantum, IBM, Gadzoox Networks, Brocade Communications, Hewlett-Packard, Seagate Software, Computer Associates, and many, many others, who have contributed their time and insights to help to make the work useful to the reader.

The author also acknowledges the patience, encouragement, and support of editor Tim Moore and the production editors at Prentice Hall. Without their firm-but-flexible management, this project might not have seen the printed page.

Margaret Romao Toigo, my wife and business partner, is owed an enormous debt for her many contributions to this project. A fellow technologist, she has been my sounding board and my personal organizer—skillfully managing interview schedules, aiding in the preparation of manuscript pages, helping to generate artwork, policing contracts and approvals, and controlling accounts receivable. In short, she enabled our business to stay on track while I was completely consumed in writing.

As if that wasn't enough, Margaret also maintained the health and sanity of our family while I was otherwise occupied. Life goes on while we attempt to document its passage: daughter Alexandra Etienne became a teenager, son Maximilian Christopher's voice began to change, Mercedes entered the terrible twos, and Vincent Xavier was born—all during this project! Margaret ensured that I did not miss the important events around me while I labored over this manuscript.

The author also wishes to acknowledge the support of other family members, whose intervention and participation helped to smooth the path for this effort. Heartfelt thanks to Lori and Tony Romao, who "borrowed" Mercedes from us at strategic times and who facilitated Margaret's adjustment to the requirements of mothering an infant and a toddler. Special thanks also to Denice and Garry Riley, for going above and beyond the responsibilities of god parenting, and to Bill and Esther Toigo, my parents, who contributed their support and encouragement without limits.

Finally, this book recognizes the folks behind the Public Broadcasting System's "Teletubbies" program, which occasionally allowed us a respite from the storm and provided relative quiet in which work could be accomplished. Thank you, Tinky Winky, Dipsy, Laa-Laa, and Po.

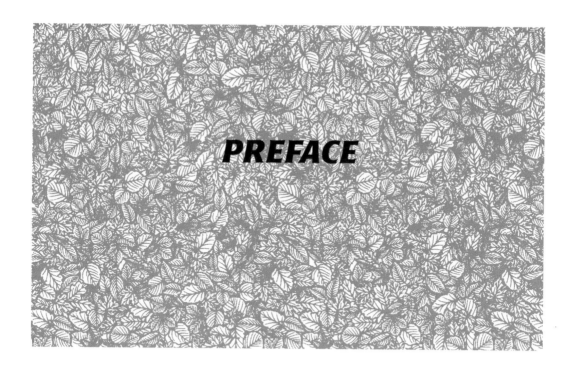

PREFACE

Data storage and its management are rapidly becoming key issues for modern corporate information technology. While the job title *storage manager* may be commonplace in the glass house of the traditional mainframe environment, such a title rarely exists in the realm of distributed computing. In the distributed world, responsibilities for managing storage have been largely distributed with the servers to which storage devices have been attached.

A system administrator, with or without software tools beyond those provided as part of the operating system, is typically responsible for managing server storage. He or she provides storage planning, grooming, and other management tasks as a subset of general system maintenance effort.

This arrangement may have proven adequate as long as distributed servers were not tasked with hosting mission-critical applications. However, with the evolution of client/server computing as a trusted platform for mission-critical work, the emergence of Storage Area Networks (SANs) and other nontraditional storage configurations, and the new storage-centric focus of enterprise IT, such casual handling of storage management responsibilities is increasingly less appropriate.

Case in point: A number of SAN product vendors have observed that product sales have been somewhat impeded by the job skills requirements inherent in SAN management. The job title most involved in SAN acquisition decisions is that of system administrator, rather than network manager. Understanding and managing SANs (as well as their cousin technologies such as Network Attached Storage [NAS] devices) requires a blending of skills from the network, system, and storage management disciplines. In the absence of personnel possessed of a such "hybrid" skills sets, most SAN sales have been driven by demonstrations of specific applications, such as faster backups, rather than by presentations of the design and capabilities of the technology itself.[1]

In short, the acquisition of newer storage technologies such as SANs is being delegated to nonnetwork savvy system administrators, many of whom do not even possess the knowledge, skills, or tools required to manage even traditional server–captive storage configurations effectively. It is the argument of this book that the situation reflects a potential disaster inherent in unmanaged storage within the corporate IT enterprise.

PURPOSE OF THIS BOOK

The purpose of this book is to provide a primer of sorts that will enable readers to begin cultivating the hybrid knowledge and skills they require to serve as storage managers within the modern IT enterprise. The scope of the book is large and its chapters address a broad range of subjects—from the particulars of storage devices themselves, to the fundamentals of interface and interconnect technologies, to the principles of effective management, to industry "best practices" in planning and analysis.

The book also endeavors to present the current "politics" behind storage technologies. Storage technologies do not develop in an apolitical vacuum, but in a competitive market where vendors vie constantly for a share of the customer base.

Generally speaking, vendor attitudes manifest more a *kammeralist* than a *merchantilist* bent. This means that vendors tend to perceive markets for their goods as fixed in size and dollar volume. Sales is a "zero sum game" in which my success is your loss. Only in cases of new technologies that create entirely new markets does the merchantilist worldview of expanding markets prevail.

Against this backdrop, the language of marketing, rather than technology, tends to obfuscate efforts to understand what products are appropriate for a given set of requirements. To the extent possible, this book endeavors to acquaint readers with the code words and buzz phrases of storage "market speak" in order to assist them in separating the kernels of practical information from the chaff of hyperbole and spin doctoring that often accompanies marketing communications.

It is expected that some material will be familiar to the reader, while other content will be new. This reflects the specific background and experience that the reader brings to the text.

Readers of this book are expected to have either a systems-specific or a networking-specific background: Enterprise storage management requires a mixture of skills from both disciplines.

This book is based on extensive research in the evolving area of enterprise storage technology and includes information taken from hundreds of hours of interviews with vendors and consumers of storage products. It is profusely illustrated with line drawings, product photos, charts, and graphs to aid in communicating complex concepts simply and to facilitate understanding.

ORGANIZATION OF THE BOOK

The book is divided into three main parts. Part One provides a context for thinking about storage management and introduces some of the central themes explored in greater detail in subsequent parts of the book. Also provided in this section are several "generic" distributed storage models. These models are intended for use by the reader as a starting point in conceptualizing, planning, integrating, and managing storage capabilities in a distributed environment.

Part Two provides a detailed discussion of storage technologies themselves. The perpetuation of magnetic disk–based storage is considered at length. Beginning with an evolutionary overview of the technology underlying the magnetic hard disk, the latest engineering advancements in hard disk media, controller, and interface technology are examined.

From the *micro-level* focus on hard disk technology, we shift to a *macro-level* view and consider disk storage subsystems. Array technologies based on open and proprietary RAID implementations are considered in detail.

By the late 1990s, these array architectures comprised the preponderance of "tethered" (server-attached) storage subsystems. According to analysts, these arrays will be detached from servers over the next decade and migrated to storage area networks (SANs). How this is being accomplished and what capabilities SAN switches and hubs add to the enterprise storage platform will be considered in detail.

This section also includes a detailed examination of another, evolving, disk-based, storage architecture: network-attached storage (NAS). The untethering of storage and its related I/O operations and wait states from the server supports an "appliance view" of storage in an distributed computing context. We will conclude our examination of magnetic disk–based storage by looking at the "thin–server storage appliance" concept, initial products, and the problems that this approach solves (and creates) for IT planners.

In addition to magnetic disk and disk-based arrays, enterprise storage also includes tape and optical storage technologies. Technologies for near-online storage—including tape and optical storage subsystems—continue to have valuable roles to play in enterprise storage platforms. Their traditional missions in disaster recovery and system backup will be evaluated, together with evolving roles in production applications.

Part Three of the book is entitled Storage Management Techniques. Far from being an exhaustive manual for managing the many varieties of storage that are likely to be deployed within the corporate IT enterprise, this section seeks to provide the reader with a framework for analyzing and assessing the relevance of management approaches.

The section begins with an overview of a "project" whose objective is the implementation of an effective storage management capability. While highly simplified, the project model set forth introduces the generic objectives and tasks that need to be considered as IT professionals endeavor to take control of storage and its management within the corporate enterprise.

Core to defining effective storage solutions is the cultivation of a "storage infrastructure perspective." Looking at storage requirements from such a perspective helps to define the application-specific data layout and data movement requirements that a storage solution must support. This concept is illustrated using examples that range from very large databases (VLDBs), which undergird most of today's mission-critical client/server applications, to large-scale data streaming applications, such as digital video and audio editing, which are the harbingers of the next wave of "killer multimedia applications."

Some traditional applications and data movements persist, including hierarchical storage management (HSM) and backup/restore, which are discussed in detail as the third section concludes. Traditional HSM was a technique for optimizing storage capacity by migrating less-used data from "hot," "online," disk-based media to "near-online" (automated tape library or optical library media) or "off-line" (removable or archival tape) storage. This approach failed to catch on in the distributed environment for a number of reasons, including the falling price of disk storage, the distribution of data and lack of network infrastructure to support large data movements over production networks, and the desire of companies to keep all data online all of the time, particularly for applications such as data warehousing. As with traditional backup/restore applications, HSM is currently experiencing a renaissance of interest within the corporate environment, especially as the effects of unmanaged storage, especially increased downtime, begin to be felt. This chapter looks at the impact of new technologies for remote mirroring and the use of SANs to recast these traditional applications for modern service.

The conclusion of this book has two parts. First, it examines the major, competing initiatives in the storage industry to realize a goal of a "storage nirvana" in which all storage is easily managed, scaled, and shared to meet application and end user requirements. Each of these contending approaches, and the many others that will likely follow, reflect a vendor-sponsor's preferences and product orientation. At present, vendors show little inclination to reach an accommodation that will deliver an "open" approach, appropriate to all companies.

Despite the failure of vendors to deliver a common storage infrastructure, this book concludes that the pace of advancement of storage technology continues to stay ahead of the "storage pain curve" for IT organizations. As the market has demanded more storage, faster storage, and greater storage capacity, vendors have been ready with products to meet the need. While this may be regarded as a good thing, it has also supported the cultivation of *a laissez-faire* attitude among IT professionals based largely on an unstated belief that the situation will continue indefinitely.

This view, however, is a fallacy. As the unplanned deployment of storage capabilities continues, IT organizations are creating an environment that is prone both to dramatic increases in total cost of ownership and to disastrous interruptions of mission-critical business applications.

Inevitably, companies will be forced to begin a quest for the "Holy Grail" of rational storage resource planning. It is better that proactive steps be taken today than expensive and reactive ones tomorrow. The first step is education.

A LIVING APPENDIX

Even as this book goes to press, changes are happening in storage-related technology. To keep readers apprised of these changes, a site has been created on the World Wide Web to serve as a "living appendix" to the book. Visit the site at http://www.stormgt.org to remain current with the latest trends, products, and thinking about storage technology and storage management.

A FINAL NOTE TO READERS

A book of this type is sure to draw criticisms as well as (hopefully) some applause. Advocates of competing technologies have a tendency to engage in "religious" wars over the merits of their preferred vision, approach, or protocol.

Some are more subtle than others. For example, in a recent interview with a Microsoft product manager, the author was advised that there are no problems of heterogeneous file system access if everyone simply abandons UNIX servers and moves to a completely Microsoft-standard server environment. The same sort of message has been received by representatives of Sun Microsystems, vendor of several popular UNIX platforms.

The author harbors no particular preference for one technology over another. It is the position of this book, based on hundreds of hours of interviews conducted with industry experts, end users, and analysts, that heterogeneous computing will continue to be a fact of life for at least as long as this book is likely to remain in print.

One bias that the author does embrace is a sort of *real politik* when it comes to enterprise IT. As in Hobbes' state of nature, life in an unmanaged IT environment is nasty, brutish, and short. Readers are asked to set to one side any idealistic views they may have of a perfect IT environment where self-directing and responsible end users, IT professionals, and vendors work together harmoniously to realize business goals. Real life suggests that management, while imperfect, is the best hedge we have against an unpredictable and chaotic future.

The Holy Grail, referenced in the title of this book, symbolizes a vision or quest that can never be fully actualized or concluded. This is not to say that IT professionals must engage in a pointless struggle to accomplish what can never be accomplished. Such an existential viewpoint would also make this book a pointless undertaking.

Rather, storage management, like so many other aspects of business technology management, seeks to anticipate what is within our ability to anticipate, so it can be controlled. Secondly, storage management seeks to minimize the harmful consequences of events that are beyond our ability to anticipate.

Given the pace of change in business and in technology, management must flexible and open to new opportunities. Effective management is constantly reinventing itself and redefining its objectives and strategies. It is in this context that the symbol of the Holy Grail is invoked. A well-managed enterprise storage platform is a worthwhile objective that requires constant attention and proactive effort on the part of skilled personnel. It is not, and can never be, a task that is completed once and for all.

ENDNOTES

1. Interview with Bill Lozoff, Director of Marketing, Gadzoox Networks, Inc., San Jose, CA. 1998.

PART

1

THEORY OF STORAGE MANAGEMENT

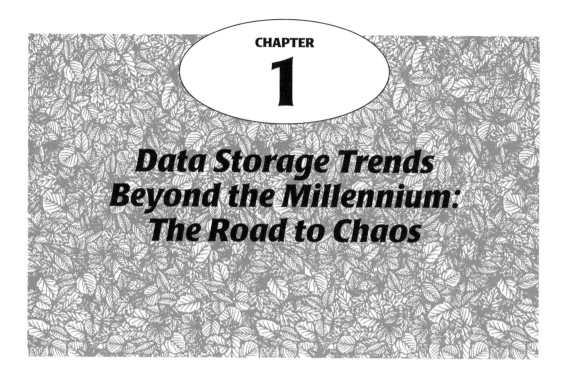

Data Storage Trends Beyond the Millennium: The Road to Chaos

A new millennium dawns as this book is being written. Yet, from the standpoint of information systems technology, industry analysts anticipate little deviation in the coming decade from the well-plotted trends and directions of modern business enterprise computing.

The preceding two decades have witnessed numerous technological advances:

- Processor speeds in mainframes, minicomputer servers, and desktop workstations have nearly doubled every three to four years.
- Networks are now commonplace in the business landscape, providing robust and capable intersystem access to distributed applications for geographically dispersed end users.
- The Internet is a *de riguer* component of most business networking strategies, providing ubiquitous access to corporate applications and services both to internal employees and corporate customers worldwide.
- Operating systems, too, have settled into smooth, relatively predictable development paths, with vendors of competing operating

system architectures at least grudgingly accepting the need, and providing the instrumentation, for cross-platform integration.

Against this backdrop, data storage technology has kept pace with the requirements of corporate information system development. In some respects, storage technology vendors have anticipated business information technology (IT) needs with products featuring increased capacity, faster access rates, smaller physical sizes and new deployment architectures.

A PARADIGM SHIFT

One could argue that declining storage device cost and increased storage capacity has been as much a driver as it is a consequence of the often-cited explosive growth in business data. Whatever the causal relationship between storage demand and storage technology, by the end of the 1990s data storage had become the center of the modern computing universe.

While it went largely unnoticed, the shift from a processor-centric to a storage-centric computing paradigm was nothing less than revolutionary—tantamount to the replacement of Ptolemy's Earth-centric view of the universe by the sun-centric astronomy of Copernicus in 1543. From the earliest days of computing, processors had garnered the attention of systems developers, with storage and other input/output (I/O) functions surrounding the processor like so many satellites. The preoccupation with the technology used to process information, however, concealed for a long time the underlying truth that data itself, and not data processing, was the actual stuff of business IT. When this was finally recognized, a fundamental shift occurred toward a more data-centric, hence a more storage-centric, view of business IT.

The new, storage-centric orientation of corporate information systems design evolved from two basic trends. One was the rise of local area networks, a key enabler of distributed computing environments. From a network perspective, data storage no longer needed to be a local I/O function. With the advent of stable information networks, data stored anywhere in the business enterprise could be accessed by anyone who needed it.

Supporting the trend toward a storage-centric computing paradigm was the rhetoric of client/server computing advocates throughout the 1980s and 1990s and the development of distributed relational databases. Client/server advocates assailed traditional, centralized, mainframe-centered computing architectures, accusing them of holding data hostage. The key to successful business computing, they argued, was to place information directly in the hands of decision makers who needed it to perform useful work.

Following the stabilization and integration of distributed (and often isolated) "islands of automation"—first-generation PCs and servers— using local area networks, attention turned to organizing and "managing" the distributed data used by client/server applications to facilitate fast access. Relational databases were introduced to provide a rational data storage approach. From that point on, data was conceived as a resource to be used by a network of processors.

The shift to a storage-centric view in corporate IT soon gave rise to a number of storage innovations. One was network-attached storage (NAS). Anticipating the need for expeditious access to data by client/server applications installed on heterogeneous platforms (mainly, servers operating UNIX and Microsoft Windows-based operating systems), some vendors sought to untether file storage from server platforms altogether and create the industry's first "operating system-agnostic" network-attached storage products.

Early efforts at server-free, network-attached storage configurations were spearheaded by the optical storage products industry. It was not long before interest spread to the magnetic disk products sector. New NAS disk array products are being developed on an ongoing basis. One product category—the filer—serves as multiprotocol, network-based "file cabinet" (see Figure 1–1) storing end user and application files for retrieval by either UNIX or Microsoft Windows hosts. Converting and storing files in a native format, then restoring them to the format of the host

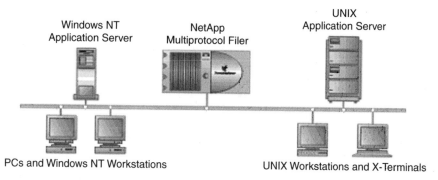

Figure 1–1   Network-Attached Storage System. (*Source:* Network Appliance, Inc., Santa Clara, CA.)

requesting access is an approach to cross-platform data sharing that has established Network Appliance as an early leader in this product segment (see Figure 1–2).

Another innovative strategy is the storage area network (SAN). SAN technology evolved from the proposition that large data transfers did not need to consume precious bandwidth resources of production networks—a concern voiced in connection with traditional, network server-tethered storage configurations and with newer NAS products as well. Instead of deploying storage products attached to production networks, SAN pioneers proposed the creation of "back-end networks" consisting of storage devices interconnected via intelligent hubs and switches, as shown in Figure 1–3.

Such a strategy, they suggested, would surmount the constraints imposed by the Small Computer Systems Interface (SCSI) protocol, which was widely used for deploying server-tethered disk arrays. With SANs, storage resources would be much more scalable, more fault tolerant and more open, enabling the deployment and concurrent use of nearly any disk, tape or optical storage product from any vendor in the market.

While debates continue over the appropriate protocol for use within SANs themselves—whether SCSI, Internet Protocol (IP), Intel Next Generation I/O (NGIO), or some other protocol should be used to interconnect the members of a gigabit-speed storage network—industry experts regard the architecture as an increasingly viable alternative to server-tethered storage. As depicted in Figure 1–4, SANs and NAS products are expected to enjoy enormous growth during the first decade of the new century, while server-tethered storage products are expected to lose considerable market share. According to one senior analyst at Dataquest,

Figure 1–2   Network Appliance F700 Series Filer. (*Source:* Network Appliance, Inc., Santa Clara, CA.)

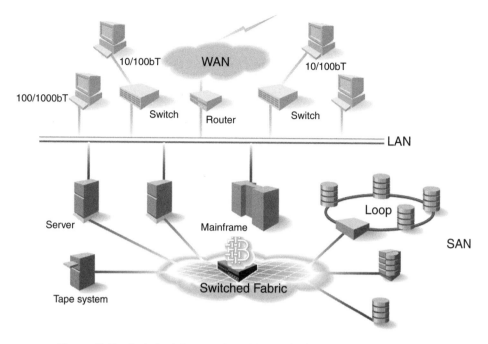

Figure 1–3   Switched Storage Area Network. (*Source:* Brocade Communications Systems, San Jose, CA. www.brocade.com.)

EXTERNAL ARRAY REVENUE FORECAST

In Non-Mainframe Applications

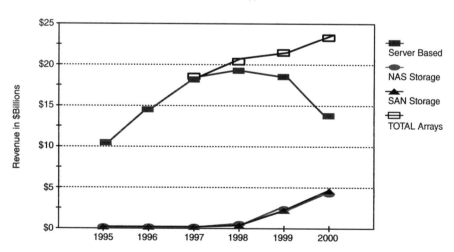

Figure 1–4   SAN, NAS, and Server-Tethered Storage Futures. (*Source:* Strategic Research Corporation, Inc., Santa Barbara, CA.)

In 1998, about 98 percent of the storage in distributed environments is attached directly to servers in the form of Ultra SCSI or Fibre Channel hard disks and disk arrays. This will shrink to about 10 percent by the year 2002. We see Storage Area Networks and Network Attached Storage devices replacing traditional server-attached storage in most cases.[1]

Few trends offer a clearer view of the shift to a storage-centric computing model than do NAS/SAN market projections. These technologies establish repositories for data that can be shared among multiple processors and multiple end users. As the new architectures take hold, it is the servers and workstations that become the satellites of the storage resource.

THE ROAD TO CHAOS

One promise of technologies such as SANs and NAS devices is an overall reduction in the per gigabyte price of storage product acquisitions. Prior to the advent of these technologies, IT organizations that required additional storage capacity typically needed to purchase, together with the storage array, a server to which the storage array would be tethered. The few "shared" storage platforms that existed—so-called multiported array products—were either prohibitively expensive for deployment in an open systems environment, proprietary in design, or both.

One promise of SANs in particular is that the technology will, in a single move,

- Eliminate potential server I/O bottlenecks
- Enable the deployment of storage products based on price rather than brand name
- Eliminate the need to add servers to control storage
- Provide scalability to support growing storage appetites within modern corporations

Obviously, it is difficult for vendors of traditional server-tethered and multiported storage products to compete with such a value proposition. Indeed, as of this writing, most storage vendors have articulated support for SANs and are working to make their products SAN-ready. Those few vendors who have withheld endorsement have sought to discriminate their products based on "superior intelligence," usually in the form of storage management software. For many of these companies, brand loyalty has been a major component of sales. SAN advocates argue that storage networks recast disk arrays and other storage products as commodity products, eliminating the importance of brand. In response, vendors of non-SAN-compatible products paraphrase the old axiom: "The road to chaos is paved with cheap technology."

Whether these vendors' claims of superior storage manageability are supported by fact is beside the point for now. The implied messages contained in their statements—that storage is being poorly managed and that the lack of effective storage management has potentially negative ramifications for the business automation infrastructure—are exactly the issues addressed by this book.

Just as many IT organizations are beginning to recover from the impact of the Y2K bug, the next great challenge for corporate IT may already be looming on the horizon in the form of storage management. Three trends, taken together, suggest that this may well be the case.

- **The current explosive growth in business data will continue into the next decade**. Companies are generating data at a phenomenal rate. Analysts claim that Fortune 500 companies are increasing their requirements for data storage by 100 percent or more per year. This trend is expected to continue, and the volume of data to be stored will increase, well into the next decade. Data warehouses, the dynamics of distributed systems, and replicated databases are some of the factors cited for continued data growth.

- **Businesses will continue to deploy storage platforms to provide on-line or "near on-line" access to corporate data**. Depending on the analyst one reads, corporate information technology departments will spend between 75 and 90 cents of every hardware dollar over the next five years on data storage products. Magnetic disk and automated tape products top the list of preferred technologies because they deliver speedy data accessibility to decision makers, customers, and other global end users on a 24-hour basis. While off-line or archival storage media markets continue to show growth, the preponderance of corporate spending is on highly accessible, magnetic disk–based storage media, reflecting the preference of most large companies to keep all data on-line and readily available for access by end users and applications.

- **Most companies lack a rational storage plan or strategies for managing data or acquiring storage device platforms themselves**. Today, most data growth is unplanned in distributed computing enterprises. So, too, is the acquisition of storage technology itself. Storage products—including disk drives, arrays, tape libraries and optical media—are typically acquired on an as-needed basis with little attention paid to future growth and with only casual concern for architectural considerations. Issues such as scalability and investment protection that are almost always emphasized in system and network technology acquisitions are often hardly considered in storage purchases. This trend promises to continue, according to some observers, because the "threshold of pain" in storage management has not been reached. New technologies, such as storage area networks (SANs), may well serve to push back the pain threshold for many companies. They enable the acquisition and deployment of increasing amounts of physical storage at a low cost and do not introduce any significant motivation for sound, proactive planning.

Given the trends identified above, today's storage boom may well lead to tomorrow's storage bust. Of course, there is more to justify this position than the marketing pronouncements several disgruntled vendors of non-SAN–compliant storage hardware.

Some groundbreaking studies have been performed by industry analysts endeavoring model the costs for managing enterprise storage. While methods differ, an industry guideline has evolved: For every dollar that a company spends in storage hardware, it can expect to spend ten times that sum in management costs. As with so many other components of IT, storage hardware acquisition costs comprise only a minute percentage of the total cost of ownership (TCO) for storage technology.

Storage TCO was only beginning to attract the interest of industry analysts in the mid-1990s when SANs burst onto the stage. Presumably, the storage area network, which is an enterprise-wide storage architecture, delivers new economies of scale to storage management. It does so mainly by centralizing physical storage, thereby facilitating storage administration without staff increases.

Prior to the widespread deployment of SANs, however, International Data Corporation offered the opinion that "spending nearly twice as much for a consolidated enterprise storage architecture" would yield companies significant improvements in the cost of managing storage, in many cases, "improve application availability, avoid costly losses, and add business value."[2]

At the time of the IDC study, SANs were still primordial technologies. Other enterprise-level storage architectures, presumably based on expensive, multiported, multiprotocol, storage products, were the basis

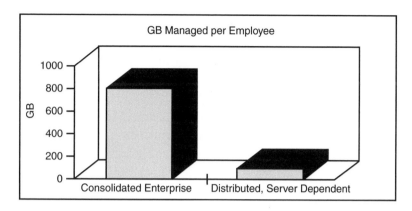

Figure 1–5 Gigabytes of Storage That Can Be Managed per Employee. (*Source:* International Data Corporation, Framingham, MA.)

for analysis. The costs to manage this type of centralized storage were contrasted with the costs to manage decentralized, server-tethered storage with the predictable result. Centralized storage was manageable by fewer staff resulting in fewer unplanned interruptions of service. Hence, costs were dramatically different (see Figure 1–5).

With the increasing deployment of SAN and NAS products, the results of such analyses would probably be even more cost-advantageous. Of course, TCO cost reductions accruing to SANs would reflect their reduced hardware costs rather than any improvements in storage management efficiency. SAN and NAS merely push back the threshold of pain in terms of operational costs of ownership. These technologies do not, in and of themselves, do anything to encourage efficient storage planning and management.

STORAGE MANAGEMENT DEFINED

What is effective storage planning and management? A simple definition may be derived from the discipline that evolved over several decades in the realm of mainframes. *Storage management is the application of procedures and processes to ensure the availability, accessibility, performance, and protection of stored data and storage devices.* Effective storage management is a process that includes several activities:

- The analysis of storage technology options and storage requirements
- The selection and implementation of appropriate storage platforms
- The testing and monitoring of the storage platform performance
- The development, implementation, and testing of storage archive and backup plans
- The development, implementation, and monitoring of high-availability techniques (disk mirroring, file mirroring, etc.)
- The development and implementation of capacity plans and storage migration strategies
- Disaster recovery planning

In addition to the above, which have been traditional components of storage management in a mainframe environment, modern distributed computing carries with it additional prerequisites for effective storage management. Storage management must also concern itself with:

- Planning and implementing strategies for file access by and data sharing among heterogeneous platforms.
- Planning and implementing techniques for data storage and replication across multiple storage devices to enhance accessibility and performance.
- Planning and designing storage networks to optimize performance (throughput) and bandwidth utilization.
- Monitoring storage networks for proper device and network operation and establishing capabilities to respond, proactively if possible, to detected error conditions.

In short, storage management involves a broad range of activities that contribute directly to the availability, accessibility, performance, and protection of the corporate data resource. Effective storage management stands in stark contrast to the current *laissez faire* attitude of many IT organizations. Asked about storage management, many IT professionals will launch into discussions about backup and recovery software that is deployed or planned for deployment in their environments. The correlation between storage management and backup and recovery derives partly from vendor marketing. Most of the so-called storage management vendors actually provide applications only for server- or network-based backup. The implication is that backup and recovery software is all the storage management that a company requires.

Common sense should argue otherwise. Storage management is a multifaceted and complicated undertaking that promises to become even more important as companies continue to migrate business-critical applications onto distributed computing platforms, increasing in the process the complexity of data storage and accessibility requirements. Poor storage management, in turn, impacts other IT processes. For example, IT and network professionals must know where data physically resides and how applications and end users will access and use stored data in order to make intelligent design decisions with respect to networks and systems. Such efforts are greatly aided by the presence of an up-to-date storage plan—one outcome of effective storage management.

ENDNOTES

1. Jon William Toigo, "Will SANs Be the Giant Slayers?" *Solutions Integrator*, 2(16), October 1, 1998.
2. John McArthur, "Demonstrating the Value of Enterprise Storage," IDC White Paper, International Data Corporation, Framingham, MA, 1997.

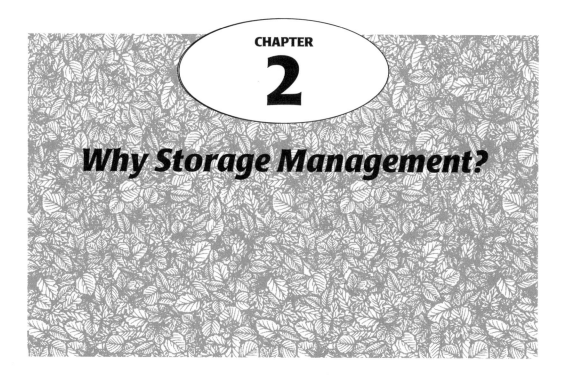

CHAPTER 2

Why Storage Management?

Storage management provides the glue that binds together a diverse and sometimes disparate assortment of storage products so that they begin to form a unified storage infrastructure. In a very real sense, storage management creates order from disorder.

Without storage management, organizations are left with a collection of hardware, software, and interconnects that do not return the value that was the basis for their acquisition. In its absence, IT professionals have little choice but to persist in the acquisition of additional storage resources based on limited tactical assessments of immediate needs. Worse yet, storage acquisitions may be made on the basis of what a vendor, a research analyst, or a trade press writer finds interesting or provocative at the moment.

To these theoretical considerations can be added other more practical outcomes of the failure to develop a proactive storage management strategy. Based on anecdotal evidence gathered from interviews and case studies, there are at least seven cross-cutting consequences of a lack of effective storage management. The following pages address these consequences in some detail.

INCREASED RISK OF DATA LOSS

Failing to manage storage effectively increases exposure to data loss in several ways. For one, unmanaged data is rarely backed up.

The lack of attention to data backups may result from a failure to appreciate the value of the data based upon a lack of knowledge about the data (its very existence may not be known) or its importance to an application or to the organization as a whole. Failure to back up data may also reflect a misapprehension of the need for backup if other mirroring or hierarchical storage management capabilities exist. Additionally, failure to perform backups may reflect a lack of time, software, or personnel required to perform the procedure. Finally, backups may be taken but not verified, resulting in backups that cannot be used to restore data if a catastrophic event—such as a fire, software bug, computer virus, or disk failure—occurs.

Regardless of the reason, the failure to take backups places all other IT activities, and the business itself, at risk. It is a fundamental prerequisite for business continuity and disaster recovery that data be backed up and available for immediate restoral if the business is to function following an unplanned interruption.[1]

Numerous estimates are forwarded by research institutes indicating the dollar value of downtime (i.e., time spent recovering purposeful computing activity in the wake of an unplanned outage). One, from the Fibre Channel Association, places hourly downtime costs at values ranging from $6.5 million for brokerage operations to $14,500 for ATM systems (see Table 2–1). These estimates should suggest how important it is to ensure that data backups are taken and that restoral of data is tested on a periodic basis. Without data backups, other recovery activities are pointless.

In addition to the failure to take backups and to ensure restorability of data, the failure to make adequate provisions for data security—also a function of effective storage management—can create a loss exposure for a company. Intellectual property, trade secrets, and even sensitive memoranda and e-mail, when misappropriated or misused, can have consequences ranging from far-reaching erosion in company market position to temporary disruption of normal day-to-day operations. As suggested by the wry axiom, "NFS also stands for No Freaking Security," storage management must concern itself with the security provisions associated with shared files, particularly as file systems become increasingly shared through network attached storage and storage area network product deployments.

Table 2–1   Downtime Costs for Select Applications

Business	Industry	Hourly Downtime Costs
Brokerage operations	Finance	$6,450,000
Credit card/sales authorizations	Finance	$2,600,000
Pay-per-view	Media	$150,000
Home shopping	Retail	$113,000
Catalog sales	Retail	$90,000
Airline reservations	Transportation	$90,000
Tele-ticket sales	Media	$69,000
Package shipping	Transportation	$28,000
ATM fees	Finance	$14,500

Source: Fibre Channel Association, Maintainview, CA. www.fibrechannel.com

INCREASED PERSONNEL COST

The signature of poor storage management is the requirement to hire additional human resources to manage growing storage assets. An industry guideline holds that for every dollar spent to acquire storage, five to seven dollars must be budgeted annually for its maintenance.[2] According to International Data Corporation, 55 percent of distributed storage management costs are administrative—a number that can be reduced to 15 percent through the physical or *logical* consolidation of storage resources for more effective management.[3]

Robert Gray, IDC's research manager for storage systems, underscores the point,

> There are two ways to lower the cost of storage. One is to put resources together in the same physical location; the other is to put them together in the same virtual location. The advantage of the new architectures is that you can buy built arrays in bulk at the most favorable cost per megabyte and allocate them [virtually] out to various servers as you need them. You can deploy the type of RAID and the type of performance that matches the application a little more easily. You also can have a single set of software tools to do the managing—which increases efficiency and lowers training costs.[4]

Both physical consolidation (the use of SANs, for example) and logical consolidation (the use of automated, centralized, storage management tools) facilitate the management of more storage by fewer personnel. Storage management activities involve both the specification of consolidated frameworks for more cost-effective storage management and the selection and use of appropriate management software tools to increase the amount of storage that IT personnel can effectively manage. In the absence of storage management, personnel must be added together with storage. This is tantamount to hiring many monks instead of buying a copying machine.

INCREASED STORAGE ACQUISITION COSTS

In the absence of storage management, storage acquisition costs typically comprise a higher percentage of the IT budget. Unmanaged storage is a driver of new storage acquisitions. Without disciplined storage management, disk and tape storage media are used inefficiently and additional capacity is required sooner to handle growing amounts of end-user and application data.

According to some industry watchers, the hard disk has become a much-abused resource since prices relative to capacity have steadily declined. As much as 80 percent of the data written to hard disks in a network is rarely, if ever, accessed again once it has been committed to storage.[5]

It is a similar story for tape. An IBM study of tape systems, for example, found that 79 percent of multi-gigabyte tapes in contained data sets less than 400 MB in size. Low cartridge utilization resulted from the common practice of placing a single backup (save set) on a tape, despite its capacity.[6]

In addition to poor grooming of existing storage, the lack of effective storage management leads to tactical purchases of storage hardware, which sets the stage for additional storage purchases. For example, if products are purchased on an "as-needed" basis, product selection may ignore compatibility requirements for future data sharing in a heterogeneous server environment. This, in turn, drives the acquisition of additional storage products for use in replicating datasets so they are accessible to hosts that cannot interface with existing storage platforms. There are many valid reasons to replicate data sets and to distribute them across networks. Storage hardware limitations should not be one of them, however.

INCREASED DOWNTIME DUE TO STORAGE-RELATED ISSUES

System downtime costs money and storage-related downtime occurs more frequently in an environment that lacks an effective storage management capability. One explanation for this phenomenon is the storage

Table 2–2   Annual Failure Rates of Storage Devices

Storage System	Integral Media	Annual Failure Rate (AFR; %)
Hard Disk Systems	Disk Drives	3.8
	Large RAID Systems (>50 Drives)	60.0
Tape Drives	4mm DAT	11.1
	8mm Exabyte	6.9
	DLTtape	11.0
Tape Library Systems	Multiple Driver Systems	20–51

Source: Michael Peterson, "De-Mystifying Tape Reliability," *Storage Management Solutions,* 1997. Copyright © 1999 Westworld Productions, Inc. All rights reserved. Reprinted with permission.

product acquisition methods used in an unmanaged environment. While some storage platforms are designed for greater resilience than others, selection in an ad hoc storage acquisitions environment is often made on the basis of factors unrelated to resilience, such as capacity, performance, and price. IT professionals may purchase RAID storage believing that RAID will afford maximum resilience and deliver maximum uptime.

Michael Peterson, President of Strategic Research Corporation, uses the measure Annual Failure Rate (AFR) to describe the likelihood of storage product failures. His findings, which are summarized in Table 2–2, suggest that a 50-drive RAID disk array will lose an average of three drives per year, while a 1000-drive RAID will experience weekly drive failures. Peterson observes that "RAID does not stop failures. . . . Failures still occur and high availability architectures are required to prevent downtime, protect data and insure [sic] continued performance."[7]

INCREASED DOWNTIME DUE TO ABSENCE OF AN AVAILABILITY-OPTIMIZED ARCHITECTURE

Peterson further observes that architectures, and not product mean time between failure statistics, define availability. Using statistics derived from the LAN industry, he defines several levels of availability, ranging from unmanaged to ultra-available. Unmanaged storage architectures experience downtime approaching 50,000 minutes per year (90 percent uptime), while ultra-availability storage architectures incur 0.05 minutes of downtime per year (99.99999 percent uptime).[8]

Costs for an ultra-high availability storage architecture are significantly greater than those for less available architectures, of course. Availability costs must be balanced against the company's costs for unplanned downtime in order to establish a cost-optimized solution. Few, if any, unmanaged storage environments base storage product acquisitions and deployment architectures on such analyses.

DECREASED PERFORMANCE IN APPLICATIONS

Storage management is key to application performance in several ways. One way that storage management directly impacts application performance is through its focus on storage tuning.

As discussed in later chapters, databases can be extremely sensitive to the layout of their segments across RAID disk arrays and may demonstrate significant performance improvements in multiaccess environments through the application of different RAID levels to different segments. The same is true for the large streaming files typical in multimedia applications. The block layout of digitized audio or video *clips* has a direct relationship to their jitter-free playback in networked environments. Failure to address these factors (and many others) through effective storage tuning can reduce application throughput.

Effective storage management is also required to facilitate transaction-oriented applications. Its attention to the details of data movements associated with an application enables the design of a balanced storage architecture that facilitates multiple, concurrent, transaction-oriented accesses.

Only from a storage management perspective can the complex relationships between host bus bandwidth, interconnect bandwidth, and storage controller bandwidth be understood and applied to deliver a balanced solution. In the absence of storage management, unbalanced architectures can and do proliferate, and one bad choice often leads to another.

For example, one far-too-common scenario involves host systems with extremely fast CPUs and gigabyte memory capacities that become I/O-bound, saturating disks and bringing response time to a grinding halt. Without the tools to adequately assess the situation, many system administrators seek to address the problem by using faster disk drives. What may, in fact, be required is a solid state disk (SSD) solution that addresses fast I/O requests in microseconds, using dynamic RAM, rather than in milliseconds, using the best and most expensive mechanical disk drives currently available.[9]

In addition to improving application performance by balancing host bus and storage controller speeds, a disciplined storage management approach is also needed to assess the benefits and drawbacks of distributing (or consolidating) data. A large part of the "explosion of data" cited by analysts and trade press pundits is, in fact, replicated data that is physically distributed across enterprise networks with the intention of improving application performance for remote end users. Such replicated data sets often require significant, network-borne data transfers to synchronize them with the original data set. The impact of these transfers on network bandwidth and on the performance of unrelated applications that also use the production network needs to be understood clearly. Effective storage management addresses this application performance issue through the use of tools that enable the modeling of data movements and the prediction of impact on network resources. Unmanaged storage leaves the entire matter to the network administrator, who may not understand the purpose or importance of the synchronizing data flows and, by consequence, may afford them a lower priority and lesser access to network resources than they require.

DIMINISHED END USER CONFIDENCE AND SATISFACTION

Considering the impact of the other consequences of a lack of storage management described above, it should be clear that unmanaged storage does not cultivate satisfaction with, or confidence in, an IT organization or its capability to deliver solutions that address business needs. Unmanaged storage will result in higher costs, lower reliability, reduced application performance, and increased downtime. These are the outcomes that the business end user or manager—or worse yet, the customer—will see and care about. None of these people will see or care about any of the wonderful storage technologies that have been deployed. In this, the situation can be likened to another technology: the telephone. In its prebreakup days, AT&T used the motto, "It all begins with a dial tone" to signify its appreciation of the fact that most customers were unaware of—and largely uninterested in knowing about—the complex network of transmission lines, satellites, and switches that provided their phone service. All of the sophisticated technology and careful planning and management that enabled the user to "reach out and touch someone" were meaningless if a dial tone did not buzz through the earpiece when the telephone handset was lifted off the cradle.

It is much the same with storage technology. Only one vendor among the many network, systems, and storage management software vendors interviewed for this book emphasized this point.[10] While others spoke of neural networking-enhanced agents, correlation engines based on deep mathematics, and integrated management platforms, Candle Corporation stated that the mainstay of its storage management product offering was a client agent that monitored how much time transpired between the press of a key (or click of a mouse) by the end user and the repainting of his display screen with data returned by an application. That is, in the final analysis, where the rubber of the storage management wheel meets the proverbial road.

IMPEDIMENTS TO STORAGE MANAGEMENT

Given all of the negative consequences of failing to manage storage effectively, one might wonder why more companies don't manage their storage effectively. There are several reasons. Many have to do with the simple fact that storage management isn't glamorous. It is rarely regarded as a high-profile task that will attract the appreciative attention of management. Nor does it make one popular with network administrators, database administrators, systems administrators, application programmers, or systems architects, all of whom will likely perceive the requirements associated with a storage infrastructure to be yet another pesky consideration affecting their work. Storage management certainly won't make great conversation on a date and it won't cure baldness.

Moreover, it isn't easy. Establishing a storage management capability requires "mental bandwidth" that may be short in coming against a backdrop of daily operational fire drills. It takes time and research and resources that may be in short supply. Additionally, no one software tool exists that provides a comprehensive storage management solution. One must integrate several tools, including both system management framework products and point products capable of providing discrete functions or managing discrete elements of the storage infrastructure, and possibly write a few tools that are not offered commercially, to get the job done.

These are all factors that militate against doing the job of storage management. It is hardly surprising, therefore, that everyone in the IT organization is not knocking on the manager's door and nominating themselves for the job.

The growing need to develop a storage management capability, however, will likely see an unfortunate cadre "volunteered" to take up the task by their superiors. While the project may seem to be a cruel joke at first, or a case of bad karma catching up, an honest and unbiased examination of the state of distributed storage within the business enterprise will quickly underscore the importance of the undertaking.

ENDNOTES

1. See my books, *Disaster Recovery Planning: Managing Risk and Catastrophe in Information Systems* (2nd ed.) (New York: Prentice Hall, 1999) and *Disaster Recovery Planning for Computer and Communications Resources* (New York: Wiley, 1996), for more information about disaster recovery planning, exposure windows, and backup strategies.
2. Mike Peterson, president of research firm Peripheral Strategies (Santa Barbara, CA), says: "The big myth is that storage in PC LANs is free; it may cost only $1 per megabyte, but the labor cost of managing that is pushing $8 per megabyte per year." From "Managing Storage," Andy Reinhardt, *Byte Magazine,* June 1994.
3. Don Lundell, "Assessing a Storage Resource," *Storage Management Solutions,* July 1998.
4. Randall D. Cronk, "Best of Both Worlds," from "Storage Moves Into The Networked World," Advertising Supplement, *Network World,* 1998.
5. Ranga Rangachari, "Selection Criteria for HSM and Archive Storage Solutions," *Computer Technology Review,* June 1995.
6. "Demystifying Tape Performance," Strategic Profile, Strategic Resource Corporation, Santa Barbara, CA, 1996, provided as marketing collateral for IBM's Magstar MP.
7. Michael Peterson, "De-Mystifying Tape Reliability," *Storage Management Solutions,* 1997.
8. *Ibid.*
9. Todd Coopee, "Excellerator Ultra Excels at Mass Storage," *InfoWorld,* February 15, 1999.
10. Candle Corporation, Santa Monica, CA.

CHAPTER

3

Storage in the Modern Distributed Enterprise

DATA DISTRIBUTION MODELS EVOLVE

When Xerox Corporation, Digital Equipment Corporation and Intel Corporation rolled out the first ethernet network in 1976, they may not have anticipated how successful LAN technology would become. Within a few years, customer concerns regarding the "isolated islands of automation" that had been created by the pervasive deployment of PCs and departmental minicomputers drove the nearly universal adoption of local area networks and set the stage for client/server computing.

While the benefits of LANs—such as improved communications, resource sharing, and enhanced coordination of group work activities—were certainly factors in their success, vendors of networking products also played to the fears, uncertainties, and doubts that had been cultivated by the critics of distributed computing. A recurring theme in the debate over centralized and decentralized computing architectures was a *lack of mainframe-style management discipline* in the distributed environment. In its absence, critics argued, companies were putting their most precious information assets at risk.

Mainframe-centric computing had been at the heart of corporate automation efforts since the late 1950s. Over time, the information systems support organization had evolved a hierarchical and specialized structure. Discipline was a buzzword, referring to a set of established job descriptions with well-defined areas of responsibility and carefully documented tasks and procedures. Discipline created an orderly operations milieu within the data center "glass house" and ensured that all of the requirements for mission-critical IS services were being met.

By the 1970s, however, huge backlogs of application development requests, timeliness issues with reports and other information outputs, and massive costs in mainframe data centers sent many business managers on a quest for alternatives. The minicomputer, and later the PC, provided less expensive (from the standpoint of hardware and software costs, at least) approaches for moving information processing closer to the decision makers who needed it.

The backlash against the mainframe data center, embodied in distributed computing, found expression in the desktop computers and departmental servers that sprung up virtually overnight throughout most major companies. Curiously, LANs found a case with both detractors and advocates of this phenomenon. LANs enabled the concept of distributed computing to become a reality, vendors argued to distributed computing advocates. Rugged individualists could possess their own desktop processing capabilities, instead of being slaves to mainframe processing schedules, as they were in older mainframe terminal networks. With a LAN, they could share resources—use hard disks and modems and other peripherals installed on remote machines. They could use e-mail and collaborate on projects. When it was desirable to do so, they could just as easily disconnect from the network and work in privacy and isolation.

To detractors of distributed computing, vendors presented another rationale. By interconnecting PCs and departmental computers with networks, the stage was set for centralizing the control and management of these distributed computing resources. Most importantly, data could be safeguarded using the infrastructure of the LAN in conjunction with centrally administered backup and restore software. Where mainframe data centers persisted, argued some vendors, they might even become central repositories for backed-up data. Network-based backup and restore solutions might further cost-justify expensive mainframe storage peripherals and recentralize the corporate information asset for disciplined management by data center personnel, even if processing remained distributed.

Over the two decades that followed, a wide range of data distribution architectures arose. For the purposes of this book, the models can be grouped into three supersets, defined by storage location and degree of management. These three high-level data distribution models are distributed-anarchical, regionalized-managed, and centralized-managed.

DISTRIBUTED-ANARCHICAL DATA DISTRIBUTION

Shown in Figure 3–1, the distributed-anarchical model for storage management is represented by a straightforward and familiar network topology in which a production network interconnects subnetworks of PC workstations, departmental (or functionally tasked) servers and corporate mainframes. Each computing platform has local storage components, which may include hard disk and tape drives.

The responsibility for managing data on the disks resides with the local administrator of the system (the end user in the case of a PC or other intelligent workstation). There is no centralized storage management capability, so the model is described as anarchical. Local administrators are responsible for ensuring the availability, accessibility, performance, and protection of stored data and storage devices. Data remains at the site of origin. If backups are taken, they may be removed to another location for safekeeping and rotated periodically.

This data distribution model embodies the idealism of some of the original distributed computing advocates, who claimed that distributing processing and storage management functions across the enterprise

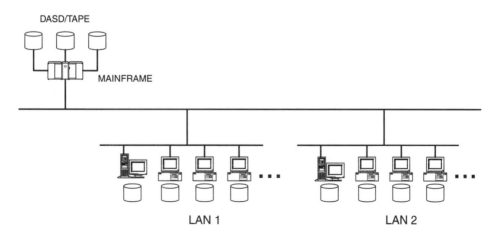

Figure 3–1   Distributed-Anarchical Data Distribution Model.

would yield the practical benefits of reduced cost and more efficient network bandwidth utilization. Since data is locally managed and not migrated across the network to centralized storage repositories, network congestion is not an issue. The strategy also obviates issues of "backup windows"—the amount of time available within a mainframe-based data center processing schedule to perform tasks such as data backup—that may arise when the mainframe or some regional storage server is used as a centralized data repository.

Over time, experience with the decentralized-anarchical model has demonstrated its many limitations. The criticisms lodged against this model may be summarized succinctly as a lack of disciplined management and high cost. With this model, independent administrators and end users are required to manage the storage associated with their individual servers or workstations. Experience suggests that this is not done well, if at all.

Nontechnical end users often lack the skills and training to perform storage management tasks efficiently. Even when prerequisite skills and knowledge are present, often storage management functions are left undone or are treated as low-priority, get-to-it-when-you-can tasks. Moreover, asking high-salaried business professionals to manage the storage of their own desktop systems has proven to be a cost-multiplier in PC total cost of ownership.

Some organizations have sought workarounds for these limitations that would not require imposing centralized control. Automated storage replication, mirroring, and vaulting solutions have been designed into some distributed environments to remove the responsibility for storage management from the end user. Such strategies move companies closer to the second data distribution model, the regionalized-managed model.

REGIONALIZED-MANAGED DATA DISTRIBUTION

As depicted in Figure 3–2, the regionalized-managed model reassigns storage management responsibilities from end users and departmental server administrators to one or more regional storage managers. These IT-trained personnel utilize storage management software products, typically from centralized consoles, to migrate data from distributed platforms to regional storage servers. In other words, the data stored on several PCs and departmental servers is periodically copied and migrated to regional repositories, where fewer and better trained administrators ex-

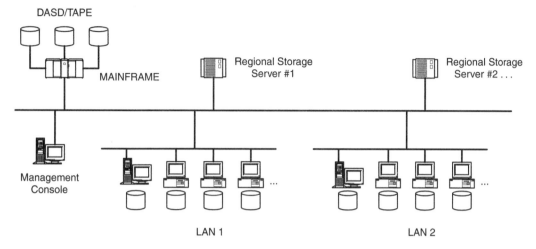

Figure 3–2   Distributed-Managed Data Distribution Model.

ercise "disciplined" management techniques to ensure data availability, accessibility, performance, and protection.

Numerous software vendors have capitalized on this model to deliver "enterprise storage management solutions" (i.e., centrally managed data backup and restore products). According to Dataquest, the worldwide sales of "distributed backup software" rose 46 percent to $1.33 billion in 1997, with products from Computer Associates International, Seagate Technology, Inc., and Hewlett Packard Company leading the market. Dataquest further projects that the overall market for "software that backs up data, checks the integrity of disk drives, and maintains file systems" will grow at a robust 21 percent per year, topping $4.8 billion by 2002.

The regionalized-managed data distribution model has the potential to improve the quality of storage management and to reduce some of its costs in a distributed environment, but it is not without its own set of limitations. For one, software used to manage distributed storage carries with it licensing and training costs. Secondly, few products offer full support of multiple, heterogeneous operating systems. Thirdly, most products do not offer storage management capabilities that go much beyond backup and restore functions.

At a design level, this model depends on storage replication for its success. Replicated storage entails hardware costs and imposes network burdens as production networks are used to transfer data from departmental servers and workstations to "regional" repositories. To address these concerns, storage vendors, including those offering network attached storage (NAS) devices, multi-ported storage arrays, and storage area networking (SAN) solutions, are proposing alternative topologies.

Installing a storage repository on a production network "near" to the subnetwork of workgroup devices that originate data is one way to contain and limit the network congestion that may result from large data transfers. In the past, many companies deployed storage servers with captive storage arrays to implement this solution. However, such deployments may be costly to administer in a large enterprise with many subnetworks.

Vendors of NAS products claim that the use of general purpose servers is less cost-effective than using NAS devices. They point out that NAS devices have operating system kernels that have been "optimized" for I/O specifically, making them more efficient and better suited than general purpose servers to a storage repository role. Other features of NAS products include their "plug-and-play" operation (e.g., many products autodiscover their own IP addresses, advertise their storage volumes automatically to network members, etc.) and ease of management. Vendors observe that NAS products are readily maintained using Simple Network Management Protocol (SNMP) management software, equipment-generated web page interfaces, or specialized management utilities that may be used from anywhere in the network. Some NAS devices also provide heterogeneous file system support, facilitating data restore operations to mixed operating system platforms.

NAS and other network-based storage repositories will likely benefit from improved class of service (COS) and quality of service (QOS) provisioning capabilities, which are being added by vendors to their switches, routers, and other networking products. By taking advantage of traffic prioritization schemes, network designers may be able to minimize the disruption of, or interference with, other mission-critical application traffic on production networks that might result from large storage data migrations.

Another way to minimize the burden of storage management traffic on production networks is to remove the traffic from the production network altogether. Another trend in corporate computing has set the stage for such a solution. In an effort to reduce server administration costs, many companies in recent years have been re-centralizing and consolidating previously distributed servers. The adoption of a "server farm" architecture has enabled the recentralization of server storage resources as well.

CLARiiON Vice President of Technology Bob Solomon observes that the term "SAN" originated in the server industry,

As recently as a year ago, when someone used the term SAN, I had to stop to ask them whether they were referring to a Server Area Network, which was the original meaning of the acronym, or a Storage Area Network. The storage industry stole the term, which originally referred to the interconnection of servers through a [back-end] switch fabric. In fact, it doesn't make any difference. SANs provide a switched environment to interconnect servers and storage devices, whether the network is a collection of SAN-attached storage devices or stand-alone, intelligent, disk arrays.[1]

SAN advocates have been leveraging data migration and backup/restore as ideal applications for their back-end storage network topology since it was first conceived. The objective of SAN vendors has been to untether captive storage from servers and to place it in a highly accessible network capable of operating at gigabit speed. In so doing, the problems of production network congestion due to storage management-related traffic would largely disappear.

Multiported disk array manufacturers settled on a similar concept prior to the emergence of SANs. EMC Corporation, a vendor of multiported, high-capacity, intelligent storage arrays, was an early pioneer of consolidated storage. Their storage architecture, called an Enterprise Storage Network, is based upon a self-contained, sharable, storage array product, with "intelligent storage management software" that serves as a centralized storage pool for an organization.

Like a SAN, an EMC array is not captive to any one server, but instead supplies storage services to multiple servers via a back-end network of high-speed interconnects. The company now foresees the evolution of this concept to a networked set of EMC arrays communicating through a sophisticated switch fabric with production servers (see Figure 3–3). By configuring storage resources in their own network fabric, data migrations may be performed without using production network resources.

EMC discriminates its architectural vision from that of "open" SAN vendors by referring to its all-in-one-cabinet design and integrated management software (see Figure 3–4). In effect, the vendor's pitch is that they offer a "SAN in a box" that works equally well to support evolving server farms, data warehouses integrating server and mainframe data, and in other large scale, centralized, data storage applications, especially where limited staff are available to manage terabytes of data.

EMC's Enterprise Storage Network is by the company's own admission an expensive solution targeted to the upper tier of Global 1000 companies. Because of the Symmetrix product family's proprietary architecture,

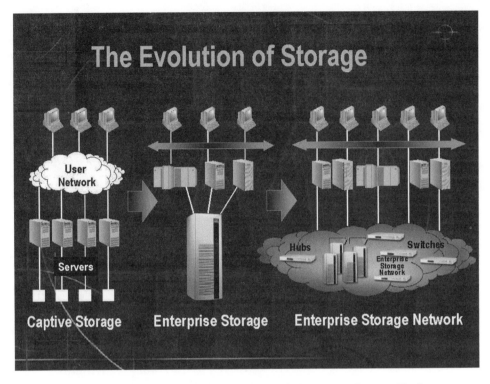

Figure 3–3   EMC Corporation's Vision of Enterprise Storage Evolution. (*Source:* EMC Corporation, Hopkinton, MA.)

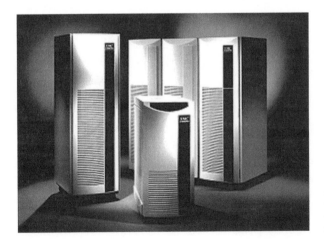

Figure 3–4   EMC Symmetrix Storage Systems. (*Source:* EMC Corporation, Hopkinton, MA.)

EMC is able to position its solution as a comprehensive one, featuring not only capacity and performance, but superior storage management capabilities as well.

Like many multiport storage array vendors, EMC claims that SAN vendors offer an overly complex storage network that requires substantial reeducation of IT and network personnel and lacks refined management tools. SAN vendors concede that their solution is more decentralized, thereby imposing a somewhat greater management burden. However, they point out that SANs are more "open" than are array product offerings. Like EMC's products, the SAN can be connected to virtually any server platform; unlike EMC, SANs permit the interconnection of a broad range of storage devices from nearly any manufacturer. According to one vendor, as companies deploy SANs, they are bound to discover that they have been paying too much for brand-name storage solutions.[2]

CENTRALIZED-MANAGED DATA DISTRIBUTION

The multiported array and the SAN constitute storage topologies that bridge the distributed-managed and the centralized-managed data distribution models introduced at the outset. In its purest form, the centralized-managed model (see Figure 3–5) envisions the migration of data from all distributed platforms in the enterprise back to a centralized repository. Traditionally, the repository was configured from mainframe DASD, but other large-scale enterprise storage arrays may be substituted as readily.

As shown in Figure 3–5, this data distribution model creates a centralized data store that can be subjected to disciplined management by IT personnel. The approach has been suggested from time to time (through never very successfully) by vendors of mainframe peripherals and channel extenders as a way to leverage both trained data center staff and the corporate investment in mainframe storage subsystems.

Advocates represent this approach as an embodiment of the three fundamental principles of effective management: standardization, centralization and simplification. According to Jeff Held, Director of Ernst & Young's Center for Technology Enablement, centralizing storage is a vastly superior alternative to managing decentralized storage via software. Says Held,

> You can either treat the symptom or the disease. [Distributed storage] management software addresses the symptoms and companies find that trying to manage 300-plus of anything is impossible. Treating the

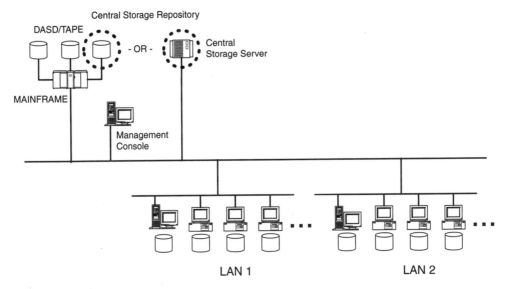

Figure 3–5   The Centralized-Managed Data Distribution Model.

disease means centralizing storage. While it is possible to manage decentralized storage, it requires replication and synchronization of data in multiple locations. You will be using up all server processing cycles just doing that.[3]

Detractors of the solution point to shrinking backup windows in mainframe data centers, network bandwidth requirements to support large and frequent data transfers, and problems with processing data restoral requests on a per file basis from a central repository. Even IBM's ADSTAR[TM] Distributed Storage Manager (ADSM) marketing organization observes that the centralized storage model, whether it involves using mainframe-attached or non-mainframe-attached storage peripherals, is not a solution that customers are clamoring to deploy.

A CONTINUUM OF OPTIONS

Arranged on a continuum, the three models of data storage distribution described above resemble Figure 3–6. In general, the more managed and centralized the model, the more costly the model from a design and hard-

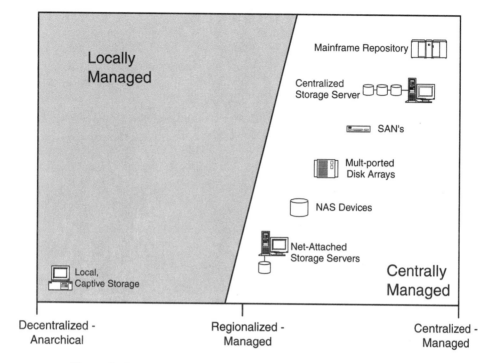

Figure 3–6   A Continuum of Data Storage Distribution Alternatives.

ware/software cost perspective. However, studies by Strategic Research Corporation, International Data Corporation, and a number of other firms suggest that the total cost of ownership to the organization for more managed, more centralized storage models is actually lower than decentralized alternatives, owing in large part to lower labor costs and reduced storage downtime.

For the foreseeable future, according to analysts, enterprise storage will continue to comprise a mixture of topologies and devices as companies deploy storage solutions with less regard to strategic than to tactical requirements. Managing storage in such an environment will continue to be a challenge for IT professionals concerned about safeguarding mission-critical business information assets.

ENDNOTES

1. Interview with Bob Solomon, Vice President of Technology, CLARiiON Advanced Storage Division of Data General Corporation, Southboro, MA, 1999.
2. Interview with A. J. Casamento, Solutioneer, Brocade Communications Systems, Inc., San Jose, CA, 1998.
3. Interview with Jeff Held, Director of the Center for Technology Enablement, Ernst & Young, New York, NY, 1998.

STORAGE TECHNOLOGIES

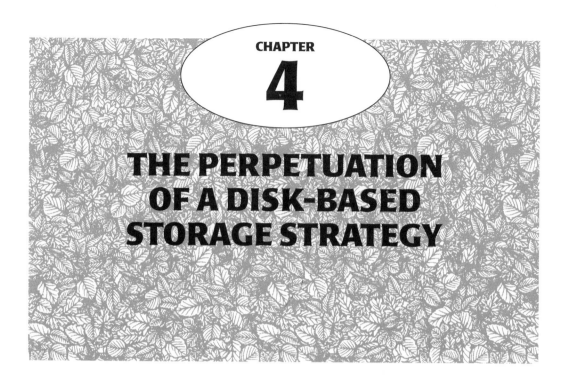

THE PERPETUATION OF A DISK-BASED STORAGE STRATEGY

Data storage, of course, is a generic term, encompassing a broad range of devices and media. Current popular storage media include random access memory (RAM), solid state disk, hard disk drives, magneto-optical (MO) disc, Near Field Recording (NFR) drives (a hybrid magnetic optical disk technology), CD-ROM and DVD, and magnetic tape. Each technology has capabilities and limitations that need to be understood when designing a storage architecture or managing storage deployments that are already in place.

Given the preference in modern business organizations to keep all data highly accessible to end users, customers, and decision makers, the hard disk drive has become the preferred data storage device in production systems. To facilitate an understanding of current hard disk technology, a brief overview of its evolution may be useful.

EVOLUTION OF HARD DISK TECHNOLOGY

The earliest mode of data storage, dating back to the 1800s, was the punch card and paper tape.[1] By the early 1950s, card decks or punched tapes, as well as magnetic tape, were the predominant storage technology for mainframe and minicomputers. Cards or paper tapes were loaded into reader peripherals so that their sequentially stored contents could be transferred into the random access memory of the computer.

This cumbersome storage technology underwent a significant change in May 1955, with the announcement of a new product by IBM: the RAMAC disk drive. RAMAC offered random-access storage of up to 5 million characters, weighed nearly 2000 pounds, and occupied about the same floor space as two modern refrigerators. Data was stored on fifty, 24-inch diameter, aluminum disk platters that were coated on both sides with magnetic iron oxide. The coating itself was derived from the primer used to paint the Golden Gate Bridge in San Francisco, CA.

Before the release of RAMAC, hard disk drives were considered an impossible dream. One engineering problem was a head fly height barrier. For a hard drive to write information to its media (typically a metallic disk coated with iron oxide), the media needs to rotate under the read–write head, which is positioned at the end of an actuator arm. Data is written to the media using an electrical field generated in the head, which, in turn, produces a magnetic pattern on media surface. Before RAMAC, engineers believed that to accomplish this function, heads needed to be spaced (to "fly") within 800 microinches of the media surface. This seemed an impossibility because irregularities in the media itself, and "runout" or "wobble" of disk media when rotating at 1200 rpm, necessitated that heads fly at least 20,000 microinches above the platter. Clearly, the head fly height required to make a drive work would also cause the heads to crash into the disk media during operation.

A group of IBM engineers, known as the "Dirty Dozen," succeeded in surmounting this barrier and the RAMAC drive was the result. IBM became the sole supplier of disk drives for several more years.

The cost for the new storage medium was steep. At $35,000 for a year's lease of a RAMAC 305, companies embracing the new technology had to spend about $7,000 per megabyte of storage for the privilege.[2] Despite the costs, RAMAC and its successors at IBM defined a new market. In a fascinating chain of events, the "Dirty Dozen" left IBM in 1967 and created a new company, Information Storage Systems, with the objective of creating competitive, plug-compatible, disk-drive products for IBM mainframes. Two years after their exodus, another IBM manager, Alan F. Shugart, left IBM, first to work with Memorex, then to form his own company dedicated to the perfection of the hard disk drive. Ultimately, his company, Shugart Technology, was renamed Seagate Technology.

Over the years, the hard disk drive went from being an expensive peripheral found only in mainframe data centers to becoming an integral, inexpensive, and ubiquitous component of server and desktop systems. Table 4–1 provides a summary of some of the firsts in hard disk drive technology.

The modern hard disk drive enjoys the distinction of being one of the most quickly advancing technologies in computing. Generational improvements have been made in hard disk technology on an almost annual basis since the early 1980s.

Introduced for the PC market by Seagate Technology in 1980, the first 5.25-inch hard disk drives offered 5 to 10 MB of storage—equalling, then doubling, the capacity of the RAMAC—in a form factor that was a small fraction of RAMAC's massive dimensions. The adjective "hard" became a part of the device description "disk drive" because the product needed to be discriminated from "floppy" disk drives already used in personal computers. Floppy drives derived their name from the metal oxide-coated Mylar used as a storage medium. The platter inside a Seagate hard disk drive (and most drives since that time) was a coated, rigid, aluminum alloy.

Another point of departure of the hard disk drive from earlier PC floppy drives was head design. In floppy disk drives, read–write heads made direct contact with media. The Seagate hard disk represented a return to the RAMAC design, since heads did not contact the media, but flew above it. This feature, combined with a durable disk media, gave hard disks a longer life expectancy than floppy media and soon made them a trusted medium for long-term data storage.

After the Seagate innovation, the market for disk drive technology exploded and product prices declined dramatically. Competition drove innovation—in head technology, platter coating, actuator arm control, and form factor. Within five years, 5.25-inch form factor drives were only three inches high and weighed a few pounds, while lower capacity "half-height" drives measured only 1.6 inches in height.

The 3.5-inch form factor hard drives appeared in 1987. Smaller than a paperback book and weighing only a pound, they enabled the laptop computer and later became standard components in both desktop and portable PCs, offering up to 500 MB of storage. They were soon challenged by 2.5-inch form factor drives weighing only four ounces and offering the same capacity as their larger cousins. Eventually, this miniaturization spiral resulted in IBM's 1998 announcement of a microdrive, which offered a capacity of 340 MB on a single disk platter the size of a small coin, weighing only 20 grams.[3]

Table 4–1 Firsts in Disk Technology

Vendor	Model	Name	Year	MB	Mb/in2	MB/s	Fly Ht	Comments
IBM	RAMAC	RAMAC	1956	5	0.002	0.0088	800	First disk drive
IBM	1301	Advanced Disk File	1962	28	0.026	0.068	250	First disk drive with air bearing heads
IBM	1311	Low Cost File	1963	2.68	0.05	0.068	125	First disk drive with removable disk pack
IBM	2310	Ramkit	1965	1.024	0.111	0.155	125	First disk cartridge drive
IBM	2311		1965	7.25	0.111	0.156	125	First disk pack drive
IBM	2314		1966	29.2	0.22	0.3125	85	First disk drive with ferrite core heads
IBM	3330-1	Merlin	1971	100	0.776	0.806	50	First track-following servo system
IBM	3340	Winchester	1973	70	1.69	0.886	17	First disk drive with low mass heads, lubricated disks, sealed
IBM	43FD	Crystal	1976	0.568	0.163	0.031	0	First flexible disk drive with two-sided recording
Shugart Associates	SA400		1976	0.2188	0.248	0.031	0	First 5.25" flexible disk drive
IBM	3370	New File Project	1979	571.4	7.7	1.859	13	First disk drive with thin film heads
IBM	3310	Piccolo	1979	64.5	3.838	1.031	13	First 8" rigid disk drive
Seagate Technology	ST506		1980	5	1.96	0.625		First 5.25" rigid disk drive
Sony	OA-D30V		1981	0.4375	1.027	0.062	0	First 3.5" flexible disk drive
Fujitsu	F6421	Eagle	1981	446	11.3	1.859		First 10.5" rigid disk drive

Company	Model	Codename	Year					Notes
SyQuest Technology	SQ306F		1982	5	5.2	0.625		First 3.9" disk cartridge drive
Control Data	9715-160	FSD	1982	150	5.5	1.2		First 9" disk drive
Rodime	RO352		1983	10	6.6	0.625		First 3.5" rigid disk drive
Maxtor	XT-1140		1983	126	9.678	0.625		First 8 disk 5.25" disk drive with in-hub motor
DMA Systems	360		1984	10	6.7	0.625		First 5.25" disk cartridge drive
Hitachi	DK815-5		1984	460	12.9	1.8		First 8.8" disk drive
Quantum	Hard-card		1985	10.5	11.3	0.625		First disk drive mounted on card
Conner Peripherals	CP340		1986	40	21.4	1		First voice coil actuator 3.5" disk drive
Conner Peripherals	CP3022		1988	21	24.8	1.25		First one inch high 3.5" disk drive
PrairieTek	220		1988	20	25.9	0.625		First 2.5" disk drive
Hitachi	DKU-86I		1988	1890		3		First 9.5" disk drive
IBM	681	Redwing	1990	857	50.8	3	7.6	First disk drive to use MR heads and PRML
IBM	3390-3	Pacifica	1991	5676	89.5	4.2		First IBM mainframe drive with thin film disks
Integral Peripherals	1820	Mustang	1991	21.4	89.5	1.9		First 1.8" disk drive
Integral Peripherals	1841PA	Ranger	1992	42.5	140.9	2.2		First 1.8" PCMCIA card disk drive
Hewlett Packard	C3013A	Kittyhawk	1992	21.4	134.4	1		First 1.3" disk drive

(cont.)

Table 4–1 *Continued*

Vendor	Model	Name	Year	MB	Mb/in2	MB/s	Fly Ht	Comments
SyQuest Technology	SQ3105		1992	110	84	1.95		First 3.5" disk cartridge drive
IBM	3390-9	Eureka	1993	17028	268.6	3.9		First large diameter drive with MR heads
Seagate Technology	ST11950	Barracuda	1993	1689	159	7.1		First 7200 RPM disk drive
Hitachi	H-6588-314		1993	2920	119.2	4.2		First 6.5" disk drive
IBM	DPRA-21215	Presto	1995	1215	700.4	7.1		First 2.5" drive over 1 gigabyte
IBM	DSOA-21-9	Sonata	1995	1080	923.1	6.7		Highest areal density for any drive
SyQuest Technology	SQ1080		1995	80	230.4	1.3		First PCMCIA drive with removable disk
IBM	DLGA-23080	Legato	1996	3080	1358	10.0		Highest 1996 areal density for any drive
IBM	DGHS-318220	Marlin	1997	18,220	1253	22.4		First 18 gigabyte 3.5" server drive
IBM	DYKA-23240	Yukon	1997	3240	3123	11.7		Highest 1997 areal density for any drive
IBM	DTTA-351680	Titan	1997	16,800	2687	20.5		Highest 1997 areal density 3.5" disk drive First drive with GMR heads
Calluna Technology	CT-520RM		1997	520	709.7	6.4		First 520 MB 1.8" disk drive

Company	Model number	Model name	Year	Capacity (MB)			Description
Seagate Technology	ST19101	Cheetah 9	1997	9100	935.8	22.1	First 10,000 RPM disk drive
Seagate Technology	ST446452	Elite 47	1997	47,063	1491	23.0	Highest capacity disk drive in 1998
IBM	DBCA-206480	Biscayne	1998	6400	5693	14.8	Highest 1998 areal density for any drive
IBM	DCYA-214000	Cypress	1998	14,100	4976	15.7	Highest current capacity for 2.5" disk drive
Calluna Technology	CT-1040RM		1998	1040	1403	6.6	First 1 gigabyte 1.8" disk drive
Seagate Technology	ST118202	Cheetah 18	1998	18,200	1518	28.4	First 10,000 RPM drive with 3" disks
Hitachi	DK3E1T-91		1998	9200	2490	27.3	First 12,000 RPM disk drive
IBM		Micro-drive	1999	340		6.1	First 1" disk drive
Seagate Technology	ST150176	Barracuda 50	1999	50,000	3225	25.7	Highest capacity 3.5" disk drive announced to date
Hitachi	DK229A-10		1999	10,000	6299	16.6	Highest current areal density for any drive

Source: DISK/TREND, 1999.

ENABLING TECHNOLOGY FOR DISK DRIVE ADVANCEMENT

Form factor miniaturization is not, in and of itself, a meaningful gauge of disk drive advancement. What is important are the underlying technologies that enable more data to be stored and accessed reliably in the same recording area of the magnetic media.

In 1956, the areal density (a measurement of the amount of data that can be stored in a media recording area) of the RAMAC disk was 0.002 million bits per square inch (.002 Mb/inch^2). On February 3, 1999, Seagate Technology announced that it had achieved a world record in disk drive technology by demonstrating areal density of greater than 16 billion bits per square inch (16 Gb/in^2). This areal density was achieved using merged read-write giant magneto-resistive (GMR) heads and an ultra-smooth alloy media designed and manufactured by Seagate. According to the vendor, "Recording information at an areal density of greater than 16 Gb/in^2 would allow a user to store more than 2500 copies of Homer's *Iliad* in the space of a thumbprint."[4]

Historically, the hard disk industry had been increasing the areal density storage capacity of hard drives at a rate of roughly 27 percent per year. In recent years, the growth rate has increased to as much as 60 percent per year, resulting in a current generation of drives that store information in the 600 to 700 Mb/in^2 range. By the year 2000, according to Seagate Technology, the areal density capabilities are expected to reach 10 Gb/in^2.[5]

READ–WRITE HEADS

A major contributor to meeting the areal density objectives of disk makers is read–write head technology. The current generation of disk drive products uses an inductive recording head design, with the reading and writing of data accomplished through the interpretation of the inductive voltage produced when a permanent magnet—the disk platter—moves past a wire-wrapped magnetic core—the head.

To write information to a hard drive, an electrical current flowing through an inductive structure in the read–write head produces a magnetic pattern in the coating on the media's surface corresponding to the data being written. To be more specific, microscopic areas, called domains, in the magnetic coating on the media platter are oriented to positive or negative states (corresponding to binary 1s and 0s) by the action of the read–write head when data is recorded to the disk. To read data back from the disk, the read–write head converts these magnetic states into an electrical current, which is amplified and processed to reconstruct the stored data pattern.

Over a forty-year period, many variations and enhancements in inductive recording heads were introduced to improve areal density and other disk performance characteristics. Monolithic ferrite heads—composed a single block of ferrite, a magnetic ceramic material—were part of the earliest disk drives. Gradually, this design was improved through the use of "composite" heads, consisting primarily of nonmagnetic material with a small ferrite structure added. Building on composite designs were metal-in-gap, or MIG, heads, which featured very thin metal layers added inside a small gap in the head to improve magnetic performance. Finally, head technologies were enhanced through the application of thin-film technology.

With thin-film heads, the structures of an inductive head are deposited on a substrate material through a process closely resembling the manufacture of microchips. Thin-film technology allows head vendors to achieve much smaller physical dimensions and to control the fabrication process more exactly, both of which result in higher-performance head products.

More than 500 million thin-film heads were produced in 1997 to meet the enormous demands of the computer industry for data storage. However, industry sources claim that further improvements in processes by which thin-film inductive heads are manufactured, as well as refinements in the technology to support increasing areal density objectives, cannot be made cost-effectively. This prediction sent most major drive manufacturers back to their engineering departments in search of an alternative technology in the early 1990s. As the IBM microdrive and Seagate areal density records demonstrate, the new direction targeted by vendors is magnetoresistive (MR) head technology.

In a white paper on MR technology, disk maker Quantum Corporation summarized the situation succinctly. According to the author, the recognition of the need for a new head technology was

> spurred by a simple fact: As areal densities increase, the bit patterns recorded on the surface of the disk grow smaller, which weakens the signal generated by the head. That, in turn, makes it difficult for the disk drive's read channel electronics to identify the bit patterns that produced the signal.[6]

According to the white-paper authors, drive designers tried to circumvent the problem by harnessing several techniques to produce a stronger read signal. Techniques included flying the head closer to the disk and adding "turns" (the number of wire wraps coiled around the magnetic core of the head).

Reducing head-fly heights to better detect and read bit patterns was a typical enhancement method for a time. Shrinking the current fly heights of two to three microinches, however, seemed a dangerous proposition. In the words of one observer, it is already like flying a 747 jet at a very high speed just inches above the ground. Attention turned to the practicality of adding turns to the inductive head.

Adding turns increased both the read signal—a good thing—and the inductance of the head itself—a not-so-good thing. Limits exist in the amount of inductance a head can tolerate and still perform read–write operations reliably. This was especially true for thin-film heads, which used the same head element for both reading and writing data.

Disk drive engineers also examined the feasibility of increasing signal strength by increasing the linear speed at which recorded data bits moved under the head. With thin-film inductive heads, the faster the speed, the stronger the signal. However, faster rotational speeds also increased the data frequencies—the rate at which the magnetic transitions, which encode the data, pass the head—beyond the capabilities of inductance heads and channel electronics to handle.

Like Quantum, many other vendors, including Seagate Technology and IBM, came to the conclusion that MR technology held an answer. At the heart of the technology is a magnetoresistive material (a ferromagnetic alloy) whose electrical resistance changes in the presence of a magnetic field.[7] By applying such a material to a disk drive read head, it is possible to detect and read weaker magnetic fields generated by bits stored at greater areal densities.

The concept took shape in vendor laboratories. Soon, most major vendors had designs for MR heads that supported Gb/in^2 areal storage capacities on hard disks.

A signature of MR head technology is a "two-heads-in-one" design, claimed by Seagate Technology. Prepared as a combined head component, the read head element contains a small stripe of MR material. As it passes over the magnetic patterns on the disk, it senses the strength of the magnetic field and creates electrical pulses corresponding to the flux reversals.

Since MR heads cannot be used to write data to hard disk media, heads employing this technology have a second thin-film inductive element, closely spaced but separate from the MR read element. This element is used to write data bits onto the disk surface. According to

Seagate, "This fundamental change in read–write technology will enable advances [in areal density] capable of carrying the disc drive industry well into the 21st century."[8]

OTHER DRIVE IMPROVEMENTS

From the previous discussion of MR heads, it should be clear that the overall capacity of a drive depends on how densely information (i.e., bits) can be recorded on the disk media. This is a function of many components of a disk drive operating in concert with each other. Figure 4–1 depicts typical disk components.

One can more clearly see the relationships between components by considering the many factors that contribute to the areal density of a disk drive. The areal density of a drive, its bits per square inch, is calculated by taking the number of bits per inch (BPI) that can be written to and read from each track and multiplying that number by the number of tracks per inch (TPI) that can be "etched" on the disk media.

The bits per inch (BPI) possible on a disk depends on the read–write head, recording media, disk RPM, and the speed at which the electronics

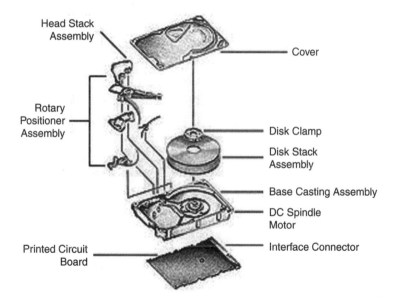

Figure 4–1   Components of a Hard Disk Drive. (*Source:* Quantum Corporation, Milpitas, CA.)

can accept bits. Similarly, tracks per inch is a function of the read–write head, recording media, the mechanical accuracy with which the head can be positioned on its actuator arm, and the ability of the disk to spin in a perfect circle. An increase in areal density is accomplished by increasing either or both BPI and TPI.

MR head technology enables the use of high areal density media by providing the capability to read information from more densely packed disks. To understand how increased storage densities are achieved requires more information about disk components.

Most of the current generation of hard disk drives feature two or more platters configured as a disk stack assembly with a common spindle. A spindle motor rotates the platters counter-clockwise at speeds of between 3600 to 10,000 revolutions per minute (RPM).

As previously mentioned, data stored on a disk is actually recorded as a magnetic pattern of bits in the magnetic coating on the platter. Read–write heads generate these patterns when writing data to the disk platters. When reading from the disk, the read–write head converts the stored magnetic patterns into electrical signals to represent stored data.

The writing of data to the disk platter occurs in accordance with the format geometry of the disk drive. Hard disk platters are divided into tracks, cylinders, and sectors to create a structure for data storage. A track is a concentric ring around the platter. In a disk stack assembly, tracks on each platter surface are identically positioned about 300 microinches apart. Identical tracks on multiple platters create cylinders.

Additionally, each track is subdivided into sectors that aid in expediting read–write operations. Sectors are given their identities during formatting when sector numbers are written to the beginning (prefix) and the end (suffix) of each sector. These identities consume hard disk space, accounting for the difference between a hard disk's formatted and unformatted capacity.

During write operations, data is recorded on the outermost track of all platters first. Once the outside track is filled with data, the heads move inward and begin writing on the next free track. This recording strategy greatly boosts performance since the read–write heads have considerable room to write data before they must be repositioned.

Since most hard disks enable the storage of data on both surfaces of a platter, drives are usually equipped with a read–write head for each platter face. Each head is held at an optimal head fly height by an actuator arm. Both the actuator arms and the read–write heads are moved over the platters by a positioning motor, which is, in turn, controlled by the disk controller.

The disk controller "knows" where to move heads to retrieve information by referring to the formatting information and sector addresses. Without formatting instructions, neither the controller nor the operating system would know where to store or retrieve data.

Early hard drive designs fixed a limit on the number of sectors per track. This, in turn, limited storage capacity since the number of sectors that would fit on the innermost track constrained the number of sectors that could be set for outer tracks that had a larger circumference. To address this issue, a number of vendors adopted a formatting technique called Multiple Zone Recording that allowed the number of sectors per track to be adjusted. By dividing the outer tracks into more sectors, data could be packed uniformly across the surface of a platter. Disk surfaces could be used more efficiently, and higher capacities could be achieved with fewer platters. With Multiple Zone Recording, effective storage capacity increased by as much as 25 percent. Additionally, disk-to-buffer transfer rates improved: With more bytes per track, data in the outer zones can be read at a faster rate.

The ability of read–write heads to fly directly to a new location once the CPU provides an address is central to its ability to randomly store and retrieve data. This capability, more than any other, explains the rapid displacement by hard disk of tape media as the primary computer storage technology after 1956.

Precise control of head positioning is a major factor in the areal density that can be achieved with disk drives. Drives are subject to many factors, including temperature-induced platter expansion and sudden movements that militate against precise head alignment. To counter these factors, most modern drives incorporate an electromechanical technique called embedded servo positioning.

Embedded servo positioning is a method that uses special data patterns, prerecorded on each track of a platter, to update drive electronics regarding head position. In fact, the strength of the signal is interpreted by the drive electronics to indicate how far the head has strayed from the center of the track. In response to the signals, the drive electronics adjust the position of the actuator motor, which repositions the heads until the maximum signal is from the bursts. This technology provides the most accurate, error-free, and cost-effective head positioning technique for small form factor drives.

Some difficulties have arisen when applying embedded servo technology in drives that use Multiple Zone Recording techniques. The varying number of sectors on tracks in different zones complicates the task of reading servo data. Quantum Corporation claims to have addressed this problem effectively by developing specialized servo feedback and controller ASICs that efficiently handle the task of separating the servo information from the user data.

The signals that a read–write head picks up from a platter are very weak. The read preamplifier and write driver circuit, typically mounted on a flexible circuit inside the hard disk assembly, increases the strength of the signals so that drive electronics can convert electrical impulses into digital signals. Drive electronics themselves are typically contained on a printed circuit board attached to the drive itself and include

- A digital signal processor (DSP) to convert the incoming electrical signals to digital signals
- Motor controllers for the spindle and actuator motors that ensure that the platters spin at the correct speed and that the actuator arms precisely position the read–write heads over the platter
- Interface electronics to communicate with the central processing unit of the system where the drive is installed

Many drives also have a microprocessor, ASICs, and memory chips on the printed circuit board to support functionality such as drive caching, embedded servo head positioning, and multiple zone recording. The circuit board also provides the physical connector for the drive, enabling the connection of the drive to the I/O bus of the system (PC, server, NAS, intelligent array, etc.) in which it is installed.

NEW INITIATIVES IN DRIVE TECHNOLOGY

Before examining interfaces, it is important to reiterate that the components of the hard drive, operating in concert, are what account for the capacity and much of the performance delivered by the drive itself. The storage manager needs to keep up-to-date with the initiatives of vendors that are constantly seeking to enhance disk drive components and to enable greater product performance and capacity.

For example, a number of vendors are working on ways to increase areal density by further reducing head fly heights. One approach, suggested by Seagate Technology's areal density record, is to create a smoother platter with fewer flaws that could cause a disk crash. Seagate used a homegrown alloy in its demonstration drive. Others are looking at alternative platter substrate materials, including glass, as a replacement for aluminum alloys in the disk substrate.

Another approach being pursued by Quantum and others is to eliminate flying heads altogether. Some researchers are looking at contact recording, a technology in which the head rides directly on the surface of the platter but does not generate friction that would quickly destroy both the head and platter surface at normal operating speeds. Liquid lubricants, "wet disk" technology, and low-friction, wear-resistant platter materials are all areas of research that may yield tomorrow's drive capacity breakthroughs.

PRML CHANNEL TECHNOLOGY AND ENHANCED MANAGEMENT FEATURES

Until the research initiatives above yield practical results, MR head technology will continue to provide a product development path for many vendors, supporting their efforts to deliver drives with increasing areal densities. Enhancing the capabilities of MR head technology is Partial Response Maximum Likelihood (PRML) technology. Briefly, PRML is a replacement for a read technique common in pre-MR head drives called peak detection. Peak detection, which served well for many years as a means for interpreting data from the read head, is less effective as bit density increases, read signal strength diminishes, and background noise begins to confound the drive electronics' efforts to distinguish individual bits by their voltage peaks.

PRML technology first converts the MR head's analog "read" signals into digital signals, then samples and filters the digital signals using sophisticated algorithms to eliminate noise and detect data bits. The result is that PRML can properly interpret more densely packed bits than can peak detection.

The efficiency of PRML, especially when used in drives with MR head technology, contributes directly to faster transfer of data as well as more accurate data. According to evaluations of PRML-enhanced MR head drives from Seagate, Quantum, and IBM, the technology is a must-have for anyone using high density drives.

Other enhancements being made to drives have little to do with areal density, but contribute a great deal to drive monitoring, management, and longevity. IBM and others have already begun to add temperature sensing capabilities to their drives that will allow storage managers to identify potentially damaging conditions before data is lost. IBM, Seagate, and others have also added head parking capabilities to the drives, ensuring that heads will not crash platters if power is discontinued suddenly.

Disk drives have been termed commodity products by some analysts, but they are in fact among the most complex components of the computing infrastructure. The definition of a reliable and manageable mass storage architecture begins with an understanding of drive technology. The enhancements and safeguards built into some disk drives by their manufacturers make them excellent choices to store mission critical information assets. Conversely, deploying disk drives that lack the features that contribute to stable, long-term storage can be an Achilles heel for any storage-management strategy.

INTERFACES: CONNECTING STORAGE FOR EFFICIENT USE

For a disk drive to become a part of a storage strategy, it must be interfaced to the bus of an intelligent system. In a "captive storage" configuration, the disk device is cabled directly to the I/O bus of a server, PC, or workstation. This is typically accomplished by cabling the bus connector on the drive's electronics (usually a printed circuit board mounted to the hard disk assembly) to a I/O interface adapter installed on the bus of the "host" system.

In such configurations, the drive is accessed by the CPU of the host as part of a cyclical process of CPU interrogations. I/O requests transfer along the bus of the host system and are passed through the I/O interface adapter to the drive electronics. Responses from the drive take the same path back to the CPU.

The performance of the disk drive itself is only one factor in the performance of I/O processing in this configuration. The speed of data transfers along the host system bus, which are determined by the bus width and cycle time, have the greatest effect on overall I/O performance. The bus cycle time is proportional to the number of "words" of data that can be transferred per second. Bus width determines the width of the transfers and whether words of data are transferred in a single cycle or multiple cycles.

Older system bus architectures had bus widths of 4 or 8 bits and transferred data at rates of up to 1 MB/s. Today, system bus architectures typically feature 16- or 32-bit bus widths and data transfers speeds of 10, 20, and up to 132 MB/s in Peripheral Components Interface (PCI) bus architectures are very possible. The next logical development for the server system bus is a 64-bit wide interface, which will allow drives and other peripherals to reach even higher data transfer speeds.

The rate at which the disk can transfer data onto a system bus is a function of its interface. A number of interfaces have been offered for hard disk drives over the years, but since the early 1990s, only two have emerged as industry leaders: IDE and SCSI.

ADVANCED TECHNOLOGY ATTACHMENT/INTELLIGENT DISK ELECTRONICS (ATA/IDE) INTERFACE

When the Intelligent Disk Electronics (IDE) interface, which is now called the Advanced Technology Attachment (ATA) interface, was first released, it was welcomed by PC end users as a "high-speed" replacement for a "motley crew" of competing interfaces for earlier PC disk drives. The ATA interface was designed specifically for disk drives and for Intel AT/IDE bus PCs and delivered disk buffer-to-host data transfer rates of 4.1 MB/s.

Over time, the ATA industry standards committee extended the capabilities of the interface to keep pace with other computer platform advancements. Among those improvements was the introduction of Fast ATA in late 1993, which supported an accelerated data transfer rate to capitalize on the new, faster, local bus architecture in Intel PCs.

Fast ATA enabled a disk drive to be connected directly to the CPU bus in the new Intel PC bus architecture, completely bypassing the slower expansion bus, held over from the days of the PC/AT. End users and the industry applauded the change, which provided for data transfer speeds limited only by the speed of the local bus and the disk drive itself. Approximately 90 percent of desktop PCs used ATA or Fast ATA disk interface adapters in 1996.

The applause, however, soon quieted as desktop system application requirements exceeded the support provided by Fast ATA. According to Quantum, an early supporter of Ultra ATA, end users of Fast ATA drive interfaces were encountering bottlenecks during sequential transfers of large files such as system boot-up, the loading of increasingly large programs, and especially desktop video applications. Stated simply, the faster internal transfer rates in newer disk drives combined with the poor utilization of the ATA bus by PC CPUs were causing disk drives to fill their data transfer buffers much faster than system CPUs could unload them. The result was I/O bottlenecking and a need for a data transfer rate doubling Fast ATA's burst data rate of 16.7 MB/s.

Recognizing that part of the bottleneck problem was beyond the ability of disk makers to control, Quantum and other vendors assisted in the refinement of the Fast ATA protocol within a set of known constraints. The Ultra ATA interface employed a new signaling and timing method that increased the speed of data buffer unloading and added a raft of additional features (plug-and-play support, CRC checking, etc.) Ultra ATA interface became an industry-recognized standard virtually overnight and drives tailored to the interface began shipping in late 1996 and early 1997.

While ATA continues to enjoy tremendous success in the PC market, the need for higher performance and multiple device support have driven many PC users to the Small Computer System Interface (SCSI). Today, SCSI is the second most common disk drive interface in Intel PCs, but it is the most widely used interface in both the workstation and server markets.

SMALL COMPUTER SYSTEM INTERFACE (SCSI)

Like ATA, SCSI is a family of protocols. The various implementations share in common a parallel interface definition used to connect host systems and peripheral devices, including disk drives. From a simple, twenty-page specification introduced to the American National Standards Institute (ANSI) in 1980, SCSI has grown into a 600-page specification for a veritable hydra of alternative implementations (see Table 4–2).

In 1985, the handwriting was already on the wall. Just as the first SCSI draft was being finalized as an ANSI standard, a group of manufacturers approached the X3T9.2 Task Group seeking to increase the mandatory requirements of SCSI and define further features for direct-access devices. Rather than delay the first iteration of the standard, the Task Group formed an ad hoc group to develop a working paper that was eventually called the Common Command Set (CCS).

The main problem with SCSI-1, according to some observers, was that the standard was too permissive, and allowed too many "vendor specific" options. It was feared that variations in implementations would result in serious compatibility problems between products from different vendors. The Common Command Set (CCS) was proposed in an effort to address compatibility problems before they created havoc, mainly for tape and disk drive products. It became a de facto component of the SCSI-1 standard for anyone serious about deploying the interface.

SCSI-1 and the CCS defined a number of basic command operations, an 8-bit wide bus with transfer rates of up to 5 MB/s, and a cable with several connector options. According to the initial "CCS-enhanced" SCSI-1 standard, up to seven devices could be connected to the bus, not

Table 4–2   SCSI Standards and Drafts and Key Features

SCSI Type	Bus Speed, Mb/s Max	Bus Width Bits	Maximum Bus Length, Meters [1]			Maximum Device Support
			Single-ended	Diff.	LVD	
SCSI-1[2]	5	8	6	25	[3]	8
Fast SCSI[2]	10	8	3	25	[3]	8
Fast Wide SCSI	20	16	3	25	[3]	16
Ultra SCSI[2]	20	8	1.5	25	[3]	8
Ultra SCSI[2]	20	8	3	25	[3]	4
Wide Ultra SCSI	40	16	—	25	[3]	16
Wide Ultra SCSI	40	16	1.5	—	—	8
Wide Ultra SCSI	40	16	3	—	—	4
Ultra2 SCSI[2,4]	40	8	[4]	25	12	8
Wide Ultra2 SCSI[4]	80	16	[4]	25	12	16

Notes:

[1] The listed maximum bus lengths may be exceeded in point-to-point and engineered applications.

[2] Use of the word "narrow", preceding SCSI, Ultra SCSI, or Ultra2 SCSI is optional.

[3] LVD was not defined in the original SCSI standards for this speed. If all devices on the bus support LVD, then 12-meter operation is possible at this speed. However, if any device on the bus is single-ended only, then the entire bus switches to single-ended mode and the distances in the single-ended column apply.

[4] Single-ended is not defined at Ultra2 speeds.

Source: SCSI Trade Association, San Francisco, CA.

including the host system. Asynchronous data transfers between the host computer and a given peripheral could occur in at speeds up to 2 MB/s, while synchronous transfers were supported at speeds of up to 5 MB/s.

Work on the new SCSI-2 standard began while ANSI was preparing to publish the standard it had ratified in 1986 (ANSI X3.131-1986, commonly referred to as SCSI-1). The original premise of SCSI-2 was to create a superset of SCSI-1 and the CCS. Later, the scope of the effort expanded and by the time that the draft standard for SCSI-2 was submitted for ANSI approval in 1990, the document had grown to more than double the size of SCSI-1. (The final draft was nearly 600 pages when issued in 1993.)

Nevertheless, SCSI-2 advanced several meaningful improvements to the SCSI-1 standard, including:

- Higher performance
- Increased data transfer rates
- Lower overhead
- New definitions for single-ended and differential interfaces
- New bus definitions
- Support for new peripheral types
- Support for new functions such as command queuing and disconnect
- Enhanced reliability through the implementation of functions such as parity and error checking and arbitration

Backward compatibility was a touchstone of SCSI-2 standards development, as with later iterations of the standard. "Single-ended" SCSI devices defined in SCSI-2 were backward compatible with single-ended devices conforming to the SCSI-1 standard in order to facilitate a smooth transition between the standards. Single-ended refers to an implementation of signal transmission wiring in which all data and handshaking signals to draw necessary current through common ground.

The SCSI-2 specification also defined a differential signaling implementation that was not backwards compatible with SCSI-1, but which did promise improvements such as noise reduction and longer bus cable lengths of up to 25 meters.

SCSI-2 also established two interface variations that have become synonymous with the standard.

- Fast SCSI-2 allows faster bus timing (10 MHz instead of 5 MHz in SCSI-1). The theoretical result on an 8-bit wide bus is a data transfer speed of up to 10 MB/s.
- Fast Wide SCSI-2, another variant, enables still faster data transfer rates through the use of 16-bit or 32-bit cables. Transfer speeds of up to 20 MB/s for a 16-bit bus, or 40 MB/s for a 32-bit bus are theoretically possible. Up to fifteen devices may be connected concurrently to the host under this configuration.

SCSI-2 became an official ANSI standard in 1994 (ANSI X3.131-1994)—almost a year after development had begun on a SCSI-3 standard.

Before one has a bout of déjà vu, it should be pointed out that SCSI-3 was actually intended to work on a number of separate enhancements to SCSI-2 rather than provide an entirely new standard. With SCSI-3, the draft standard was broken up from a single document into several smaller documents focused on different objectives. This was done, in part, to facilitate efforts to specify SCSI implementations over different physical transport layers, including Fibre Channel and IBM's Serial Storage Architecture. It was also believed that breaking the standards development effort into smaller projects would result in faster completion. Subprojects included

- *SCSI-3 Parallel Interface (SPI):* This project sought to further define the mechanical attributes, timing, phases, and electrical parameters of the parallel cable. Some of the electrical and cable parameters were tightened and improved from SCSI-2 specifications.
- *SCSI-3 Interlock Protocol (SIP):* New messages were added to the existing definition.
- *SCSI-3 Architectural Model (SAM):* This project endeavored to define a common set of functions, services, and definitions to explain a physical transport handles commands, data, and status exchanges between two devices. Error handling and queuing are also described.

The balance of the projects dealt with refining specific command sets associated with disk, tape, RAID, and CD-ROM devices, and with the use of SCSI over different physical transports including Fibre Channel, IEEE 1394 High Speed Serial Bus ("Firewire"), and the Serial Storage Architecture from IBM.

ULTRA SCSI

Significant outcomes of SCSI-3 development efforts included industry proposals for "narrow" and "wide" Ultra SCSI implementations. In 1996, Quantum Corporation termed Ultra SCSI "the next major performance advancement to the Small Computer System Interface and . . . a lower cost alternative to serial [interfaces]." According to the vendor, Ultra SCSI's proposed doubling of data transfer rates from the specified limits of 10 MB/s for Fast SCSI-2 and 20 MB/s for Fast Wide SCSI-2 promised to "create the bandwidth necessary to support the data intensive applications to be used in the coming generations of servers, workstations, and high-end personal computers."[9]

Even as Quantum's prognostications were hitting the trade press, Ultra2 SCSI proposals began to be heard. Ultra2 and Wide Ultra2 draft specifications were driven by growing interest in differential signaling technology and increased popularity of serial interfaces, such as Fibre Channel, as a potential replacement for SCSI.

The use of low voltage differentials (LVD) to optimize bus through-put had been addressed initially in SCSI-2. With Ultra2 SCSI, LVD trans-ceivers were being applied to the task of providing better use of SCSI bus media. Testing suggested that LVD-enhanced interfaces could deliver data transfer speeds of 80 MB/s—doubling the fastest SCSI-2 transfer speed of 40 MB/s. Increased bandwidth translated to improved server performance as large files are moved between devices quickly and effort-lessly.

As vendors readied Ultra2 devices for market, yet another pro-posal—Ultra160/m—was placed before the ANSI standards T10 Commit-tee by seven vendors "representing a broad cross-section of the computer and storage industry." Like its predecessor, Ultra160m again doubled the data transfer speed possible with the SCSI interface. Ultra160/m raised the bar to 160 MB/s by furthering the use of LVD, combined with im-proved timing techniques, cyclical redundancy checking (CRC), and "do-main validation" (i.e., verification of network integrity on the SCSI bus).

Taken together with the earlier SCSI interface alternatives, Ultra160/m SCSI helps to complete a picture of SCSI as a robust, evolu-tionary storage bus technology with adequate room for growth to meet the storage scalability requirements of many companies into the next mil-lennium (see Figure 4–2). However, SCSI does have its limitations and it presently confronts challenges for hegemony in the multidrive interface market from two rival interface standards. One is IBM's Serial Storage Ar-chitecture (SSA). The other is an open standard gaining particular atten-tion because of its use in storage area networks: Fibre Channel.

SERIAL STORAGE ARCHITECTURE (SSA)

According to IBM, the present growth of data bases and data-intensive applications within corporations signals a need for a storage technology that is robust, reliable, and scalable. Acting on this premise, the company introduced one of the first serial storage technologies in 1992, called Serial Storage Architecture (SSA). Products based on the technology began ship-ping in 1995, while IBM engaged in efforts to have the technology ap-proved as an ANSI standard.

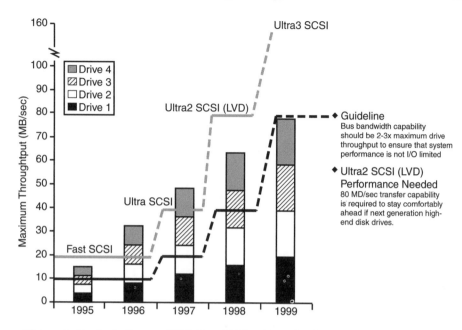

Figure 4–2   Evolutionary SCSI Capabilities Growth. (*Source:* Quantum Corporation, Milipitas, CA.)

By November 1996, ANSI ratified proposed standards covering the SSA Physical Layer (ANSI X3.293-1996), Upper Level Protocol—SCSI-2 Mapping (ANSI X3.294-1996), and Transport Layer (ANSI X3.295-1996). By February 1997, the success of SSA appeared to be confirmed with an announcement by IBM that more than one petabyte of Serial Storage Architecture (SSA) products had been shipped to customers in only 18 months.[10] Additional components of SSA were made ANSI standards in December of the same year (see Table 4–3).

SSA is the first serial storage technology to achieve such market acceptance, and IBM has leveraged its early success to argue the case for deploying SSA as a replacement for SCSI. The company also insists that its serial interface offers advantages that make it superior even to emerging Fibre Channel interfaces for connecting storage devices, storage subsystems, servers and workstations.

SSA provides serial disk interface using bidirectional cabling to establish a drive "loop." Data and commands sent from the SSA adapter can travel in either direction around the loop to their destination devices, or nodes. If interruptions are detected in the loop (e.g., a hard disk node

Table 4–3 ANSI Standards for SSA

STANDARD	TITLE	SUMMARY	APPROVAL DATE
ANSI X3.293-1996	Information Technology- Serial Storage Architecture- Physical Layer 1 (SSA-PH1)	Defines the physical layer of the Serial Storage Architecture (SSA). SSA defines a serial interface hierarchy to be used for purposes within its distance and performance characteristics, including, but not limited to, storage subsystems. This standard is intended to be used with an upper layer protocol (e.g., SCSI-2 Protocol (SSA-S2P)) and a transport layer (e.g., SSA Transport Layer 1 (SSA-TL1)). A major goal of the SSA-PH1 standard is to define a physical layer acceptable to device vendors, looking for an evolution from parallel SCSI, and systems designers looking for opportunities to more fully exploit the capabilities inherent to a serial bus.	11/29/96
ANSI X3.294-1996	Information Technology- Serial Storage Architecture- SCSI-2 Protocol (SSA-S2P)	Describes an upper-level protocol of Serial Storage Architecture. SSA-S2P is a mapping of the existing SCSI-2 protocol, described in American National Standard for Information Systems—Small Computer Systems Interface-2 (SCSI-2), ANSI X3.131-1994, with extensions to map SCSI-2 to the SSA serial link.	11/29/96
ANSI X3.295-1996	Information Technology- Serial Storage Architecture- Transport Layer 1 (SSA-TL1)	Defines the transport layer of the Serial Architecture (SSA). SSA defines a serial interface hierarchy to be used for purposes within its distance and performance characteristics, including, but not limited to, storage subsystems. This standard is intended to be used with an upper layer protocol (e.g., SCSI-2 Protocol (SSA-S2p)) and a physical layer (e.g., SSA Physical Layer 1 (SSA-PH1)). A major goal of the SSA-TL1 standard is to define a transport layer acceptable to vendors, looking for an evolution from parallel SCSI,	11/29/96

and systems designers looking for opportunities to more fully exploit the capabilities inherent to a serial bus.

| ANSI NCITS 307-1997 | Information Technology-Serial Storage Architecture-Physical Layer 2 (SSA-PH2) | The SSA-PH2 standard defines a physical layer that support the SSA transport layer 2 (see SSA-TL2) and any protocols supported by SSA-TL2. The goals of SSA-PH2 are: (a) extend the cable distance; (b) copper cable operation at 40 MB/s; (c) full duplex operation to achieve an aggregate 80 MB/s between two ports; (d) and other capabilities that fit within the scope of SSA-PH2 that may be proposed during the development phase by the participants in the project. This document defines the physical layer 2 (SSA-PH2) of the Serial Storage Architecture (SSA). SSA defines a serial interface hierarchy to be used for purposes within its distance and performance characteristics, including but not limited to storage subsystems. This standard is intended to be used with an upper layer protocol [e.g., SCSI-2 Protocol (SSA-S2P) or SCSI-3 Protocol (SSA-S3P)] and a transport layer [e.g., SSA Transport Layer 2 (SSA-TL2)]. A major goal of the SSA-PH2 standard is to define a physical layer acceptable to device vendors, looking for an evolution from parallel SCSI or SSA-PH1, and systems designers looking for opportunities to more fully exploit the capabilities inherent to a serial bus. | 12/2/97 |
| ANSI NCITS 308-1997 | Information Technology-Serial Storage Architecture-Transport Layer 2 (SSA-TL2) | Defines a transport layer of the Serial Storage Architecture (SSA) that runs SSA-S2P and SSA-S3P (BSR NCITS 309) while running on SSA-PH2 (BSR NCITS 307). The goals of SSA-TL2 are to: (a) provide an Extended Distance Option; (b) provide support for higher data rates in the physical layer 2 (SSA-PH2); (c) enhance packet formats and addressing methods; (d) define a transport layer acceptable to vendors looking for an evolution from parallel SCSI and systems | 12/12/97 |

(cont.)

Table 4–3 *Continued*

STANDARD	TITLE	SUMMARY	APPROVAL DATE
		designers looking for opportunities to more fully exploit the capabilities inherent to a serial bus; and (e) cover other capabilities that fit within the scope of SSA-TL2 that may be proposed during the development phase by the participants in the project.	
ANSI NCITS 309-1997	Information Technology- Serial Storage Architecture- SCSI-3 Protocol	Defines a protocol layer of the Serial Storage Architecture (SSA) that runs on SSA-TL2 (BSR NCITS 308) while running on SSA-PH2 (BSR NCITS 307). The goals of SSA-S3P are to: (a) map the SAM services and terminology to SSA; (b) define the data field format of the SSA-S3P SMSs; (c) support for dual port and alternate pathing; (d) provide support for auto-sense; (e) provide support for third-party operations; and (f) cover other capabilities that fit within the scope of SSA-S3P that may be proposed during the development phase by the participants in the project.	12/1/97

fails), SSA can automatically reconfigure the system to maintain connectivity with other nodes until the interruption is repaired.

SSA's loop configuration enables the addition and replacement of disk drives without interrupting normal operations. Users can configure the SSA array initially with only a few hard disk drives, then add more drives to the loop when needed. SSA hard disk drives are described as self-configuring. This capability obviates the addressing limitations and complexity of SCSI drive installation.

An SSA Adapter supports up to 192 hot-swappable hard disk drives per system. If desired, drives can be preconfigured for use as "installed spares" to be used by the host only if a failure occurs. Drives with capacities of 4.51 GB, 9.1 GB, and 18.2 GB capacities are available for use in SSA arrays. Storage capacities of up to 291 GB per tower or drawer or 1.752 TB per host adapter are possible (see Figure 4–3).

SSA provides for a maximum distance of 25 meters between hard disk drives and server host(s). Cabling consists of thin, low-cost copper wires. With a fiber optic extender, arrays can be positioned up to 2.4 kilometers distant from the server, if desired. SSA arrays can also be attached to up to four concurrently attached SCSI-based servers via an Ultra SCSI Host to SSA Loop Attachment. The host's standard SCSI driver and hard-

Figure 4.3   IBM 7133 Serial Disk Systems. (*Source:* IBM.)

ware are used to make the attachment, so no modification to server hardware or software is required.

The SSA subsystem supports both RAID and non-RAID configurations. Disks can be mirrored across servers to provide a hedge against unplanned downtime and data loss. According to the vendor, the subsystem provides up to 80 MB/s of maximum throughput, which is described as sustained data rates as high as 60 MB/s in non-RAID mode and 35 MB/s in RAID mode.

IBM positions SSA as an open, standards-based product and emphasizes the support that SSA subsystems offer for attachment to a broad range of system hosts. Critics point to the fact that both the array and disk drives bear the IBM moniker to suggest that this is IBM's proprietary architecture. While SSA has experienced substantial success, concerns about its proprietary nature do not appear to have been offset by ANSI standard approvals. SSA represents a very small segment of an interface technology market that is dominated by variants of SCSI.

As a serial storage architecture, SSA does offer many advantages over even Ultra SCSI. Tests of Ultra SCSI and SSA published on the IBM Storage Division website show that SSA clearly provides greater performance under identical loads. An SSA array also scales better than an Ultra SCSI, providing consistently high performance numbers while Ultra SCSI performance declines. IBM claims, based on the tests, that SSA's serial bus has between 18 and 33 percent less overhead than SCSI's parallel bus and that this is a major factor in the superior SSA performance numbers.

Head-to-head comparisons must top out, however, at sixteen drives, which is the maximum number of drives that can be connected to an Ultra SCSI bus. SSA's connectivity capabilities exceed this number by a factor of 10.

SSA, says IBM's marketing literature, "addresses SCSI's throughput bottleneck with its fundamental building block—the SSA connection, or node." An SSA node (an IBM SSA disk drive) has two ports that can each be used to carry on two 20 MB/s conversations at once (one inbound and one outbound), thereby enabling a total of 80 MB/s of throughput. By contrast, a single SCSI bus, "can easily be saturated by just one high-performance disk running at 12 MB/s."

Even though SSA is an entirely different architecture than SCSI, it still maps the SCSI command set, observes the vendor, so existing applications can migrate seamlessly to SSA-based subsystems. This saves the user the time and cost of rewriting applications while giving applications a performance boost.

Table 4–4 provides IBM's suggested review criteria for prospective customers who are evaluating SSA and other drive interface technologies.

Table 4–4 A Comparison of Interface Technologies

	EIDE/Ultra ATA	SCSI	SSA
Environment	Offers low cost and performance equal to SCSI in most desktop and mobile environments.	Delivers excellent performance for network computers with Intel-based processors. Data-intensive applications and large numbers of users in LAN environments.	An ideal solution for PC servers: combination of high storage capacity, data protection, extensibility, and affordability.
Performance	In a single-user environment, EIDE (Ultra ATA) and SCSI perform comparably.	A SCSI interface offers the performance edge, especially when coupled with Windows NT.	Greatly reduces the risk of downtime from communication failure. 80MB/s maximum throughput ensures data transfer rates will not be a problem.
Price	Generally least expensive. The controller is standard on the system board chipset.	Drives are a little more expensive for the same capacity and rotational speed as EIDE. May also require a SCSI adapter.	
Expandability	Can support high hard disk drive capacity, as well as CD-ROM and tape devices—up to four devices in all.	Holds more than 9 GB. Offers high capacity and performance for multiple hard disk drives, a wide variety of devices and long cable connectors for more convenient attachment of external devices. Backward-compatible.	Adapter supports allow for up to 192 hot-swappable hard disk drives per system. Hard disk drives are available in 4.51 and 9.1GB sizes.
Ease of Installation	Although most PCs ship with an EIDE (Ultra ATA) interface, ensure that your system's EIDE (Ultra ATA) interface and BIOS support all the functions of the new hard disk drive.	You may need to install a SCSI adapter.	SSA makes hard disk drives self-configuring, avoiding SCSI addressing limitations and complexity.

Source: IBM.

FIBRE CHANNEL

SSA, like SCSI, are more than drive interface technologies. They are also an interconnect specifications for mass storage disk arrays. Fibre Channel is another serial interface/interconnect technology.

Fibre Channel is a 1 GB/s data transfer interface that maps several common transport protocols including IP and SCSI, allowing it to merge high-speed I/O and networking functionality in a single connectivity technology. Like SSA, it is a standard ratified by ANSI (ANSI X.3230-1994 is the core standard) and operates over copper and fiber optic cabling at distances of up to 10 kilometers.

However, Fibre Channel is different from SSA in its support of multiple interoperable topologies, including point-to-point, arbitrated-loop, and switching. Additionally, Fibre Channel offers several qualities of service for network optimization. With its large packet sizes, Fibre Channel is ideal for storage, video, graphic, and mass data transfer applications.

Fibre Channel's developers have achieved the majority of their original goals in defining the technology, which included:

- Performance from 266 MB/s to over 4 GB/s
- Support for distances up to 10 kilometers
- Small connectors
- High-bandwidth utilization with distance insensitivity
- Greater connectivity than existing multidrop channels
- Broad availability (i.e., standard components)
- Support for multiple cost/performance levels, from small systems to supercomputers
- The ability to carry multiple existing interface command sets, including Internet Protocol (IP), SCSI, IPI, HIPPI-FP, and audio/video

Today, Fibre Channel stands out as a leading contender to become the dominant channel/network standard. As a drive interface technology, it combines high speeds with SCSI-3 command language support. As a network interface, it provides the required connectivity, distance, and protocol multiplexing. It also supports traditional channel features for simplicity, repeatable performance, and guaranteed delivery. And Fibre Channel also works as a generic transport mechanism.

As a true channel/network integration, Fibre Channel supports an active, intelligent interconnection among devices. All that a Fibre Channel port must do is to manage a point-to-point connection. The transmission is isolated from the control protocol, so point-to-point links, arbitrated loops, and switched topologies are used to meet the specific needs of an application. The fabric is self-managing. Nodes do not need station management, which greatly simplifies implementation.

Most current thinking in storage area networking involves the deployment of Fibre Channel between end stations (hosts and devices) in an arbitrated loop configuration or a switched environment containing several loops. Fibre Channel-Arbitrated Loop (FC-AL) was developed with peripheral connectivity in mind. It natively maps SCSI (as SCSI FCP), making it an ideal technology for high speed I/O connectivity. Native Fibre Channel Arbitrated Loop (FC-AL) disk drives will allow storage applications to take full advantage of Fibre Channel's gigabaud bandwidth, passing SCSI data directly onto the channel with access to multiple servers or nodes.

FC-AL supports 127-node addressability and 10 KM cabling ranges between nodes. The peak transfer rate of a Fibre Channel port is 1.062 GB/s, or 100 Mbytes/second, which is the link rate of the full-speed interface. A Fibre Channel adapter can burst a 2048-byte frame at the link rate.

IBM discriminates SSA from Fibre Channel by pointing to SSA's greater cost efficiency and comparable performance. This view is echoed by SSA advocates, who have raised several points intended to sell their preferred serial interface.

One often voiced concern is that the performance of a Fibre Channel-Arbitrated Loop may fall short of expectations because of Arbitration. FC-AL developers promise bandwidth of 200 MB/s, while current implementations of SSA provide bandwidth of 80 MB/s. This fact would appear to favor FC-AL.

However, in actual field implementations, SSA advocates hypothesize, data transfer rates for FC-AL are likely to be considerably slower than 200 MB/s because of the technology's loop arbitration scheme. Arbitration effectively cancels out any advantage arising from its larger theoretical bandwidth.

This concern has been voiced since the earliest days of Fibre Channel development. It was even on the minds of International Data Corporation analysts in the mid-1990s, "One must fully consider the impact of various overheads and arbitration schemes. As such, SSA implementations will frequently outperform FC-AL, depending upon workload and configurations."[11]

Fibre Channel-Arbitrated Loop, as the name suggests, is an all-or-nothing or first-come, first-served technology. The arbitrated loop is "owned" by the end station initiating a transfer until the transfer is complete. Others must wait in a queue until the communication is complete. By contrast, SSA provides four, full-duplex, frame-multiplexed, channels. In the field, SSA advocates charge, the greater the number of disks in an SSA loop, the better the array actually performs. In a simple, unswitched FC-AL implementation, the more disks in a loop, the greater the possibility of an I/O bottleneck.

The answer to this concern, according to Fibre Channel enthusiasts, is twofold. The larger frame sizes supported by Fibre Channel and the greater bandwidth it offers makes loop arbitration less of an issue. If more data can be moved faster, enabling shorter communications sessions, then greater loop availability should be the result.

An alternative is to use a switched fabric, rather than a straight loop or hub-attached loop topology. Switching between multiple loops is a straightforward means for increasing the number of devices that can be included in a Fibre Channel network—well beyond the specified loop limits.

An SSA connection consists of two ports conducting four concurrent conversations at 20 MB/s, thereby generating a total bandwidth of 80 MB/s. The topology is a series of point-to-point links, with ports connected between nodes by three-way routers. Point-to-point duplex connections establish the means for every SSA node to communicate with every other SSA node in either direction on the loop. This topology accounts for the high reliability of SSA systems. By contrast, critics say, a FC-AL topology provides opportunities for single points of failure.

Fibre Channel backers respond that FC-AL can be made fault tolerant by cabling two fully independent, redundant loops. This cabling scheme provides two independent paths for data with fully redundant hardware. Most disk drives and disk arrays targeted for high availability environments have dual ports specifically for the purpose. Alternatively, cabling an arbitrated loop through a hub or concentrator will isolate/protect the rest of the nodes on the loop from the failure of an individual node.

Fibre Channel nodes can be directly connected to one another in a point-to-point topology or can be cabled through a concentrator/hub or switch. Because each Fibre Channel node acts as a repeater for every other node on a loop, one down or disconnected node can take the entire loop down. Concentrators, with their ability to automatically bypass a node that has gone out of service, are an essential availability tool in many Fibre Channel networks.

For disk subsystems and RAID subsystems connected to a arbitrated loop, the Fibre Channel Association, an industry group backing the technology, is strongly recommending that each device or node within the subsystem have a port bypass circuit associated with it so that any node may be bypassed and allow for "hot swapping" of a device. With the use of the PBC, if a device failure occurs, the failed device can be bypassed automatically, eliminating any disruption of data transfers or data integrity.

Many have observed that Fibre Channel is a relatively unique application of networking technology to peripherals and thus presents a new challenge for IT professionals concerned with storage. While connecting peripherals through a concentrator is a somewhat foreign concept, with the networking of peripherals comes the need for protecting the availability of networked peripherals. This can require redundancy or the use of concentrators in peripheral networks.

THINKING OUTSIDE THE BOX

Because of their roles as both device interfaces and peripheral networking technologies, Fibre Channel, SSA, and SCSI force server administrators to "think outside the box"—to develop a view of storage that goes beyond the disk drive installed on a ribbon cable in the cabinet of a general purpose server. According to many analysts, while captive storage will likely remain a part of the corporate computing landscape for the foreseeable future, new mass storage arrays and storage area networks will become increasingly prevalent as companies seek to build a more manageable enterprise storage architecture. The next chapter examines array technologies in greater detail.

ENDNOTES

1. Magnetic tape was also an early form of sequential data storage and has persisted to the present as a preferred medium for archival and backup data storage.
2. Quantum Corporation, *Storage Basics*, Milpitas, CA, 1998.
3. "IBM Introduces World's Smallest Hard Disk Drive," IBM News Release, September 9, 1998.
4. "Data Storage Breakthrough: Seagate Demonstrates World's Highest Disc Drive Areal Density," Seagate Technology Press Release, February 3, 1999.
5. "MR Heads: The Next Step in Capacity and Performance," Seagate Technology White Paper, 1998.

6. "Magnetoresistive Head Technology: A Quantum White Paper," Quantum Corporation, 1998.

7. This phenomenon was discovered by Lord Kelvin in 1857 and today is called the anisotropic magnetoresistance (AMR) effect.

8. "MR Heads: The Next Step in Capacity and Performance," Seagate Technology White Paper, op. cit.

9. "Ultra SCSI White Paper," Quantum Corporation, Milpitas, CA, 1996.

10. "IBM Reaches One Petabyte Milestone in Serial Storage Architecture Shipments," IBM Press Release, San Jose, CA, February 25, 1997.

11. "The Case for Serial Interfaces," International Data Corporation, Framingham, MA, September 1995.

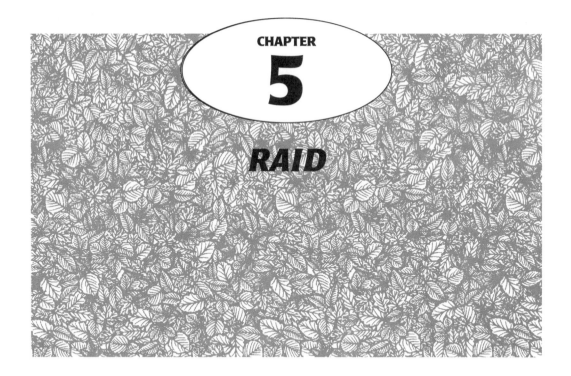

Al Loundsbury, Director of Technology Strategies for integrator, MCI Systemhouse, is concerned about the vulnerability of businesses that depend on information technology to potentially disastrous interruptions. Says the integrator, "Business continuance is no longer about access to a network or server. It is about access to information."[1]

Loundsbury goes on to say, "The problem is that people still think about business continuance in tactical terms. They haven't developed a strategic view of IT in which storage is more than something that is tethered to a server on a network. They think of business continuance in terms of replacing failed servers and repairing networks, not about designing a storage infrastructure that will ensure continued access to information."

The integrator echoes the view of many in the industry when he acknowledges that he is "warming up to Storage Area Networks very quickly." SANs, together with stand-alone storage arrays and network-attached storage devices, constitute a significant departure from the traditional view of storage as a server component. These technologies are enablers of a storage-centric approach to corporate IT that underscores the primacy of information rather than processing. In practical terms, these technologies create new opportunities for assuring business continuation in the event of a system or network failure.

DISK STORAGE SUBSYSTEMS: CUTTING THE TETHER

In a very real sense, intelligent storage devices, NAS devices, and SANs are the latest manifestation of trends that have been building since distributed computers were first interconnected by local area networks and became a platform for more and more mission-critical business applications. A brief historical survey helps to illustrate this point.

Since the mid-1980s, the dominant model for increasing online storage has been to add disk drives—either to server or workstation drive bays directly, or by installing additional drives in an external "array"[2] cabinet. In the latter case, the external array is "captive." That is, the array is tethered to an I/O bus adapter installed on the server or workstation bus, thereby extending the I/O channel of the host system to the array's bus.

Among the earliest implementations of the array approach to increasing storage was the JBOD array. In a JBOD, an acronym for "just a bunch of disks," multiple disk drives were attached along an array bus in an external cabinet. Once the array bus was tethered to the host system I/O adapter, each drive in the array appeared as a separate volume to the operating system of the host system.

By the late 1980s, storage architectures were beset by new demands from corporate IT organizations. JBODs and other early arrays enabled an increase in the numbers of disk drives and the total capacity of storage available to a system host, but they contributed little to offsetting the cost of storage—by enhancing its performance or ensuring its availability. With emerging needs for storage performance and reliability in mind, scientists at the University of California, Berkeley, sought to develop a new array architecture. They set forth a description of their solution, called Redundant Array of Inexpensive Disks (RAID), in a 1987 whitepaper.[3]

The RAID concept originally comprised a cluster of small inexpensive disks that appeared to the system host as a single, large, and expensive disk drive (SLED). Initial tests of this configuration demonstrated that a RAID array could deliver the same or better performance than a traditional individual hard disk drive.

However, simple RAIDs also manifested a fundamental problem associated with all arrays to that point. Increasing the number of drives decreased the mean time before failure (MTBF) characteristics of the overall array. In other words, by multiplying the number of drives comprising a single logical volume, the probability of a single drive-related outage increased.

In response to this concern, the Berkeley scientists proposed five levels or methods of RAID to provide a balance of performance and data protection. These methods involved techniques for providing redundancy (through mirroring and/or enhanced error checking) and performance (through disk striping).

RAID LEVELS

It is valuable to review the original RAID specifications in order to sift through the confusing descriptions that pervade much of present-day RAID product marketing literature. The original five RAID levels articulated in the RAID white paper were:

- Simple disk mirroring (RAID 1)
- Mirroring augmented with Hamming Error Correction Code (ECC) (RAID 2)
- Byte striping with dedicated parity (RAID 3)
- Block striping with dedicated parity (RAID 4)
- Block striping with distributed parity (RAID 5)

Some commentators add RAID 0 to the above list as one of the original RAID specifications, while others protest its inclusion. RAID 0 arrays are characterized by disk striping, a technique for spreading data across multiple disk drives and enabling the fast retrieval of data from disk storage, but make no provisions for array resilience. While RAID 0 is not, strictly speaking, a RAID level (RAID levels are, by definition, methods used to bolster array reliability), it may be thought of as the prototype array to which various RAID methods are applied. With respect to RAID purists, RAID 0 is included in this discussion to facilitate the understanding of other concepts that are central to "true" RAID architectures.

As depicted in Figure 5–1, a RAID 0 array is essentially a collection of striped disks lacking any particular fault tolerance enhancements. Data transfers from the host system are split up by an array controller ("controller" as used here may refer to host-based RAID software working in connection with a host I/O adapter, a server bus-based RAID-enabled

RAID 0

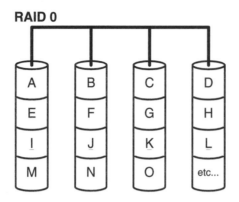

Figure 5–1   RAID 0.

adapter, or an external RAID controller—see below), then written into segments called "stripes," across each disk drive. *Stripe size*, a common descriptor of RAID array products, refers to the smallest block of data that can be read from or written to a physical drive. Many RAID array controllers provide end users with the ability to tune block sizes to better meet the typical access patterns of the applications that use the array.

Stripe size is often confused with another common descriptor used with RAID arrays: *stripe width*. Stripe width refers to the number of physical drives used for a stripe. As a rule, the wider the stripe, the better the performance.

In a RAID 0 array, short data transfers may require only one or two disk drives, while longer transfers may require and use a larger drive group. Reads and writes to the drives can be performed either in parallel or independently of each other, allowing for concurrency of disk accesses. With many RAID 0 implementations, several small transfers can be processed simultaneously to realize an increase in I/O rate, since each group of disk drives can be working on a different I/O operation concurrently.

Generally, when I/O operations involve mixed-length data transfers from the host, all required disk drives must be available to execute the longer transfers. Longer data transfers to an array are placed in a queue until all disk drives become available to process them.

By spreading the I/O load across many channels and drives, read performance in a RAID 0 array is greatly enhanced. Another performance enhancement is derived from the low overhead of RAID 0 in processing I/O operations. With RAID 0, there is no error checking or data duplication during drive operation. Thus, full use can be made of the I/O channel for data reads and writes.

This same performance advantage also accounts for the main drawback of RAID 0 arrays: They lack fault tolerance. Because of their nonredundant striping, the failure of just one drive will result in all data in an array being lost. For this reason, most experts agree that RAID 0 should never be entrusted with mission critical data.

RAID 1

This conclusion was also reached by the Berkeley scientists, who first sought to address storage fault tolerance through the mirroring and duplexing techniques incorporated in RAID 1 (see Figure 5–2). *Disk mirroring*, as the name implies, involves the copying of data on one disk drive to another disk drive. There are a number of ways to accomplish disk mirroring, but all entail the processing of data transfers and subsequent writing of original and copied data to (at least) two separate disks, predefined as a mirrored pair.

Duplexing refers to the capability of the RAID 1 configuration to read and write data to the mirrored drive pair concurrently. This is typically accomplished using two I/O connections between the host system and the disk array. The highest performance level is achieved when the mirrored disk pair can be accessed concurrently for I/O operations.

RAID 1 configurations are highly fault tolerant. With RAID 1 arrays, I/O activity can continue uninterrupted in the event of a drive failure by shifting read and write operations to the mirrored drive. This mode of op-

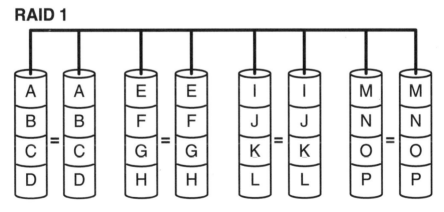

Figure 5–2   RAID 1.

eration can continue until the faulty drive is replaced, data is copied from the mirror to the new drive, and the two drives comprising the mirrored pair are resynchronized.

In some array products, drive replacement and resynchronization require a temporary shutdown and restart of the array. Other products permit "hot swapping" of drives for online recovery, and duplicate not only drives themselves, but also the bus and other array components, including power supplies and cooling systems. Vendors tout these features as additional safeguards against unplanned downtime and guarantors of high availability.

An obvious disadvantage of disk mirroring is the cost of duplicating the disk drives, which makes the effective cost per megabyte in RAID 1 arrays twice that of non-mirrored solutions. (When RAID 1 was proposed in 1987, storage was substantially more expensive on a per megabyte basis than it is today. However, price remains a frequently cited criticism of RAID 1 products by many vendors.)

Additionally, with most RAID 1 arrays, error checking and correction (ECC) is used to guarantee the accuracy of data writes to mirrored disk pairs. Since ECC is required for data writes to both original and mirrored media, RAID 1 with ECC has the highest processing overhead of all RAID types, compromising its performance in some cases.

Additionally, most implementations of RAID 1 are software-based—that is, RAID functionality is provided by software operating in host operating system environment. Software-based RAID is often criticized for the load it places on server CPUs and for its tendency to provide degraded throughput during periods of high activity.

From a design standpoint, RAID 1 configurations also impose a drive size limitation. While a RAID 1 array can consist of multiple pairs of mirrored drives of varying capacities, the drives making up a specific pair must be of the same capacity. If drives within a mirrored pair have different capacities, the smaller capacity drive dictates the maximum capacity of both mirrored drives.

For all of its potential drawbacks, RAID 1 remains an array architecture used by many companies that seek total redundancy in disk storage. Improvements in the performance of the server bus and CPU components, as well as declining per megabyte storage media costs, are often cited as contributors to the continuation of RAID 1. Moreover, some vendors have integrated RAID 1 and other RAID levels to create hybrid RAID definitions that capitalize on the strengths of the architecture, while minimizing some of its limitations (see below).

RAID 2

In contrast to RAID 1, which persists in part because of technology advances, RAID 2 has virtually disappeared for almost the same reason. RAID 2 was originally conceived as another method to ensure that data was protected in the event that drives in the array ever failed. This level builds a fault tolerance solution around the Hamming error correction code, which is used as a means of maintaining data integrity.

As depicted in Figure 5–3, a special checksum algorithm is used to tabulate the numerical values of data stored on specific blocks in the virtual drive (the collection of disks in a RAID array constitutes a single drive volume or virtual drive). The checksum is then appended to the end of the data block for verification of data integrity when needed.

When data is read from the RAID 2 drive, ECC tabulations are computed again, and stored checksums are compared against the most recent tabulations. If the checksums match, the data is determined to be valid. If the checksums differ, the lost data can be reconstituted using the first or earlier checksum as a reference point.

At the time that RAID 2 was developed, its capability to deliver "on the fly" data error correction and its suitability to applications requiring extremely high data transfer rates were highly touted. However, the technology of disk drives, especially the increased use of embedded error cor-

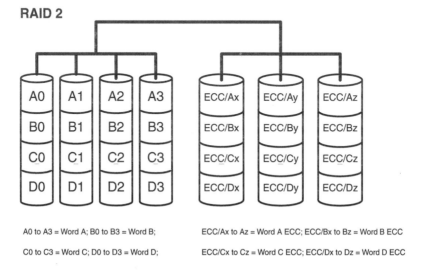

RAID 2

A0 to A3 = Word A; B0 to B3 = Word B;   ECC/Ax to Az = Word A ECC; ECC/Bx to Bz = Word B ECC

C0 to C3 = Word C; D0 to D3 = Word D;   ECC/Cx to Cz = Word C ECC; ECC/Dx to Dz = Word D ECC

Figure 5–3   RAID 2.

rection by disk drive manufacturers, soon caught up with RAID 2 and mitigated the need for the technology. Some commentators observe that the technology was never as efficient as RAID 3 and was largely superseded by the next RAID level.

RAID 3

RAID 3, like its predecessor, uses a separate data protection disk drive to store error checking data. Like RAID 0, however, it uses disk striping to achieve a high data transfer rate (see Figure 5–4).

With a RAID 3 implementation, application data is striped across all disks except for the data protection drive (sometimes called the parity drive). The parity drive stores parity information, used to maintain data integrity across all drives in the subsystem. The parity drive is itself striped, and each stripe stores parity information pertaining to corresponding application data stripes on the data disks.

In operation, each data transfer is split by the array controller and distributed on a byte-by-byte basis across all of the data disks in the array. The spindles in all disks are synchronized so that all read–write heads in the array are reading or writing on the same data sector in parallel. This configuration enables very high data transfer performance. However, the actual transfer rate achieved depends on several factors, including host bus adapter bandwidth and data patterns themselves.

It is important to note that every write operation involves all disk drives in the array, since new encoded data must be written to the data

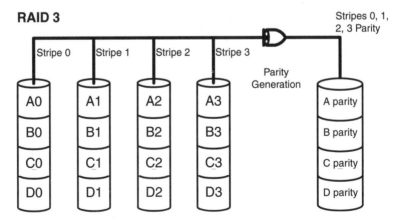

Figure 5–4   RAID 3.

protection drive at the same time as production data is written to the data disks. Reads also involve all disks in the array.

Should a data disk fail, the array controller reconstructs missing information normally stored on the failed drive using an encoded form of the data stored on the parity disk. The array can continue to operate in this mode until a second disk fails—an event that designers regard as having a low probability of occurrence.

Some arrays offer hot swappable drives, while others must be quiesced and powered down before a failed drive can be replaced. In many cases, installing a new functional drive will automatically trigger striping and data restoral processes.

The cost of this RAID approach, in terms of usable megabytes of storage, is a function of the ratio of application data disks and encoded data disks that cannot be used for application data storage. Simply put, there is a trade-off in RAID 3 between the aggregate capacity of all disk drives and the amount of storage set aside to ensure storage fault tolerance. In most applications, the cost of reserving storage for data protection represents an acceptable trade-off for increased availability and uptime.

RAID 4

RAID 4 (see Figure 5–5) is similar in concept to RAID 3, but is tailored to shorter transaction-oriented files, rather than large sequential files. RAID 4 has a larger stripe width, usually of two blocks, which allows the disks to be operated much more independently than in RAID 3. This capability

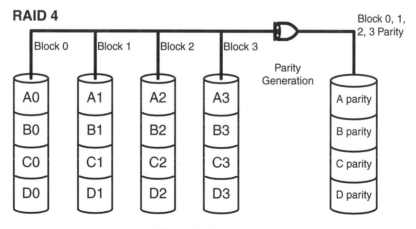

Figure 5–5 RAID 4.

reveals the intent of designers to sacrifice some of RAID 3's data through-put performance in favor of faster data access in read-intensive applications like database queries.

Critics observe that RAID 4 architecture manifests an inherent bottleneck on the parity drive. The parity encoding scheme is quite complex and creates the worst write performance of any RAID level.

It is clear that RAID 4 was aimed at read-intensive applications that had little need for write operation performance, such as historical or archival databases. This, in turn, has limited RAID 4 deployment in conventional business settings.

As previously stated, RAID 4 provides excellent read, but poor write, performance in the storage of smaller files. RAID 4 write bottlenecks derive from the concentration of error checking information onto a single parity drive. While this approach worked well in RAID 3, with its parallel drive architecture and longer file lengths, it became a hindrance in RAID 4, where disks operated independently and file sizes were smaller.

RAID 5

RAID 5 (see Figure 5–6) addresses the write bottleneck in RAID 4 by eliminating the parity drive altogether. Instead, parity block information is distributed across what were previously regarded as application data disks.

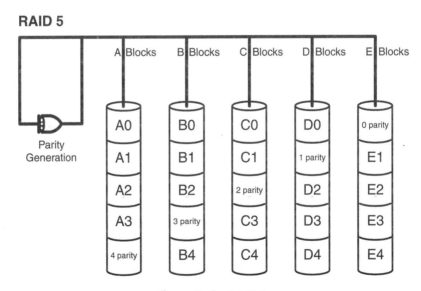

Figure 5–6   RAID 5.

It should be kept in mind that the RAID 5 parity encoding scheme is the same as is used in RAID 3 and 4 and is intended to enable the system to recover any lost data should a single drive fail. This is possible only if the parity information for a particular disk drive is not stored together with the application data on the same disk drive. Thus, with RAID 5, parity information for drive number one is stored in a parity stripe on drive number two. Number two's parity information is stored in a parity stripe on drive number three, and so forth.

This technique eliminates the parity drive bottleneck in RAID 4. In a RAID 5 array, all of the drives in the array assume write activity responsibilities and including parity information writes. This technique improves overall throughput in comparison with RAID 4 arrays.

Challenges to write performance remain in RAID 5, however, depending on the application involved. In a write operation involving a small block of data, multiple disk drives need to be accessed, new parity code calculated, and new code information rewritten to the parity stripe corresponding to the application data storage stripe of the application disk. The extra processing required to calculate and record parity information on writes represents extra overhead and incurs a performance penalty.

With some RAID 5 products, storage parameters can be tuned to better meet the needs of the applications that use it. Increasing the RAID 5 stripe size, for example, increases the array's ability to handle concurrent small reads, but reduces write performance. Decreasing the RAID 5 stripe size increases data throughput rates by increasing the likelihood of completing writes across all disks as a single event, but reduces the ability of the array to handle small reads concurrently. Determining what mix of parameters best meet the I/O requirements of applications using the storage array will probably require close monitoring over time and an iterative process of trial and error.

Since many applications generate data transfers of mixed I/O sizes, and generate different I/O profiles at differing times, there is no single RAID 5 storage parameter profile guaranteed to optimize application performance. With RAID 5, performance is as much a function of effective storage management as it is a matter of array queuing, data patterns, access types and other technical parameters.

Still, RAID 5 remains the most popular RAID implementation in current business technology environments. As with other RAID levels, the failure of a disk drive in a RAID 5 array can be handled expeditiously while the system remains in operation.

Beyond RAID 5

Over the years, RAID 3 has been characterized as well-suited to storage scenarios involving large data transfers, while RAID 5 was deemed more appropriate for data storage in online transaction processing (OLTP) environments. As OLTP has evolved, however, manifesting an increasing volume of write operations and widely varying data transfer sizes, this convenient industry guideline has been called into question.

In the last several years, additional RAID "levels" have appeared from the vendor community. The objective, to provide greater business continuity through improved storage fault tolerance, has remained the same, but the RAID designs have become somewhat more rarified—and, in some cases, very proprietary. Separating valid RAID levels from market-speak is an increasingly difficult task.

One RAID "level" that has become popular within vendor marketing literature was previously addressed. RAID 0, which entails disk striping with no provision for resilience, is not actually a RAID level at all.

In modern marketing parlance, RAID 0 is a kind of shorthand used to describe a high-throughput storage array devoid of error correction schemes, parity disks or parity stripes, or other overhead-producing characteristics. RAID 0 is an icon symbolizing perfect storage accessed at channel speeds.

A second RAID "level" sometimes discussed in the marketing literature and trade press is 0+1 or RAID 10. This is a hybrid of RAID 0 (striping) and RAID 1 (mirroring) and involves the creation of two or more pairs of mirrored arrays (see Figure 5–7). Put another way, RAID 10 is a striped array whose segments are not disks, but RAID 1 arrays.

Because disks are striped and no parity calculations are used, write operations can be very efficient. Some overhead accrues to mirroring, of course, but the overall performance is well above that of RAID 1.

The drawbacks of RAID 10 are its expense and limited scalability. Moreover, all of the drives in the RAID 10 array must operate in parallel, which can degrade performance with longer read–write operations.

Another RAID hybrid is RAID 5+3 or 53 (see Figure 5–8), which some critics argue should be termed RAID 03 given its use of striping and the fact that its segments are themselves RAID 3 arrays. Presumably, the selection of 5 and 3 was intended by a savvy marketeer as a means of capitalizing on the two most popular traditional RAID definitions.

RAID 53 proponents argue that this hybrid delivers high data transfer performance in a RAID 3 fault-tolerant configuration. High data transfer rates are obtained in part due to RAID 3 array segments, while

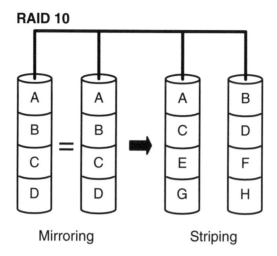

Figure 5–7   RAID 10.

high I/O rates for small requests are achieved based largely on RAID 0 striping.

The disadvantages of current RAID 53-based solutions are that they are very expensive to implement, requiring disk spindle synchronization available in only a few disk drive products. Moreover, byte striping results in poor disk utilization. The overhead associated with fault tolerance for this architecture is about the same as that of RAID 3 generally.

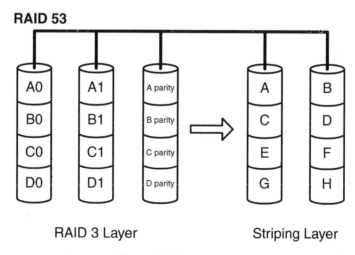

Figure 5–8   RAID 53.

Another RAID level that builds upon the technologies articulated in the 1987 RAID white paper is RAID 6 (see Figure 5–9). RAID 6, which was proposed by the Berkeley team in 1989, is characterized as an extension of RAID 5's independent disks and distributed parity scheme. The "extension" offered in RAID 6 consists of a second distributed parity scheme that, proponents claim, improves the fault tolerance of the array.

In RAID 6, data is striped on a block level across a set of drives (as in RAID 5) and a second set of parity calculation results is computed and written across all the drives as well. Proponents claim that this configuration provides extremely high fault tolerance by embuing the array with a capability to sustain multiple simultaneous drive failures and to continue operating. Disadvantages of this approach include a complex controller design, significant controller overhead to compute parity addresses, and very poor write performance.

RAID 6 has not shown up in actual commercial products. However, a number of vendors of large arrays have used RAID 6 as a jumping off point in the development of their own proprietary products. The literature from Storage Technology (StorageTek) describing their Iceberg array (which is also vended as IBM's RAMAC 2 Virtual Storage Server) provides an example.

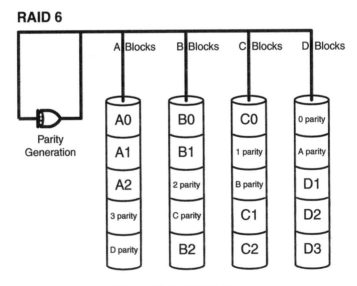

Figure 5–9   RAID 6.

The StorageTek white paper refers to the Berkeley RAID 6 definition as the basis for the RAID architecture implemented by Iceberg: "The architecture of Iceberg contains elements of the RAID 6 definition, but differs from the Berkeley RAID taxonomy by including advances specifically addressing RAID's performance penalties in commercial transaction processing environments."[4] Later in the same document, the author writes that the Iceberg product

> also implements a second extension to the Berkeley RAID 6 definition. With RAID 6, three disk failures within an array group cause data to become unavailable. To minimize the exposure to this failure scenario, Iceberg uses global disk sparing and dynamic drive reconstruction to recover a failed disk to a spare disk before a second failure is likely to occur. When a disk fails, Iceberg automatically activates a global spare and begins data reconstruction via RAID 6 dual parity. Using RAID 6 dual parity for the reconstruction process, allows data reconstruction to be completed successfully even if non-recoverable read errors are encountered during the recovery process.[5]

As an "enterprise-class" storage array product, Iceberg and similar standalone arrays (see Table 5–1) do not necessarily conform to traditional RAID definitions. RAID levels were defined by the original Berkeley group with cost, performance, and availability in mind. As larger array products are developed to meet the needs of "enterprise" storage, often

Table 5–1   A Sampling of "Enterprise-Class" Storage Arrays

Vendor/ Product	Platforms	Maximum Cache	Online Copy Software	Concurrent I/O Slots
Hitachi Data Systems/ 7700E	S/390, Unix, Windows NT	10G bytes	Shadow Image Copy (S/390 only)	32
EMC/ Symmetrix 3700	S/390, Unix, NT	4G bytes	TimeFinder (S/390, NT, Unix)	32
IBM/Ramac Virtual Array	S/390 (and Unix & NT when using the IBM Cross Platform Extension)	3G bytes	Snapshot Copy (S/390 only, unless using Cross Platform Extension)	16

the equipment cost criteria articulated by the RAID white paper authors is of less importance than the purported benefits of the storage platform to the company.[6] This is also reflected by the substitution made by many vendors of the word "independent" for "inexpensive" in the RAID acronym: Redundant Array of Inexpensive Disks.

Another example of a proprietary "RAID level" aimed at enterprise storage array class of products is RAID 7® (see Figure 5–10) from Storage Computer Corporation. RAID 7 has been described in the trade press as

> an independent striped array that reportedly achieves very high performance through extensive parallel processing, a high-speed central processor, a real-time operating system, 'advanced' caching techniques and algorithms, parity overhead minimization schemes, 'unique' memory management technology, and a no-wait asynchronous architecture. [RAID 7 arrays also use] some undisclosed 'technology and techniques' that aren't explained in the various patents. In other words, [Storage Computer] seems to be simultaneously tweaking every element it can in the entire RAID system to try to eliminate I/O bottlenecks.[7]

In this proprietary RAID implementation, all I/O transfers are asynchronous, independently controlled and cached, including host interface transfers. Reads and writes are centrally cached via a high speed, internal cache, data transfer X-bus. Error correction code storage is provided via a dedicated parity drive, which can be located on any channel, and parity generation is integrated into the cache memory. A fully implemented, process-oriented, real-time operating system is resident on an embedded array control microprocessor. Multiple attached drive devices can be configured as hot standbys.

RAID 7 ®

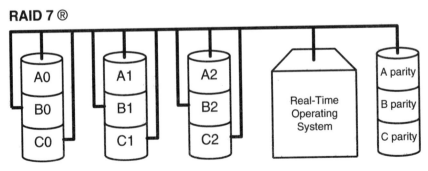

Figure 5–10   RAID 7® by Storage Computer Corporation.

According to the vendor, overall write performance is 25 to 90 percent better than single spindle performance and 1.5 to 6 times better than other RAID array levels. Small reads in a multiuser environment have a very high cache hit rate, resulting in near zero access times. Other claims include:

- Write performance improves with an increase in the number of drives in the array.
- Access times decrease with each increase in the number of actuators in the array.
- No extra data transfers are required for parity manipulation.

Critics of proprietary technology RAIDs point to a number of short-comings of RAID 7, as well. Predictably, most have to do with cost, both of the technology itself and of the proprietary nature of the product. RAID 7 arrays constitute a one-vendor proprietary solution that is not user serviceable. The arrays are covered by a very short warranty, require an expensive uninterruptible power supply to safeguard cache operations, and have an extremely high cost per megabyte of storage.

Other observers see the RAID 7 array as a sign of things to come, "There's little doubt that future RAID systems from other vendors will similarly improve performance, perhaps using some or all of these same techniques."[8]

IMPLEMENTING RAID

Since they were first articulated, RAID levels have been applied to the task of meeting storage requirements at workstation, LAN-based server, and enterprise levels. Over the same period of time, at least three implementation models have evolved that are summarized in Table 5–2.

Software RAID

The first RAIDs were software-based. As depicted in Figure 5–11, RAID functionality was controlled by the host system's central processing unit. A standard host interface adapter (typically a SCSI board) was used to provide an I/O bus for transmitting read and write commands and controlling the operation of the attached disk drives.

As a rule, software RAIDs use more host system resources than hardware-based RAIDs. This fact becomes more evident as more disk ports

Table 5–2   RAID Implementations

TYPE	DESCRIPTION	ADVANTAGES
Software-based **RAID**	Included in NOSs such as NetWare and Windows NT®. All **RAID** functions are handled by the host CPU.	Low price; only requires a standard I/O adapter card.
Bus-based RAID adapter/controller	Processor-intensive **RAID** operations are offloaded from host CPU to enhance performance.	Data protection and performance benefits of **RAID** with connectivity benefits of a standard I/O adapter card. Delivers more robust fault-tolerant features and increased performance.
External **RAID** controller	**RAID** functions are done on a microprocessor located in the external **RAID** storage subsystem. Connects to server via a standard SCSI or fibre channel card.	OS independent; works with any OS. Can build super high-capacity storage systems for high-end servers.

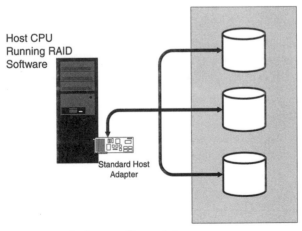

Host CPU
Running RAID
Software

Standard Host
Adapter

Software-Based Array

Figure 5–11   Software RAID.

and channels are required by the I/O processing load, and I/O processing itself impacts other aspects of host CPU performance.

Parity processing, an extremely resource-intensive task, is generally avoided in software RAID implementations. By contrast, software RAID is often a preferred implementation for RAID 1, which uses mirroring as a guarantor of data protection.

While software RAID is often touted as less expensive than hardware RAID because it does not require a dedicated RAID controller, there are numerous offsets to this cost argument. Since RAID 1 mirroring is the preferred method to achieve fault tolerance in software RAIDs, the expense for extra disks and the lack of "hot swap" capabilities (typical of software RAIDs generally) are cost multipliers in software RAIDs.

Despite these drawbacks, software RAIDs continue to enjoy support from major operating system (OS) and network operating system (NOS) vendors. For example, Microsoft Windows NT® provides software support for two fault-tolerant disk configurations: mirror sets and stripe sets with parity.

Similarly, Sun Microsystems provides the Online Disk Suite for use in implementing RAID 0 or RAID 1 arrays using the internal host processor. The UNIX system vendor takes advantage of the large cache memory available in its workstations and servers to obtain acceptable performance from software RAIDs.

Even with operating system support, some desirable RAID functions can only be efficiently provided through hardware-based RAID configurations. There are basically two types of hardware RAIDs: those that utilize a host-based bus adapter and those that utilize an external array controller.

Host-Based Adapter RAID

An alternative to software-based RAID is the bus adapter-based RAID configuration depicted in Figure 5–12.

A RAID adapter/controller plugs into a host bus slot and offloads some or all of the I/O commands and RAID operations to one or more secondary processors. The specifications of RAID adapters in vendor product literature suggest some of their typical components and functionality:

- Read–write cache memories, often with battery backup, enable the fault tolerant storage of I/O commands on the controller, freeing up the host CPU to process other interrupts.

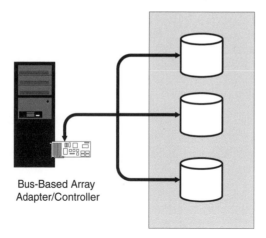

Bus-Based Array
Adapter/Controller

Figure 5–12   Bus Adapter Hardware-Based RAID.

- Interface connectors support the connection of array drives via an interface, such as SCSI or Fibre Channel.
- RAID software, embedded in the board, determines the level of RAID that the board can support across the array.
- Some boards offer subprocessors that are used to perform parity calculations, offloading this processing-intensive task from the host CPU.

From the above list, it can be surmised that bus-based RAID adapters vary from each other based on storage capacity support, data transfer rate support, scalability support, RAID level support, and interface support. They also vary in terms of caching capability and method.

The goal of disk caching, generally, is to increase system performance. This is accomplished by using fast memory to store disk I/O temporarily, rather of waiting for mechanical, and much slower, disk drives to process I/O instructions.

In software RAIDs, main system memory and cache memory on the disk itself (a small memory mounted to the disk electronic circuit board) are typically used as I/O caches. Serial I/O instructions are stored at various levels of this combined cache and are unloaded (flushed) and processed as quickly as possible by the drives in the array. Ideally, caches are balanced and fill as quickly as they unload, optimizing performance.

When this is not the case, for any of a number of reasons, I/O binding occurs and system performance is degraded.

With bus-based RAID adapters, I/O binding issues are addressed through the use of intelligent caching. "Intelligent," in this context, refers to the use of a coprocessor in conjunction with cache memory on the RAID adapter. In operation, the host system memory used for I/O caching is unloaded (flushed) at bus speed to the I/O cache on the RAID adapter. Most RAID adapters feature write-back caching. That is, the completion of a write request is signaled as soon as the data is transferred to the RAID adapter cache, enabling the flushing (and reuse) of the system I/O memory. Actual processing of the write requests stored in the RAID cache then occurs at disk processing speeds.

RAID adapter cache operations may be further optimized by the on-board coprocessor. Adaptec, for example, refers to its intelligent co-processing of I/O cache as "elevator sorted write back." In addition to signaling I/O write completion to the host I/O memory, the coprocessor on the Adaptec RAID adapter also sorts and organizes I/O requests to minimize disk read–write head movement and to make disk operations smoother and faster. This elevator sorting, says the vendor, eliminates much of the "head thrashing" commonly associated with disk-intensive applications and, in some cases, reduces average write times by 50 percent.[9]

In addition to elevator sorting, the coprocessor may also help to boost I/O performance by "prefetching" sequential blocks of data. Prefetching anticipates read requests for data sets by the operating system. When the operating system requests a specific data block, the coprocessor fulfills the request and orders the reading the next sequential block of data into its cache in advance of an anticipated follow-up request from the operating system. Called "look-ahead reads," this intelligent manipulation of cache operations can improve the read speeds of RAIDs.

In addition to cache manipulation, RAID adapter intelligence can also be applied to such functions as parity checking, fail-over management, and automatic resynchronization of replaced drives in the RAID array. Cost originally limited the use of bus-based RAID adapters to mid- to high-end servers. However, lower-cost adapters are now available that are tailored specifically to entry-level server network applications.

Adaptec product literature explains that bus-based array adapters/controllers provide connectivity functions that are similar to standard host I/O adapters. Their placement on a host PCI bus, enables them to "provide the highest performance of all [host-based] array types."[10] However, the company's "Array Guide" goes on further to say, "As newer, high-end technologies such as Fibre Channel become readily available, the performance advantage of bus-based arrays compared to external array controller solutions may diminish."[11]

External Controller-Based RAID

RAID arrays based on external RAID controllers have been available in the "enterprise storage" space (e.g., mainframes and other extremely large and centralized servers) for many years, but nearly always at a prohibitive cost. In the mid-1990s, these products began to enter the price range of the "open systems" market.

As depicted in Figure 5–13, this variant of hardware RAID implementation enables not only the logical, but also the physical, untethering of storage I/O processing from the host system. A storage array platform equipped with an external, intelligent, RAID controller has a dedicated, on-board CPU in addition to subprocessors to calculate parity, map the locations of files, and provide I/O caching. Unlike internal, bus-based adapter/controllers, which are operating system dependent and rely on software device drivers to access and configure the RAID array, an array that uses an external RAID controller is independent of the host operating system.

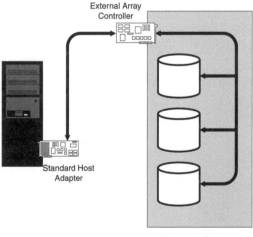

External Array
Controller

Standard Host
Adapter

External Storage
Subsystem

Figure 5–13 External Controller
Hardware-Based RAID.

To a host system, communicating with the array via a standard I/O interface adapter, the array resembles a virtual large disk drive. If the external controller fails, generally the host system does not need to be shut down and restarted to make repairs, as in the case of bus-based adapters. Arrays with external controllers are also generally easier to scale than software or bus-based hardware controlled RAIDs, can achieve capacities in excess of a terabyte, and are easier to configure for drive failover and other fault tolerance characteristics.

STAND-ALONE ARRAYS

Intelligent external array controllers are enablers of the current generation of stand-alone storage platforms. They provide a "bridge" between single- or multiple-device channels on the array and one or more I/O interfaces (typically supplied through SCSI or Fibre Channel I/O adapter cards) from servers that share the storage platform. With increasing frequency, arrays with external controllers are deployed to provide shared storage in networks of Intel-based and UNIX-based servers or in clustered server environments. They are the precursors to new storage architectures (see below) such as storage area networks and network-attached storage, and may well become the building blocks of future storage infrastructures.

According to DISK/TREND, Inc., the most popular type of disk drive array configuration is the complete subsystem, sold by the originating manufacturer with disk drives and all other necessary equipment, ready to install. Complete subsystems generated 47.1 percent of all disk drive array shipments in 1997, growing to a projected 52.3 percent share in 2001. The analyst further reports that bus-based arrays held 44.1 percent of the 1997 array total, but are expected to decline. The 2001 share for board-level array controllers is forecasted to decline to 40.1 percent as some disk drive arrays designed for personal computer networks start to use low-cost array chip sets that can be mounted on system motherboards, eliminating the need for separate array controller boards. Software-based array products are expected to hold 7.7 percent of the 2001 market, with usage concentrated in mirrored disk, or RAID-1, applications.[12]

Figure 5–14 provides DISK/TREND's forecast for disk array revenues, sorted by target environments, through the year 2001. The greatest growth is expected in the network/midrange systems market segment.

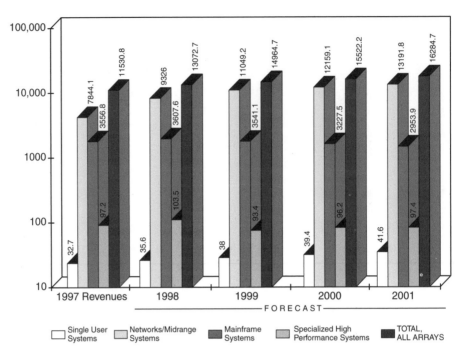

Figure 5–14 Disk Array Revenues Forecast. (*Source:* DISK/TREND, Inc., Mountain View, CA.)

RAID OBJECTIVES SCORECARD

As suggested by the DISK/TREND findings, the original objectives of the RAID authors have remained largely intact and have been expanded upon over time. RAID advocates originally sought to improve data availability by increasing the fault tolerance of disk arrays and by minimizing the amount of downtime required to recover data and to replace damaged disks.

Data Availability

Today's RAID arrays have increased data availability beyond the expectations of the RAID authors—partly as a result of the successful application of RAID levels, but also as a consequence of improvements in array component technologies themselves. Today's RAIDs are often constructed using disk drives that comply with ANSI's Self Monitoring, Analysis, and Reporting Technology (S.M.A.R.T.) specification, or similar drive health monitoring and reporting standards, such as those articulated by IBM or Compaq Computer Corporation.[13] Other components of the RAID array enclosure also feature compliance with standards, such as ANSI's SCSI Enclosure Services (SES[14]) specification, the Intelligent Platform Management Interface (IPMI[15]), and/or, the SCSI Accessed Fault Tolerant Enclosures specification (SAF-TE[16]).

Taken together, these standards enable the reporting of status and the alarming of out-of-threshold conditions in array components and provide a means establishing a program of proactive array maintenance. Companies, such as Vitesse Semiconductor Corporation,[17] have implemented standards-based monitoring systems on silicon for use with external RAID controllers and arrays.

As a further demonstration of the continued primacy of fault tolerance considerations in modern RAIDs, one need look no further than the RAID Advisory Board (RAB), an industry consortium concerned with RAID technology. For the past several years, the RAB has been working to develop a new taxonomy for array classification using fault tolerance characteristics as the primary criterion.

Concerned about the popular misconception that the higher the number of the RAID level, the more fault-tolerant the array, the RAID Advisory Board has introduced the concept of Extended Data Availability and Protection (EDAP) capabilities. The Board is seeking, though somewhat unsuccessfully according to informed observers,[18] to re-classify RAID product offerings from vendors according to the amount of EDAP capability they offer, rather than their RAID level.

While the EDAP-based taxonomy may be too complicated for industrywide adoption (and this is the kindest criticism that has been offered by the many detractors of the approach), it does underscore the point that the fault-tolerance objective remains an important one in RAID product acquisition. One vendor offers a partial RAID controller feature table (see Table 5–3) to assist customers in identifying and selecting the appropriate controller technologies to meet fault-tolerance requirements.

Table 5–3 suggests that storage availability remains the primary objective of RAID storage. Through the implementation of RAID mirroring and parity checking schemes, supplemented by fault tolerance technologies, this objective has been met by the majority RAID array products marketed today. Future enhancements in the areas of security, virus prevention, and so on will only extend the level of protection offered by this thriving storage architecture.

Table 5–3   Partial RAID Controller Feature List

Feature	Benefit and Advantage	Disadvantage
Hot Spare Drives	Ability to recover from single disk failure	Makes drive work but is not used
Warm Spare Drives	Ability to recover from single disk failure	Delay in recovering because the drive must be started
Global Spare Drive	Ability to recover from single disk failure on any rank	Requires multiple ranks running on the RAID controller
Failover (Active-Passive)	Avoids RAID controller as the single point of failure	Other controller sits idle until needed
Failover (Active-Active)	Avoids controller as the single point of failure	More expensive

Source: Kintronics, Elmsford, NY.

Performance

In addition to enhancing data availability, modern RAID has also delivered performance that conforms with or exceeds the expectations of the original RAID authors. Current RAID controller manufacturers boast speeds in excess of 12,000 I/Os per second for high-end products, while controllers for mid-sized RAID arrays routinely deliver between 3000 and 6000 I/Os per second. Moreover, every twelve to eighteen months, improvements in processors on RAID controllers are delivering performance increases of between 10 and 25 percent, expressed as I/Os per second.[19]

The reality is, of course, that RAID performance is determined by a number of factors unrelated to the controller. The time required to process an I/O request in a RAID environment is a function of three things: the time required by a host operating system to generate a request and to pass it to the RAID controller, the time required by the RAID controller and disk drives to process the request, and the time required to transfer the requested data.[20] This simple representation of the process suggests that several elements contribute to overall performance, including the bus architecture of the host, the bandwidth of the storage interconnect, the speed of the disk drives, the configuration of RAID cache memory, and, lastly, the speed and efficiency of the RAID controller. Any high-performance storage solution must balance all of these elements.

Eric Herzog, Vice President of Marketing at Mylex Corporation, describes the relative improvements in host system architecture, interconnects, and storage technology as a "ping pong game." He notes that, when the Peripheral Component Interconnect (PCI) local bus architecture was introduced in Intel-based workstations and servers (c. 1993), its throughput rate of 133 Mb/s was more than adequate for handling the I/O capabilities of the storage interfaces and disk drives of the day. However, with the emergence of high-speed interconnects, such as Ultra Wide SCSI-3 (40 MB/s), Ultra2 SCSI (80 MB/s), and Fibre Channel (100 MB/s), and with the availability of high-speed disk drives, such as 15,000 RPM drives from Seagate Technologies, it will soon be relatively easy to saturate the PCI bus.[21]

This situation, according to Herzog and others,[22] has led to a great deal of activity within the server industry to develop a higher performance bus architecture. Some contenders are I_2O (introduced in March 1996 by a special interest group of the same name, comprising five permanent member companies—Hewlett Packard, Intel, Microsoft, NetFrame Systems, and Novell) and PCIx (introduced to the PCI Special Interest Group in September 1998 by Compaq Computer Corporation, Hewlett Packard Company, and IBM).

Says Herzog, PCIx will yield significant improvements in the PCI I/O bus bandwidth by late 1999. Combined with Intel's Merced 64-bit CPU, the technology will again place host bus speeds into balance with I/O interconnect and drive performance capabilities.

However, hot on the heels of this new balance between server I/O bus and storage interconnect and drive speeds are new storage performance projections. Within 24 months of the release of PCIx-based systems, improving storage capabilities will again make saturation of the system I/O bus a possibility. In response, two forward-looking bus architectures are currently being discussed in the industry, with product deployments anticipated in the early 2000s. They are Next Generation I/O (NGIO) from the NGIO Industry Forum, helmed by Intel, Dell Computer Corporation, Hitachi Limited, NEC Corporation, Siemens Information Communication Network, Inc., and Sun Microsystems,[23] and Future I/O from a 60-member alliance of companies led by Adaptec, Compaq Computer Corporation, Hewlett-Packard, IBM, and 3COM Corporation.[24]

While the "ping pong game" of technology innovation and improvement shows little sign of ending, some characteristics of hardware RAID controller products are helping to make the most of the resources that are available at any given time. For example, intelligent, mirrored caching capabilities on many controller products offer write-back and read-ahead capabilities to optimize the rate at which storage responds to a host system.

Elevator sorting (also called "command coalescing") cache management capabilities are also being added to RAID controller processors. Such cache management capabilities enable the efficient access of data on disk drives and the reduction of disk rotation latency. Some manufacturers are also making RAID controllers smart enough to recognize repetitive functions and to store certain files in cache so that disk access is minimized.[25]

RAID performance may be influenced by the compatibility of an array product with a specific application. For example, the physical layout of data on disk drives in the array can cause the transfer rate to be increased significantly when used with certain applications. Some RAID controllers are built to account for data transfer requirements and provide a means to select among various RAID levels to permit disk array performance tuning to match the requirements of the data.

Some modern RAID controllers enable the optional synchronization all spindles in an array so that transfers of striped data occur in a parallel fashion—yielding a speed advantage in large data transfers to and from the array. Alternatively, the controller enables disks in an array operate independently, benefiting applications requiring high numbers of shorter data transfers.

Other controller feature and functionality enhancements, including intelligent file mapping and cache-based parity calculation, have also contributed to improving the performance of RAID disk arrays. Additionally, Mylex's Herzog suggests that the capability of many hardware RAID arrays to operate in duplex, as well as simplex, modes should not be overlooked.

He explains that, for fault tolerance, many arrays use two RAID controllers "configured in a failover mode" (that is, if controller 1 fails, controller 2 takes over). He goes on to say, "What some people do not realize is that newer RAID controller designs allow both the primary and secondary controllers to be used during normal operation. The array runs in a duplex mode with both controllers moving data, which provides improved performance. If one controller has a problem, the second takes over the full load in simplex mode. That is a capability called failover. [Going further,] if controllers are also designed for failback, replacing the malfunctioning controller automatically restores the two (one original, one replacement) controllers into duplex operation (see Figure 5–15). That is a definite performance-enhancing capability."[26]

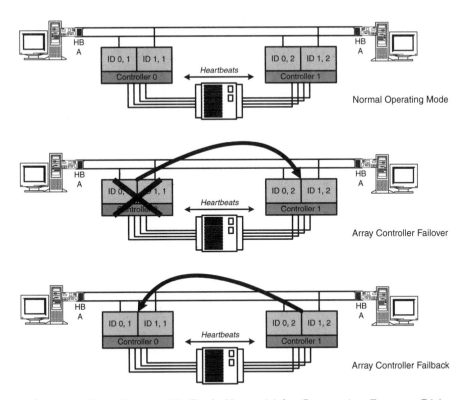

Figure 5-15   Failover and Failback. (*Source:* Mylex Corporation, Fremont, CA.)

Storage Capacity

As in the case of performance improvements, storage capacity improvements sought by the original RAID authors have also been realized. Disk drives themselves have grown in capacity as the technologies contributing to increased areal density have improved. Arrays continue to provide a means to aggregate multiple disks within a small footprint enclosure and to create an extremely large "virtual storage pool" with the same performance characteristics as a captive disk drive.

Lower Storage Cost

Lowering storage cost, the fourth objective of the original RAID team, is a problematic criterion to assess. In simplistic terms, it can be argued that RAID arrays will always have a higher cost than non-RAID arrays because some storage capacity is "sacrificed on the altar of fault tolerance."

With the declining cost of storage—according to James Porter, President of DISK/TREND, the cost per megabyte has dropped from $11.54 per megabyte in 1990 to about $.05 per megabyte in 1998[27]—one can certainly debate the relevance of the cost criteria set forth in 1987.

However, viewing storage costs from a total cost of ownership (TCO) perspective demonstrates the cost advantages of RAID by referring to the benefits of increased storage centralization and reduced risk of data loss. Using centralized, hardware-based RAID arrays to host data reduces storage management expense. This argument is advanced by one Adaptec white paper[28] that compares the management requirements of software-based RAID with local management (see Figure 5–16) and hardware-based RAID with remote management (see Figure 5–17).

With software-based RAID, Adaptec argues, array management must be performed at the host workstation or server to which the array is tethered. The illustration suggests that system administrators must physically visit each RAID installation to perform configuration, maintenance, and troubleshooting tasks. This is a multiplier of TCO costs.

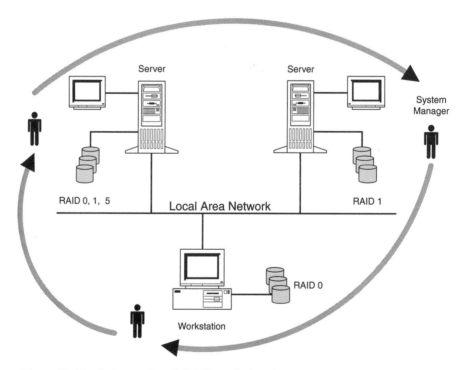

Figure 5–16   Software-Based RAID with Local Management. (*Source:* © 1999 Adaptec, Inc. All rights reserved.)

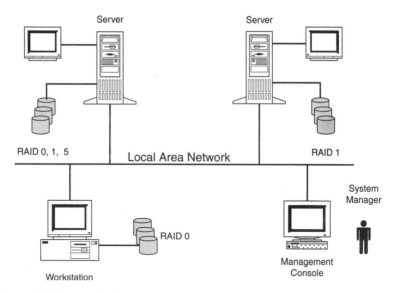

Figure 5–17   Hardware-Based RAID with Remote Management. (*Source:* ©
1999 Adaptec, Inc. All rights reserved.)

By contrast, Adaptec suggests that the amenability of hardware-based RAID arrays to remote management reduces TCO by minimizing the number of on-site visits that system (or storage) administrators must make to individual arrays.

One point that the white paper emphasizes is that storage management costs companies anywhere from five to seven dollars per dollar spent on storage hardware. This statistic alone should compel companies to do whatever they can to centrally manage storage resources in order to reduce costs. If this is not done, Adaptec, and many other storage vendors, point to statistics on the cost of downtime to justify storage management.

Clearly, storage management expense and other TCO-related costs should be included in any consideration of the cost-reduction objective set forth by the original RAID authors. Viewing the question "Have storage cost reductions accrued from RAID implementation?" from a simplistic hardware cost standpoint, the answer would have to be "No." From a TCO perspective, the answer might still be negative if appropriate storage management strategies have not been implemented together with the RAID array.

Another Objective: Storage Sharing

One objective that the RAID authors did not set for their technology was data sharing. Perhaps this was because the supporting technologies for cross-platform access to shared storage did not exist at the time that the RAID white paper was penned. Data sharing, however, has taken center stage as RAID arrays have become more "intelligent," "multiported," and "platform agnostic"—and as storage area networks (SANs) have become popular.

Some vendors of proprietary, multiported, RAID arrays boast that they invented SANs. If by SANs, one means "storage area network" in the generic sense—a pool of storage made available to multiple hosts via a "network" of high-speed interconnects, this may be an appropriate characterization.

Seeking to ride the current wave of interest in Fibre Channel SANs, some vendors claim that their multiported array products provide capabilities that are largely lacking in first-generation Fibre Channel SANs, namely

- Volume mapping capabilities to enable storage to be shared across multiple systems and servers
- A common mechanism for communicating with all devices
- Management software to ensure that the storage platform remains in top operating condition

James Staten, an analyst with Dataquest, confirms that these requirements have been met by some high-end, multiported, array products, positioning them as worthy competitors to SANs.[29]

Mylex's Eric Herzog disagrees with this assessment, stating that such comparisons ignore the fundamental problem of operating system limitations that plague both intelligent arrays and SANs. Intelligent storage arrays do offer volume mapping services in the sense that they enable segments to be allocated to specific hosts. However, the server operating system imposes restrictions on the sharing of storage among hosts.[30]

This view is echoed by Suresh Panikar, Director of Product Marketing for Mylex,

> With the operating systems of today, file systems only permit the sharing of storage subsystems in very limited ways. Windows NT, UNIX Solaris, or Novell can barely handle shared storage in a clustered server configuration. They may be able to handle two nodes with

shared access to storage, but they must develop multinodal capabilities before the sharing of common volumes will be possible.

Says Panikar, this restriction applies to both intelligent, independent RAID arrays and to SANs.

Rick Picton, Manager of Systems Engineering for MountainGate Imaging Systems Corporation, reports that his customers place storage sharing at the top of his TO DO list.[31] He notes that the act of creating a volume on a UNIX or NT host "involves formatting the disk (or array) and setting up a file system on it common to the internal operating system of a specific host. When you try to share a volume across platforms, the other hosts can't see the volume—even if they use the same operating system."[32]

Picton says that the problem of data sharing is worse in heterogeneous host environments. Operating system vendors have little interest in enabling the true data sharing between heterogeneous hosts, he notes, "so the problems with volume sharing are exacerbated in a mixed-OS environment."[33]

The marketing materials of many intelligent array vendors are confusing on this point. Many claim that their storage platforms enable heterogeneous host access to shared storage. Dissecting this claim, it quickly becomes clear that the same volumes are not shared between hosts. Rather, the array is partitioned so that storage resources are reserved to individual hosts accessing the array. Similarly, claims of heterogeneous host access are actually references to the variety of interconnects that the platform supports (e.g., SCSI variants, Fibre Channel, ESCON, etc.) between various hosts (mainframe, UNIX, and NT) and segregated storage that is reserved for their use.

This is not to minimize the accomplishments of storage array vendors in optimizing the control and management of segregated storage volumes in a single platform. Innovations like Storage Computer's "Virtual Storage Architecture" provide intelligent management of storage-related operations using an array controller that features embedded volume management software and a real-time operating system (RTOS). The vendor claims that its "logical volumes" can be shared among multiple hosts.

Similarly, EMC Corporation's high-end Symmetrix arrays offer "Hyper-Volume Extension" and "Meta Volume Addressing" features that can be used to define up to 32 logical volumes on one physical device and surmount the volume size and addressing limitations of some UNIX operating systems as well as Windows NT. Less a "SAN in a box" than a powerful server optimized for I/O processing, EMC arrays extend the capabilities of traditional OS file systems, setting the stage for true data sharing.

Intelligent, stand-alone arrays provide a bridge between the "server-captive" storage architectures of the past and the "server-independent" storage architectures of the future. The techniques for sharing dependable, high-performance, centrally managed, storage resources that were spearheaded by large-scale array manufacturers are today being applied to new technologies such as storage area networks. At the same time, the limitations of these products in terms of data sharing capabilities, complex and costly controller designs, proprietary architectures, and scalability restrictions have made the SAN the preferred architecture for storage deployment in a growing number of companies.

ENDNOTES

1. Interview with Al Loundsbury, MCI Systemhouse, Ottawa, Canada, 1999.
2. Array, as used here, is a marketing term referring to any collection of disk drives in a separate cabinet. Technical purists argue that the term array is only used properly in reference to a collection of disks that represent themselves to operating systems as a single volume.
3. D. H. Patterson, G. Gibson, and R. H. Katz, "A Case for Redundant Arrays of Inexpensive Disks, or RAID," Report Number UCB/CSO 87/391, University of California, Berkeley, 1987. (Today, RAID is more commonly referred to as "Redundant Array of Independent Disks.")
4. John Ewing, "RAID: An Overview," White Paper, Storage Technology, Inc., Boulder, CO, December 1993.
5. *Ibid.*
6. Nancy Dillon, "Open Storage Systems Help Cut Costs, Also Reduce Data-synchronization Woes," *Computerworld*, April 27, 1998.
7. Larry Loeb, "Deconstructing RAID," *Solutions Integrator*, August 1998.
8. *Ibid.*
9. "Adaptec Storage Accelerator White Paper: Performance Benefits of a Caching RAID Coprocessor in PC NT Workstations," Adaptec, Inc., Milpitas, CA, August 3, 1998.
10. "The Adaptec Array Guide," Adaptec, Inc., Milpitas, CA, 1997.
11. *Ibid.*
12. "The RAID market rises above $13 billion in sales, producing lucky winners and unlucky losers," DISK/TREND NEWS, DISK/TREND, Inc., Mountain View, CA, 1998.
13. According to "S.M.A.R.T. Phase II," a white paper by Roger T. Reich and Doyle Albee, Maxtor Corporation, Milpitas, CA, February 14, 1998, "Self Monitoring Analysis and Reporting Technology (or S.M.A.R.T.) is a technol-

ogy that enables a PC to in some cases predict the future failure of storage devices (like hard disk drives). Armed with prediction information the user or system manager in some instances has the opportunity to back up key data or replace a suspect device prior to data loss or undesired downtime. S.M.A.R.T. is a key component in improving the data integrity and data availability of the PC architecture and is now beginning to show up in the broader PC market thanks to the aggressive attention given it by many hard drive manufacturers. S.M.A.R.T. goes by a variety of names in the computer industry. IBM invented SMART technology and as implemented in their mainframe systems called it Predictive Failure Analysis (PFA). Compaq was the first PC company to implement SMART, which it initially referred to as Drive Failure Predication (DFP)."

The authors further report that S.M.A.R.T. II proposals are under review to extend the original command set to include off-line commands, "In an effort to improve failure prediction accuracy leading storage manufacturers have recently specified extensions to the SMART industry standard for hard disk drives (this document is called SFF 8035r2). These extension are referred to as OFF-LINE SMART commands are expected to one day become known as SMART phase II. The off-line commands give HDD manufacturers the opportunity to implement more advanced prediction algorithms for identifying failure modes in HDD devices and thus, improve failure prediction accuracy and customer satisfaction."

14. SES is an ANSI standard for communicating enclosure information between a subsystem and a its host. The SCSI-3 command set includes commands for sending and receiving the diagnostic information. SES can be used in parallel SCSI and Fibre Channel applications.

15. Intelligent Platform Management Interface (IPMI), an initiative started by Intel, Hewlett-Packard, Dell, and NEC, defines a common, abstracted, message-based interface to intelligent platform management hardware. By isolating the hardware implementation from the software, system designers can leverage off-the-shelf components while preserving the ability to innovate. IPMI includes a definition for an external, interchassis connection between servers and other subsystems.

16. The SAF-TE specification, co-developed by nStor Corporation, Inc. and Intel Corporation in October 1995, is an "open" specification designed to provide a comprehensive standardized method to monitor and report status information on the condition of disk drives, power supplies, and cooling systems used in high availability LAN servers and storage subsystems. The specification is independent of hardware I/O cabling, operating systems, server platforms, and RAID implementation because the enclosure itself is treated as simply another device on the SCSI bus.

17. Actually the implementation of management protocols on silica was accomplished by Serrano Systems Corporation, Boulder, CO. The company was acquired by Vitesse Semiconductor, a pioneer in high-speed chip manufacture in the Fibre Channel networking space, in early 1999.

18. Interview with James Porter, President, DISK/TREND, Inc., Mountain View, CA, 1999.

19. Interview with Eric Herzog, Vice President of Marketing, Mylex Corporation, Fremont, CA, 1999.

20. "Throughput and I/O's Within RAID Applications," Brian R. Sorby, RAID Product Marketing Manager, Artecon, Carlsbad, CA.

21. Herzog interview.

22. "Driver Support, Competing Standards Snag I_2O Adoption," Joe Wilcox, Computer Reseller News, November 29, 1998.

23. "Leading Enterprise Computing Companies Form Group to Promote New Input/Output Server Specification: Intel, Dell, Hitachi, NEC, Siemens, Sun Microsystems Chartered with Developing, Implementing Industrywide Next Generation I/O Specification for High Performing Servers," Intel Corporation Press Release, January 7, 1999. According to the release:

> Intel, Dell Computer Corporation, Hitachi Limited, NEC Corporation, Siemens Information Communication Network, Inc., and Sun Microsystems, Inc. are forming the NGIO Industry Forum and will serve on the steering committee.
>
> The NGIO Industry Forum, with broad industry participation, will ensure that the architecture is robust, broadly adopted and available for products beginning in 2000. A founding principle of the Forum is that contributions to the core specification should be licensed on a mutual royalty-free basis.
>
> In addition to the steering committee members, several companies have been involved with developing NGIO, including Adaptec Inc., Fujitsu Ltd., EMC Corp., GigaNet Inc., LSI Logic Corp., Nortel Networks, Qlogic Corp., and Sequent Computer System, Inc. Membership to the NGIO Forum is open to the industry, with more information available at www.ngioforum.org.
>
> Unveiled in November, the NGIO architecture is designed to deliver new levels of reliability, scalability, and flexibility for data flow in servers— vital in developing a complete and robust Internet connected environment. NGIO provides for a direct, high-performance, and expandable interface between main memory and the controller devices for I/O services such as network communication, storage, and processing subsystems.
>
> NGIO is designed to complement existing peripheral interconnect approaches like SCSI, Fibre Channel, and Ethernet. NGIO is also expected to coexist with PCI in the foreseeable future.

24. "Future I/O Alliance Debuts with Broad Industry Support: Over 60 New Companies Join the Future I/O Alliance; Outlines Timeline Goals; Highlights Technical Underpinnings and Announces Governance and Intellectual Property Guidelines," Compaq Computer Corporation Press Release, February 18, 1999. According to the release,

> Compaq, HP, and IBM proposed the PCI-X bus protocol to PCI Special Interest Group (SIG) during the second half of 1998. The PCI-X bus protocol

is an evolutionary design, based on, and remaining backward-compatible, with the prevalent PCI bus. PCI-X enables 64-bit, 133 MHz performance, for a total throughput of 1066 megabyte/s. These evolutionary enhancements to PCI will meet the near-term (2 to 3 years) demands for I/O performance, allowing stable and customer need driven Future I/O solutions to be delivered to the industry in a timely fashion. The PCI SIG (Special Interest Group) formed a special workgroup to review the PCI-X proposal, and the workgroup intends to complete the specification during the first half of 1999. Many industry-leading companies have already committed to deliver products that incorporate the PCI-X technology by the end of 1999. PCI, and PCI-X will continue to be deployed in systems for many years, coexisting within the same systems as higher performance Future I/O solutions.

Building on the success of this initiative, Compaq, HP, and IBM have joined with Adaptec and 3Com to develop and promote the Future I/O specification. The specification is focused on providing a longer-term solution for I/O that will meet customer performance, flexibility, and cost of ownership needs beyond the life and viability of PCI-X. The Future I/O interconnect will be based on a point-to-point, switched-fabric interconnect to provide high speed, low pin-count solutions.

The architecture has been in the specification stage for over 6 months and is currently being refined with the input of Future I/O participant companies. The overall goal, however, is to provide a single interconnect that can be used for both interprocessor communication in parallel application clusters as well as for high bandwidth technologies such as SCSI, Fibre Channel, and Gigabit Ethernet in servers. This I/O interconnect will have performance that exceeds PCI-X at an implementation cost comparable to the existing, relatively inexpensive, PCI implementation cost.

At a component level, the anticipated Future I/O specification will use a simple switch to connect existing I/O protocols (such as SCSI) to the system area network interconnect. The initial Future I/O interconnect will be capable of one gigabyte/s per link in either direction (1+1 GB/s link). The Future I/O protocol will be embedded in the peripheral device circuitry so that it can communicate with the switch effectively.

To support the ability of system area networks to connect modular building blocks (processor-to-processor, server-to-server; I/O device to I/O device, etc.), Future I/O designs are being established using three different distance models:

- >10 Meters: ASIC-to-ASIC / Board-to-Board / Chassis to Chassis. Uses parallel copper etch within boards and parallel cable between chassis.
- 10–300 Meters: Datacenter Server-to-Server. Uses optical fibre/serial copper cable with additional logic.
- > 300 Meters: Will be possible with additional buffering and logic.

25. Brian R. Sorby, "Throughput and I/O's Within RAID Applications," op. cit.
26. Herzog interview.

27. Porter interview.

28. "Hardware- or Software-Based RAID: Which Solution is Right For You?" Adaptec White Paper, Adaptec, Inc., Milpitas, CA, 1998.

29. Interview with James Staten, Senior Analyst, Dataquest, San Jose, CA, 1999.

30. Herzog interview.

31. Interview with Rick Picton, Manager of Systems Engineering, MountainGate Imaging Systems Corporation, Reno, NV, 1999.

32. *Ibid.*

33. *Ibid.*

The Advent of SANs

The discussion of storage area networks predates the formalization by ANSI of the Fibre Channel Interconnect standard in 1994 (ANSI X.3234–1994). One can trace the concept of a distributed storage pool connected to a host by means of high-speed channels to the mainframe data center.

In the late 1970s, a number of vendors, including Paradyne Corporation, Computer Network Technology, McDATA Corporation, Computerm Corporation, and others, offered "channel extension" technologies to customers seeking to go beyond IBM's distance restrictions on I/O device cabling. Channel extenders enabled the remote placement and operation of I/O devices that were normally tethered to the mainframe backplane using bus-and-tag or fiber ESCON technology. Over time, channel extension technology became more than a distance solution. Extenders gradually became more intelligent and acquired capabilities similar to network hubs or switches. They enabled the connection of multiple I/O devices to a single extended channel and delivered near-normal performance with respect to both the mainframe channel and the connected device.

The objectives of modern SANs are somewhat different than those of channel extension technology, of course. However, the advent of a high-speed serial interconnect, Fibre Channel, has contributed greatly to the enthusiasm for this storage architecture industrywide.

FIBRE CHANNEL: A SCSI REPLACEMENT?

Fibre Channel is frequently positioned in both vendor white papers and the trade press as a replacement for SCSI. One paper from CLARiiON underscores this point. The author writes that the predominance of the SCSI bus for the past fifteen years, and its widespread support by major server platforms, has made it the standard of choice for storage vendors. "As a consequence, one way of looking at the question 'Why Fibre Channel?' is really the same as asking 'Why not stay with SCSI?'"[1]

In response to this question, vendors typically point to inherent limitations of SCSI as a bus technology and the superiority of Fibre Channel. Table 6–1 summarizes these differences.

Table 6–1   Fibre Channel and SCSI Compared

Interface	Fibre Channel	SCSI
Speed	100 MB/second	20 MB/second or 40 MB/second
Media	4 wire cable or fiber optic	68 wire cable
Distance	500 meter cabling	25 meter cabling
Capacity	126 devices per loop	16 devices per bus
Cabling Considerations	Easy High Availability cabling	Complex High Availability cabling
Scalability	Non-disruptive expansion	Not supported
Termination	No terminators	Terminators required
Resilience	Signal isolation	No signal isolation
Applications	Storage and network	Storage only
Connectivity	Hubs, switches, etc.	No interconnection

Source: CLARiiON, Advanced Storage Division of Data General Corporation, Southboro, MA.

As discussed in Chapter 4, traditional SCSI-based storage involves the attachment of up to sixteen SCSI devices on a bus comprised of a 68-wire cable. To install a greater number of devices than a single SCSI bus can support, additional SCSI buses must be deployed. For each bus, special terminators must be used that can become loose or fail, causing the entire bus to cease operation. Cabling distances are restricted to 12 meters in traditional SCSI, but can be increased to about 20 meters using special extender hardware.

SCSI is a parallel interface. With traditional SCSI deployments, data transfer speeds of up to 40 MB/s are possible. Newer SCSI standards such as Ultra3 SCSI, capitalizing on low voltage differential technology, boost this capability to about 160 MB/s.

In order to add capacity (disk drives) to a traditional SCSI implementation, data accesses on the bus must first be quiesced. Implementing "hot repair" features (i.e., the capability to swap out failed disk drives while the bus is active) in SCSI remains problematic. The resultant downtime associated with upgrade and repair in a SCSI bus-based storage deployment has been criticized in many quarters.[2]

These constraints, and others, have led many observers to the conclusion that the SCSI interconnect is slowly reaching a dead end. In response, according to Bob Solomon, Vice President of Technology for RAID-array manufacturer, CLARiiON, "many system vendors have moved to serial interfaces like Fibre Channel."[3]

Fibre Channel shares some features in common with SCSI. For one, both communicate with storage devices (though Fibre Channel can also be used as a high-speed interconnect between servers and network devices such as switches and hubs). Both are based on open standards and both are capable of using the SCSI command protocol to access blocks of data on storage devices.[4] Unlike SCSI, however, Fibre Channel can serve as the physical transport for other protocols, including IP, Virtual Interconnect (VI) used in clustering Intel servers,[5] and presumably NGIO and Future I/O, once these technologies have gelled.

Fibre Channel also delivers other capabilities that have led to its adoption by the storage industry as the interconnect of choice for SANs. These include:

- *Performance:* Fibre Channel is a high-speed serial interface, capable of transferring data at 1.06 gigabaud (1,062,500,000 bits of information per second), or 106 MB/s. (The Ultra3 SCSI bus offers 160 MB/s capacity, but like SCSI, Fibre Channel speeds are expected to increase exponentially as the standard matures.)

Like other interconnects, the actual performance of a Fibre
Channel interconnect is dictated by several factors. The *peak* transfer
rate of a Fibre Channel port is bit more than 100 MB/s, which is the
link rate of the full-speed interface. A Fibre Channel adapter can
burst a 2048 byte frame at the link rate. According to the Fibre Channel Association (FCA), the ability to sustain peak flow is limited by
design trade-offs, such as frame processing overhead, and system
constraints, such as burst capabilities of the host PCI Bus Interface,
system configuration, traffic characterization, and interconnect (fab-
ric/loop) model.[6]

- *Flexible Interconnect Topology:* Fibre Channel is often used synony-
  mously with Fibre Channel-Arbitrated Loop (FC-AL), which is only
  one of three topologies for Fibre Channel implementation. The standard also supports point-to-point connections and fabric connections[7]
  (see Figure 6–1). Interconnects between hosts and devices do not have
  to be made directly, (e.g., via a parallel bus interconnect as in SCSI),
  but can be accomplished indirectly using hubs and switches arranged
  in a logical storage network. These networks can connect multiple

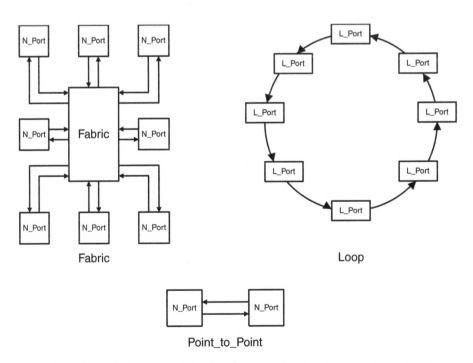

Figure 6–1   Fibre Channel Deployment Topologies. (*Source:* CERN, 1994.)

hosts and storage platforms across long distances, providing considerable flexibility in designing storage area networks.

- *Fault Tolerance:* Unlike SCSI, Fibre Channel has been developed to facilitate the removal and addition of devices while the interconnect remains in operation. Deploying dual Fibre Channel links provides aggregate data transfer bandwidth of 200 MB/s and also enables the automatic recovery of the storage area network from disruptions on one of the pathways (e.g., cable cuts, etc.)

- *Data Integrity:* As an added assurance that data integrity is retained over a Fibre Channel interconnect, all data is encoded in a special format called 8B/10B, which helps to maintain timing accuracy between devices. Moreover, checksum information is included in all data frames, which are verified by the receiver. (see Figure 6–2) In the rare cases of errors, revealed through checksum validation, senders are notified and instructed to resend the frame. When Fibre Channel is deployed using fiber optic cable, the chance of data errors resulting from electromagnetic interference (EMI) is virtually eliminated. Moreover, using fiber-optic cabling enables storage devices, network equipment and servers comprising a Fibre Channel SAN to be placed up to 500 meters apart (up to 10 kilometers with single mode fiber). This feature can be leveraged to disperse storage assets so that a single disaster potential need not put all assets at risk.

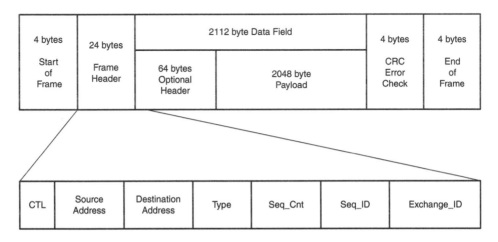

Figure 6–2   Fibre Channel Frame. (*Source:* CERN, 1994.)

- *Ease of Deployment:* Companies may choose between several varieties of copper (with a 30 meter distance cap) or fiber-optic cabling when deploying Fibre Channel (see Table 6–2). Unlike SCSI, copper cables are small and very flexible. Also unlike SCSI, no special termination is required.

  To attach fiber-optic and copper interconnects together (and to handle signal conversions), vendors have created a device called a Media Interface Adapter (MIA). Fibre Channel interconnects utilize either a 9-pin connector (copper) or a fiber-optic port for attachment. With some products, MIAs can be used to upgrade device ports from copper to fiber-optic cable if and when a customer decides to upgrade his cable plant.

  Some Fibre Channel products are equipped with Gigabit Link Modules (GLMs) or Gigabit Interface Converters (GBICs), which are used to choose if the device will be "hot swappable." GLM-equipped Fibre Channel devices can only be changed when the product is

Table 6–2   Fibre Channel Cabling Alternatives

Media Electrical		Speed	Distance
Coax/Twinax	ECL	1.0625 Gigabit	24 Meters
	ECL	266 Megabit	47 Meters
Optical			
9 Micrometer Single- Mode fiber	Longwave Laser	1.0625 Gigabit	10 Kilometers
50 Micrometer Multi- mode fiber	Shortwave Laser	1.0625 Gigabit	300 Meters
	Shortwave Laser	266 Megabit	2 Kilometer
62.5 Micrometer Multi- mode fiber	Longwave LED	266 Megabit	1 Kilometer
	Longwave LED	132 Megabit	500 Meters

- Note: In FC-AL configurations, the distance numbers represents the distance between nodes, not the total distance around the loop.

- Note: In fabric configurations, the distance numbers represent the distance from the fabric to a node, not the distance between nodes.

Source: Fibre Channel Association, Mountainview, CA. www.fibrechannel.com.

Figure 6–3   ATTO FibreBridge™. (*Source:* ATTO Technology, Inc., Amherst, NY.
www.attotech.com)

powered off. Those equipped with GBICs can be added or replaced
while the network is running. Generally speaking, GLMs and GBICs
allow the customization of the Fibre Channel implementation to
meet customer (and vendor) requirements.

It is also worth mentioning that a number of vendors have developed bridge/routers that enable the interconnection of SCSI and
UltraSCSI devices with Fibre Channel networks. Early Fibre Channel–ready products were actually older SCSI products sold with external or integrated FC bridge/routers (see Figure 6–3).

• *Scalability:* SANs will benefit tremendously from their use of Fibre
Channel from the standpoint of scaleability. A single Fibre Channel
loop supports the connection of up to 128 devices. Using hubs and
switches, more than 200 loops (about 16 million nodes) can be connected in a storage area network.

NETWORKING CONCEPTS FOR STORAGE MANAGERS

As the above suggests, Fibre Channel enables the creation of storage networks characterized by a high-performance interconnects and full independence between nodes (i.e., servers and storage devices). According to
Bill Lozoff, Director of Marketing for Gadzoox Networks, such networks
offer significant advantages to companies. Among these is improved
management. By placing storage in a back-end Fibre Channel-based net-

work, it is possible to perform tasks such as backups without impacting production ethernet networks.

The word "network," however, has proven a minor stumbling block for SAN implementation, Lozoff says, "SANs require network savvy, but network managers are rarely involved in SAN purchasing decisions. Storage is typically the responsibility of a system administrator who doesn't necessarily know a lot about local area networks. He doesn't want to hear how a SAN is put together. He wants examples of what the technology will do for him. He wants faster backups."[8]

While much vendor literature about SANs has taken a traditional "storage" focus, a knowledge of networking concepts and techniques is critical to the effective design and implementation of a SAN. For example, building an enterprise-class SAN requires at least two types of network devices: hubs and switches.

SAN Hubs

Much like Ethernet hubs in LAN environments, Fibre Channel hubs provide fault tolerance in SAN environments. A hub offers port bypass functionality that will automatically bypass a port if a problem is detected in the connected loop. This effectively isolates the problem so that an impaired device can be replaced or a new device can be added to the loop without serious consequences. Without a hub in a simple Fibre Channel loop, if one node goes down, the entire loop goes down. This is because with Fibre Channel-Arbitrated Loop each node acts as a repeater for all other nodes on the loop.

Most modern SAN hubs are Simple Network Management Protocol (SNMP) management enabled and offer an ethernet port in addition to multiple Fibre Channel ports. The ethernet port is used to forward information about the status of the hub to an SNMP-based management application. Status information may pertain specifically to the internal workings of the hub itself, or may include detailed information about the status of loops (and their nodes) that are connected to the hub's several ports. Lozoff observes that his company's hub products assist with loop monitoring and management functions and report detected faults to an SNMP-compliant manager.[9]

Typically, a hub has seven to ten ports and can be stacked to the maximum loop size of 126 ports. Hubs also support a popular cabling topology, the star topology, which makes wiring and cable management more convenient.

SAN Switches

Hubs are only part of the equipment complement required to grow SANs to enterprise-strength. Another key component is the SAN switch.

Fibre Channel switch vendors boast the best performance of any network switch available for high-bandwidth, low-latency networks—and credibly so. Some observers claim that FC switch performance derives from the fact that these switches, like the Fibre Channel protocol itself, were designed with the performance limitations of legacy channels and networks clearly in mind.

ANSI specifies three classes of service for switched Fibre Channel connections. The current generation of Fibre Channel switches support all or some of the ANSI classes.

Class 1 service is defined by a dedicated connection that is established between two devices before data transfer can take place. After the data transfer has completed, the connection can be removed by either device.

Class 2 and 3 services do not require that dedicated connections be established and terminated to transport data. These "connectionless" services allow devices to exchange data in a multiplexed fashion, utilizing the switch fabric more efficiently and eliminating the overhead and time required to set up and tear down a connection.

Class 2 service is regarded as more reliable than Class 3 for transferring data. The originating device receives delivery confirmation/acknowledgment whether or not the information has been received.

By contrast, in Class 3 service, the originator receives no confirmation/acknowledgment that the information was received. Eliminating this "chatty" traffic improves data throughput, a fact that has not been lost on Fibre Channel storage vendors, who prefer the Class 3 mode for their disk drives and subsystems. Instead of Fibre Channel–based frame acknowledgement, vendors depend on a higher-level protocol, such as SCSI, to detect transmission errors and to instruct the retransmission of erred data.

Most Fibre Channel switch products support either all three ANSI service classes (for both connection and connectionless service), or only connectionless service (Class 2 and 3). The different classes are appropriate to different applications, though connectionless services are generally preferred for switched SANs because of their efficiency in handling smaller data transfers and their ability to handle differences in the speeds of devices installed on the SAN.[10]

Switches of different classes will not interoperate, nor will host-based adapters (HBAs) and switches that have different service class capabilities. To assure interoperability, class of service support should be the same for device drivers in the server and storage subsystems; drivers, firmware, and hardware support in the HBAs; Fibre Channel protocol chips in the HBAs; and for all hubs and switches.

The typical connection-setup and frame-switching times in Fibre Channel switches are measured in fractions of microseconds. To enhance performance further, switch vendors such as Brocade Communications Systems, complement high-speed switching with other features including:

- *Cut-Through Forwarding:* With some switches, a data frame is sent to the destination by hardware without waiting for the end of a frame or waiting for a response back from the destination node. This allows the processing of more frames per second, which achieves higher bandwidth utilization and reduces delays.
- *Switch Buffering:* Buffering enables a frame of data to be stored temporarily until the device is available to receive it. Buffering frees up the channel by using the switch as a temporary storage area. However, high-speed switching mandates that this be done only as long as absolutely necessary so that data moves through the switch as quickly as possible.
- *In-Order Delivery:* While this is not mandated in the Fibre Channel standard, in-order delivery capabilities on the switch guarantee that data frames will be delivered to the destination node in order that they were originally sent. This is a practical "must-have" for storage applications.

Like hubs, switches are stackable, and like hubs, multiple switches may be required to size a switched Fibre Channel fabric that meets company needs. The address space for a Fibre Channel switch fabric allows for 16 million devices—more than adequate for large, enterprise-class, storage networks. Switch products are typically available in 8- and 16-port configurations, but can integrate many more devices via fabric loop ports attached to arbitrated loop hubs, and/or extensions to additional switches.

Why not just use hubs to build a SAN? With 126 addresses per arbitrated loop (including one address for the hub port), it is theoretically possible to cascade multiple hubs to create a 126-node loop. Practically speaking, however, such a configuration would present numerous drawbacks. With hubs, the more devices, the more latency that is introduced into the loop.

Latency results from the arbitration process inherent in Fibre Channel-Arbitrated Loop. With FC-AL, when two nodes communicate with each other, they "own" the loop until the communication is complete. The more devices communicating on the loop, the greater the latency factor against loop performance. Thus, Fibre Channel bandwidth would be more efficiently utilized by configuring multiple, less-populated loops, and employing a switching hub[11] or switch to connect them, than by building a large network using hubs alone.

Typical Arbitrated Loops contain three to twelve nodes. Tom Clark, Senior Systems Engineer for Vixel Corporation, recommends that SAN designers should not exceed a maximum of fifty to sixty nodes to ensure high bandwidth and availability. "If additional nodes are required within the same logical address space," says Clark, "a 'switching hub' can provide transparent activity between loop segments without violating bandwidth requirements for each loop segment."[12]

According to Clark and others, a single Arbitrated Loop hub can provide practical and cost-effective solution for SAN configurations of up to twelve nodes consisting of one or more servers and associated storage arrays. Additionally, reasonable bandwidth will be provided by multiple, cascaded, arbitrated loop hubs to satisfy the needs of most SANs of less than sixty nodes. If necessary, switching hubs or fabric switches may be added later to address access bottlenecks.

Gadzoox's Lozoff observes, "There is definitely a market for switching in Fibre Channel-Arbitrated Loop, but a lot of switch vendors are encouraging their customers to take a shotgun approach and to deploy switched fabric at the start. This promises to result in a lot of very expensive and underutilized SANs."[13]

As in almost every technology area, SAN vendor marketing is sometimes self-serving. Hub vendors routinely argue that switching is expensive and complex. A switch vendor may describe hubs negatively because of their lack of switch-like intelligence that places storage at the mercy of the arbitrated loop. Table 6–3 provides a comparison of hub and switch technologies from a switchmaker's perspective to illustrate this point.

The proper deployment of SANs requires a "smaller is better" approach. Beginning with pilot projects and monitoring performance as networks are utilized and are scaled is the best way to learn the differences between theory and practice in a real-world environment.

Other SAN Hardware Components

In addition to Fibre Channel hubs and switches, the Storage Area Network may also utilize other networking components. These include:

Table 6–3   Switch Vendor's Comparison of Switches and Hubs

Switch	Hub
Thousands of connections are possible via interconnected switches (support for either point-to-point fabrics or loop configurations).	A loop is limited to 126 devices (substantially fewer connections can be implemented for ideal system performance).
Bandwidth per device stays constant with increased connectivity.	Bandwidth per device diminishes with increased connectivity.
Aggregate bandwidth increases with increased connectivity.	Aggregate bandwidth stays constant with increased connectivity.
A switch has deterministic latency.	Arbitration latency increases as the number of devices increases.
Switch software includes robust capabilities for managing a topology. • Multicast—improved service for transmitting messages to groups of users simultaneously • Alias Server—support that identifies participants in a multicast group • Simple Name Server—support that identifies fabric-connected devices, and registers, and deregisters them in the fabric automatically • SNMP—a part of the management interface for networked administrative services	Hardware implementation restricts availability of management tools, making manual management of a topology necessary.

- **Extenders:** Extenders enable multimode fiber-optic cable to be used across greater distances. Essentially, they convert the multimode interface to single-mode interface and boost the power on the laser. Typically, an extender will provide a single mode cable distance of 30 Km or 18 miles

- **Host Bus Adapters**: Fibre Channel host bus adapters (HBAs) are similar to SCSI host bus adapters and network interface cards (NICs). Available for both copper and optical media, a typical FC PCI HBA is a half-length card that utilizes a Fibre Channel ASIC for processing the Fibre Channel protocol and managing the I/O with the host. Adapters are also available for SBus, PCI, MCA, EISA, GIO, HIO, PMC, and Compact PCI.

- **SCSI Bridge**: As noted above, Fibre Channel provides the ability to link existing SCSI based storage and peripherals using a SCSI bridge. SCSI-based peripherals appear to the server or workstation as if they were connected directly on the Fibre Channel interconnect.

- **SNA Gateway**: SNA gateways interface Fibre Channel to IBM's SNA. Fibre Channel host bus adapters are integrated into standard products like the Novell SAA and Microsoft SNA gateways.

- **Static Switches**: Static switches, also called link switches, provide point-to-point connections and are externally controlled. These de-

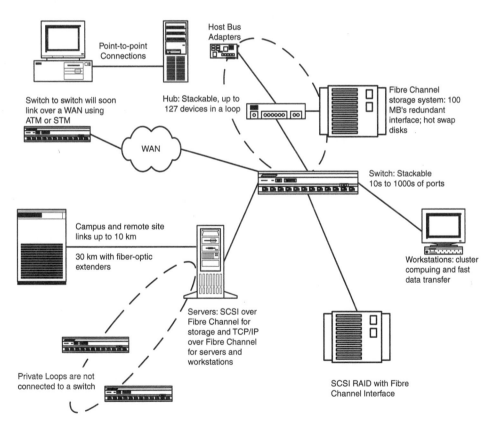

Figure 6–4   Fibre Channel Deployment Alternatives. (*Source:* Fibre Channel Association, Mountainview, CA. www.fibrechannel.com)

vices offer a low-cost option for applications not requiring the fast, dynamic switching capability inherent in the Fibre Channel protocol.

Figure 6–4 depicts a Fibre Channel interconnect incorporating a broad range of network, server, and storage devices in point-to-point, loop, and switched fabric topologies. The diagram illustrates the diversity of deployment alternatives possible with Fibre Channel and demonstrates its similarity to production networks.

SANS: PROBLEMS SOLVED, ISSUES REMAIN

Storage area networks are many things to many people. To some observers, they are an evolutionary step in storage architecture, a natural follow-on to the intelligent, stand-alone storage array products that cater to the "enterprise-class" storage requirements of Fortune Global 1000 companies. Indeed, they offer much of the same capacity, performance, and fault-tolerant features of those expensive platforms.

However, the scalability of SANs and comparatively low acquisition cost of SAN hardware makes the technology more accessible to smaller and medium-sized companies. Peter Gibbs, Director of Marketing for CLARiiON, notes that these companies are already among the early adopters of SAN technology,

> These businesses embraced [distributed computing] and are now involved in server consolidation to reduce costs and improve management. At the same time, they are looking for a way to consolidate storage. They may not need multiterabytes of capacity—yet. But they do want to rehost their storage on a platform that provides the same high-speed, high-availability, shared-storage capabilities that the big companies get from their large-scale arrays. SANs give them that.[14]

To others, SANs are an unnerving interloper in an otherwise well-ordered universe. Vendors of proprietary arrays cringe at the mention of SANs and portray them as toy box technologies that they would not trust with their least important data, let alone mission-critical business information. They emphasize every problem manifested in interoperability trials conducted by the University of New Hampshire to keep customer confidence levels in the technology as low as possible.

Says Gibbs, it has all happened before. IBM's Serial Storage Architecture, Apple Computer's FireWire, and even Gigabit Ethernet drew enormous criticism from installed vendors when they were originally introduced. Fibre Channel SANs are particularly unsettling, observes Gibbs, "because they level the playing field. They give users a choice of what storage products they want to deploy."[15]

Dataquest Senior Analyst James Staten sees storm clouds on the horizon in the storage market. He says that the "customer lock" enjoyed by some large-scale array vendors is threatened by SAN technology. He expects a "warranty lock" to quickly replace it. "A vendor will tell the customer that if he connects the vendor's platform to a Fibre Channel SAN, he will void the warranty. That would be a pretty important consideration for the customer.[16]

Gibbs responds that the initial adoption of SANs is unlikely to occur in the market space where large arrays typically sell,

> The potential market for SANs is enormous, but the technology won't become ubiquitous overnight. The market has three major segments. There are the tree-huggers, the IT practitioners from the Glass House, who want to pay money and to have the vendor do everything [with regard to the selection and implementation of a storage platform]. Then, there are the UNIX and open systems folks, who are the early adopters of SANs. They are willing to roll up their sleeves and get their fingers dirty trying a new technology. Finally, there is the plug-and-play crowd. They are not really participating at all. They are well served by tethered RAIDs.[17]

Between the extremes of vendors who back SANs as the next technology boom and those who condemn it as just another technology bust, there are the neutral observers, such as James Porter, President of DISK/TREND. Porter observes that SANs are still in their infancy, that there is still considerable room for growth in captive storage, and that coming to market early with a Fibre Channel product has already cost one array vendor considerably. Of SANs, Porter says simply, "The industry is moving that way. But right now every manufacturer has a different definition of a SAN. It is still a technology at the high talk level."[18]

On a technical level, SANs share much in common with intelligent storage arrays. With a SAN, large-capacity storage can be shared among multiple hosts at high speed. At present, SAN technology lacks the manageability of large-scale arrays, and both storage platforms face considerable challenges in the years ahead to realize the vision of data sharing in a heterogeneous operating system environment.

ENDNOTES

1. "Why Fibre Channel?," *In The Loop*, CLARiiON, A Division of Data General, Southboro, MA, 1999.
2. Interview with Bob Solomon, Vice President of Technology, CLARiiON, A Division of Data General, Southboro, MA, 1999.
3. *Ibid.*
4. By contrast, IBM's Serial Storage Architecture (SSA) uses neither the SCSI command protocol or interconnect, which is one reason why SSA is still regarded as a proprietary standard, despite the fact that it too is an "open" ANSI standard.
5. According to "The Business Advantages of an Emerging Industry Standard Approach to Clustered Communications," Intel Corporation Strategic Briefing, Intel Corporation, Santa Clara, CA, 1997: "The Virtual Interface (VI) Architecture specification is an industry initiative spearheaded by Intel Corporation, Compaq Computer Corporation and Microsoft Corporation. VI enables the building of clusters around the common building blocks of Intel Architecture (IA)-based, standard high-volume (SHV) servers and commercial, off-the-shelf operating systems ... at a fraction of the cost of traditional, proprietary mainframe and RISC-based clustering technologies. Using VI Architecture, clusters of Intel Architecture-based SHV servers can now be used to address scalability and availability solutions at all levels of the enterprise."
6. According to the Fibre Channel Association (FCA) "Frequently Asked Questions,"

> Another measure of performance is latency. In high-performance clustering environments, one of the critical performance parameters is buffer-to-buffer latency. The actual time elapsed in passing a message from one node to another bounds the minimum time for distributed lock management algorithms to establish resource ownership. The tight coupling between host DMA and hardware protocol processing results in extremely low latencies for Fibre Channel.
>
> In TCP/IP environments, if an unmodified protocol stack is used on the host system, the protocol stack overhead may become the limit to sustainable performance.
>
> The protocol assists in Fibre Channel ASICs provide considerable offload for host drivers; however, this assist is not transparent if frames are small. In other words, maximum performance, as measured in Mbytes/second, increases as Frame Size increases. Transfers should always be blocked in the largest possible Sequences to achieve maximum performance.
>
> Host bus issues can also limit performance if not understood and corrected. For example, PCI adapter performance requires running with large PCI burst sizes. Some of the other PCI-related factors affecting performance include:

- PCI Bus Access and Transfer Overhead - Latencies introduced by Req to Grant turnaround, Host Mem Reads, Burst size
- PCI Bus Loading—Number of PCI slots with active controllers (affects time from Bus Request to Grant)
- PCI Bus Loading—Host CPU activity on PCI Bus
- Host Data Blocking—Quad-word Address alignment and data blocking to take advantage of larger burst sizes
- PCI Cache Line Size and Support for Cache commands
- PCI Bridge Chip Limitations and Bridge Chip Configuration

The FCA can be found on the Internet at <u>http://www.fibrechannel.com.</u>
7. According to the Fibre Channel Association (FCA) "Frequently Asked Questions,"

> In the early days of Fibre Channel, the concept of a universal "Fabric" was popular as a means of supporting Fibre Channel's topology independence. It's value has since been enhanced with the advent of point to point and FC-AL topologies. The Fibre Channel Fabric was designed as a generic interface between each node and the physical layer. By adhering to this interface, any Fibre Channel node could communicate over the "fabric" without even knowing whether the system being attached to is a crossbar switch, a ring, a frame switch, a circuit switch, a hub, or anything else.

8. Interview with Bill Lozoff, Director of Marketing, Gadzoox Networks, Inc., San Jose, CA, 1999.
9. *Ibid*. In developing the status reporting methodology of its hub and switch products, says Lozoff, the company also created a management information communication protocol, Intracom, which he expects to eventually become an in-band management protocol for SANs.
10. "Classes of Service," Brocade Communications Systems white paper, Brocade Communications Systems, Inc., San Jose, CA, 1999.
11. In "Designing Storage Networks with Fibre Channel Switches, Switching Hubs, and Hubs," Tom Clark, Senior Systems Engineer, Vixel Corporation, Bothell, WA, 1997, Clark defines a Fibre Channel switching hub as "a hybrid technology that offers the advantages of both Arbitrated Loop and fabric switching. A switching hub manages the address space of two or more Arbitrated Loop segments to create a larger, logical loop. This allows nodes on physically separate loops to transparently communicate with one another, while maintaining higher available bandwidth on each physical loop. Switching hub products optimize extended Arbitrated Loop performance. They also give some of the benefits of fabric switching at a favorable price point. A switching hub provides concurrent 100 MBps access between multiple physical Arbitrated Loops."
12. *Ibid*. Clark also notes that loop device counts should include the internal configuration of some disk arrays. If a disk array (e.g., JBOD) uses Arbitrated

Loop as an internal architecture for linking disks, and the internal loop is connected to the external loop port, then each disk within an enclosure should be
counted as a node.

13. Lozoff interview.
14. Interview with Peter Gibbs, Director of Marketing, CLARiiON, a Division of
Data General, Southboro, MA, 1999.
15. *Ibid*.
16. Staten interview.
17. Gibbs interview.
18. Porter interview.

Network-Attached Storage (NAS) and Storage Appliances

Pat McGarrah, Technology Program Director at Quantum Corporation, is a self-described conservative. He believes that, despite the quick pace of technological change in the storage industry, the market doesn't move very quickly.[1] "Heterogeneous SANs are at least three years away," says McGarrah. The reasons are several.

On a technical level, the greatest impediment to the SAN is the server operating system. In particular, it is the file system and how it deals with the concept of a volume. "To the file system," McGarrah observes, "a disk volume doesn't change size. How many blocks are on the disk is determined when the volume is formatted. To change the volume size, you must back up all of the data that is stored there, then add it back on [after the volume has been reformatted]. This is a problem that needs to be addressed."

Another obstacle to SANs, but one that should be resolved in the near term according to McGarrah, is the file-addressing limit imposed by 32-bit file systems. He notes that current 32-bit file systems in popular server operating systems fix a 1.5 terabyte limit[2] on addressable disk space, "In 1998, that was equal to about 84 high-end disk drives. In the year 2000, it will take only 42 drives reach the limit. Disk drive capacities double about every 18 to 24 months, so by 2002, only 21 drives will be required to hit 1.5 terabytes. Two years later, 10 drives will exceed in capacity what the 32-bit file system can address."

McGarrah observes, "We need to think in terms of a 64-bit file system. That will place file system addressability beyond the petabyte range—to a number without a name: a 1 followed by 18 zeros. That will solve the addressability limit. But, we will still need to do away with the concept of a \volume—decouple it from the operating system completely. The problem is that operating systems don't understand that storage can grow."

In addition to the server operating system, McGarrah sees another impediment to SAN deployment: arbitrated loops.[3] "Loops have problems, and they don't work for storage. For one, signaling needs to be retimed constantly to account for differences in drive speed. Every device is limited by the slowest drive in the loop."

In theory, he says, using a switched fabric rather than arbitrated loop architecture in a SAN resolves the problem. A Fibre Channel fabric switch enables drives in the SAN to operate at their rated speeds, "But how do you wire an array cabinet for Fibre Channel and provide for both faster and slower drives? It's a nightmare."[4]

One hypothetical solution to this problem is to use only drives with the same speed ratings. However, McGarrah observes, this solution ignores the reality of typical disk drive purchasing patterns. "Most companies purchase a certain amount of disk drives when they first deploy a storage platform, such as a RAID array, then buy more drives over a two-to-three year period. In that same amount of time, the speed, capacity, and performance of drive technology changes. This virtually guarantees that drives of mixed speeds will be included in SAN-attached arrays and ensures that FC-AL will continue to confront drive speed problems."

In addition to drive speed issues, he is also troubled by the absence of a "hot plug" [technology for adding and removing drives while the loop is operating] in Fibre Channel-Arbitrated Loop. Efficient fault management and scalability are key to the SAN value proposition, McGarrah says. Without them, SANs will remain another just another interesting niche technology.

"What happens to the bytes when a drive is moved or removed? I haven't heard a credible explanation of how that will be handled. Fabric switching seems to be all important to the success of SANs. Until these issues are worked out and cheap switches are produced, SAN deployments will be very limited. IS buyers tend to be conservative. Look at it this way: Intel servers still ship with [antiquated] ISA buses."

DISTRIBUTED STORAGE USING NAS

One technology that does excite McGarrah is network-attached storage. He defines NAS simply, "A NAS device is a cheap file server, basically a disk drive with another board that connects it directly to the ethernet network. IT shops hate them because they enable storage to be distributed again. All you need is an IP address to make the technology work. It is much simpler than a SAN."

McGarrah argues that distributing storage makes more sense than centralizing it in a number of situations, especially with respect to end-user work files. Looking at the issue from the perspective of trends in network and storage technology, he observes that network bandwidth has grown at a much slower pace than disk storage capacity. By centralizing storage, either through the centralization of servers and their tethered arrays or using a SAN, more network traffic is generated by end user file requests. This storage-related traffic, in turn, fuels the need for more network bandwidth (see Figure 7–1).

By contrast, McGarrah observes, co-locating end user file storage nearer to those who access it reduces network bandwidth demand (see Figure 7–2). "If servers and storage are centralized and end user files are located on the servers, you need high-speed network backbones like Giga-

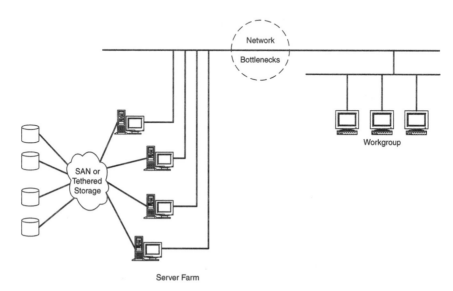

Figure 7–1   Centralized Storage Places Traffic Burden on Production Network.

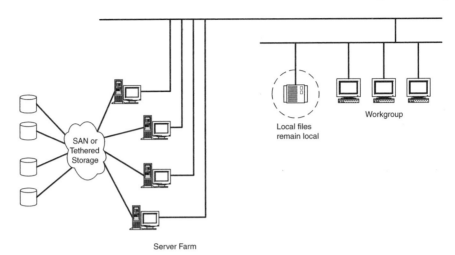

Server Farm

Figure 7–2   NAS Alleviates Backbone Network Congestion By Keeping End
User File Storage Local to Workgroup.

bit Ethernet to handle the traffic caused by file transfers to desktops. Why
solve the problem that way? I like NAS devices better. They are more distributed, and they let disk drive manufacturers do what they do best: continue to create storage capacity."

DEFINING TERMS

Thomas LaHive, a Senior Analyst with Dataquest, understands the value
proposition of NAS devices. However, in his analyses and projections, he
finds it difficult to separate NAS conceptually from the SANs of the future.
LaHive divides the storage market into three subsets (see Figure 7–3).[5]

- *Storage Directly Connected to Servers:* "This is the traditional storage
  configuration," says LaHive, "and accounts for 98 percent of the stor-
  age deployed today. We expect this segment to shrink to about 10
  percent by 2002."
- *Storage Directly Connected to Servers via Fibre Channel Hubs and
  Switches:* "We refer to these solutions as SANs without intelligence,"
  LaHive says, "and expect the configurations to claim up to 30 percent
  of the storage install base by 2002."
- *Storage Directly Connected to Networks:* "This category includes both
  NAS devices and SAN-attached storage that uses some sort of net-

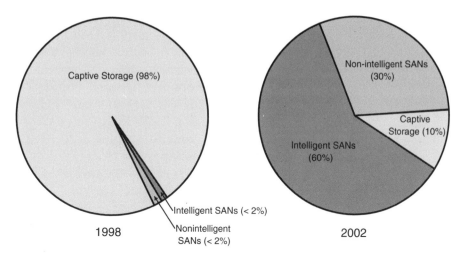

Figure 7–3   Captive Storage, Non-Intelligent SANs, and Intelligent SAN/NAS Storage Futures. (*Source:* Interviews with Thomas LaHive, Gartner Group's Dataquest, Westborough, MA, 1998.)

work protocol or enhanced switch intelligence," LaHive explains, "They will become predominant in the industry, comprising about 60 percent of the market by 2002."

LaHive argues that, while the current generation of SAN switches and hubs are manufactured by "little vendors who need the big server vendor's stamp of approval [to find a market], future SAN switches will offload more I/O intelligence from servers and the storage devices themselves will become smarter. A network I/O server will become the center of the IT universe."

NAS AND THE THIN-SERVER REVOLUTION

In certain respects, that is what network-attached storage devices deliver today. A good working definition of a NAS device is a disk array that connects directly to the messaging network via a LAN interface, such as Ethernet, using common communications protocols. A NAS device functions as a server in a client/server relationship, has a processor, an operating system or microkernel, and processes file I/O protocols such as SMB and NFS. To applications running on the network, NAS resembles an ordinary server. To any client, it looks like a large-capacity hard disk.[6]

NAS devices originated in the optical storage world, specifically in the realm of Compact Disc-Read Only Memory (CD-ROM) "tower" products.[7] CD-ROM towers, designed to facilitate access to a number of CD-ROM platters, were seized upon as a good candidate for direct network attachment for essentially economic reasons. To offset the cost of product acquisition, vendors sought a means to share their tower products among multiple workstations in a LAN. Requiring a CD-ROM tower be tethered to a network-attached, general-purpose server was viewed as a cost multiplier of an otherwise cost-effective storage solution. The concept of embedding a "thin server" directly on the tower device itself held tremendous appeal.

The success of the network-attached, thin-server–enhanced, CD-ROM tower led to similar innovations in other product areas including print, fax, Internet access, and finally dynamic (as opposed to read-only) storage. Over time, the term *thin-server* became a description of

> any specialized, network-based, hardware device designed to perform a single or specialized set of server functions and characterized by running an optimized operating architecture, requiring no per-seat network operating system license, and client access that is independent of any operating system or proprietary protocol. The [thin-server] device is a 'closed box,' delivering extreme ease of installation, minimal maintenance, and can be managed remotely by a customer with a Web browser.[8]

Modern NAS products fit the thin-server categorization. Compared with traditional "fat server"–based storage architectures, thin-server NAS devices deliver numerous advantages, as summarized in Table 7–1. Most advantages derive from the single-purpose intent of NAS products and their corresponding I/O-optimized designs.

NAS devices are routinely marketed by vendors as a cost-effective alternative to server-tethered storage products. Vendors of "enterprise-class" NAS products, which have capacities of up to approximately one-half terabyte,[10] base this claim on the reduced cost of implementation and management associated with their products. Vendors of lower-capacity, workgroup-class SANs point to acquisition costs, which are far below the combined expense for acquiring a general-purpose server and storage array of similar capacity (see Table 7–2 for a list of NAS products).

Plug-and-play products, which predominate the workgroup class NAS, are certainly less difficult to deploy and configure than are server-

Table 7–1 Server-Attached Storage versus NAS

	Server-Tethered Storage	**Network-Attached Storage (NAS)**
Acquisition Cost	General-purpose server and separate storage array must be purchased separately and configured.	Array and thin server combined in easily configured platform; plug-and-play features in most products.
Maintenance	Maintenance-intensive configurations require on-site system administrator.	Typically maintained via web browser-based software utility.
Scalability	Difficult and costly to scale.	Plug in another NAS device.
Performance	File service shares CPU cycles with other server functions. Potential I/O performance degradation with load increases.[9]	CPU and operating system optimized for I/O only.
Reliability	Mean time between failure (MBTF) increases based on device complexity. Decreasing reliability as number of applications and uses increase.	Very reliable. Dedicated application means dedicated processor and I/O functions.
Bottlenecks	Potential intra-server I/O bottlenecks resulting from multiple applications; network bottlenecks may accrue to centralization in server farms.	I/O optimized. Potential network bottlenecks alleviated through proper network placement.

tethered arrays. Procedures for installing these products generally do not include the myriad tasks involved in setting up a general-purpose server and storage array for use on a network.

To simplify network connectivity, many products feature Dynamic Host Configuration Protocol (DHCP) support. Once they are cabled to the production LAN within a company, they can discover their own TCP/IP addresses and advertise their availability on the LAN without any intervention.

Table 7–2   Selected NAS Products and Vendors

Company	Product Name	Protocol Support
Advanced Media Services Wilmington, MA www.amsstorage.com	Network Attached Media Server, JAZServer	SMB, HTTP, TCP/IP, NetBios, & NetBEUI
	DakotaStor	NFS, WebNFS, SMB, CIFS, HTTP, TCP/IP
	DakotaRAID	NFS, WebNFS, SMB, CIFS, HTTP,TCP/IP
Artecon Carlsbad, CA www.artecon.com	LynxxNSS Network Storage System	SMB, CIFS, NFS, HTTP, TCP/IP
Auspex Santa Clara, CA www.auspex.com	4Front NS2000, AS100, AS200	SMB, CIFS, NFS, HTTP, TCP/IP
Axonix Salt Lake City, UT www.axonix.com	ProLinQ Sharer	Novell (NDS), NT, 10BaseT, 100BaseT
Creative Design Solutions Santa Clara, CA www.creativedesign.com	CDS Plug-n-Stor	SMB/CIFS, HTTP, NFS, TCP/IP
Meridian Data Scotts Valley, CA www.meridian-data.com	Snap! Server	TCP/IP, IPX, NetBEUI
MTI Technology Corporation Anaheim, CA www.mti.com	MTI Gladiator NAS	NFS, SMB/CIFS, HTTP
Network Storage Solutions Chantilly, VA www.nssolutions.com	NSS100R	NFS, CIFS (SMB), HTTP
Network Appliance Santa Clara, CA www.netapp.com	Multiprotocol Filers	NFS, SMB, CIFS, HTTP, TCP/IP
Polywell Computers San Francisco, CA www.polywell.com	NetDisk	SMB, NFS, WebNFS, TCP/IP, 10BaseT, 100BaseT

Company	Product Name	Protocol Support
Procom Technology Santa Ana, CA www.procom.com	NetForce 100, 1000, 2000 and 2200	SMB, CIFS, TCP/IP, 100Base-T, 10Base-T
Raidtec Corporation Alpharetta, GA www.raidtec.com	RAIDServer	NFS, TCP/IP
REALM Information Technologies www.realminfo.com	REALM Universal Professional NAS+ Server	N/A
Unisys Corporation Mission Viejo, CA www.marketplace.unisys.com/storage/nas200	PrimeStor NAS2000	SMB, CIFS, NFS, TCP/IP

THE NAS OPERATING SYSTEM

Such features as DHCP support are functions of the embedded operating systems (sometimes called microkernels) commonly utilized on NAS products, according to James Staten, Senior Analyst at Dataquest. He observes that the preponderance of NAS products on the market today feature either licensed NAS "engines" or operating systems built by the integrators themselves.[11]

Like a general-purpose operating system, the NAS operating system has a kernel that delivers a set of standard functions. These functions include:

- An interrupt handler that handles all requests or completed I/O operations that compete for the kernel's services
- A scheduler that determines which programs share the kernel's processing time in what order
- A supervisor that actually gives use of CPU resources to each process when it is scheduled
- A manager of the operating system's address spaces in memory or storage, sharing these among all components and other users of the kernel's services

As with a general-purpose operating system, a NAS kernel's services are requested by other parts of the operating system or by applications through a specified set of program interfaces known as system calls. Additionally, kernel OS code is usually loaded into protected memory to ensure its availability on a continuous basis and to safeguard it against being accidentally overwritten by other less frequently used parts of the operating system.

DIFFERENCES IN KERNEL IMPLEMENTATION

Beyond these fundamental similarities in kernel design, NAS products are distinguishable from each other in terms of kernel implementation. Some vendors prefer to use general-purpose operating systems, such as established UNIX variants or Windows NT, as the NAS OS. They "enhance" the general-purpose operating system with additional file service–related functionality either through the addition of kernel software modules or the application of kernel-modifying software patches.

Proponents argue that such an approach embues the NAS device with the beneficial characteristics attributed to the operating system when deployed on traditional servers. For example, the Auspex 4Front NS2000 builds on the Solaris operating system from Sun Microsystems. In its descriptions of the product, Auspex endeavors to leverage this point as a product strength. The choice of Solaris as the NAS product operating system is characterized as part of the vendor's architectural vision to deliver NAS products that "combine reliable, standard components with innovative design to produce a simple, reliable platform capable of scaling to meet ever-growing network I/O and storage needs."[12] Put another way, the vendor hopes that a "Solaris connection" buys Auspex instant membership in the open systems marketplace, assuring customers that its architecture is not proprietary and is firmly grounded in established operating system technology.

Benefits of "open systems" notwithstanding, the basing of NAS devices on "enhanced" general-purpose OS kernels is an approach with as many critics as adherents. Detractors claim that the approach delivers products that are inherently inefficient.

Cheena Srinivasan, Director of Enterprise Marketing for NAS vendor Network Appliance, says that the original purpose of his company's efforts to develop their own NAS product was to "offload UNIX file services from UNIX servers."[13]

"File services tend to bog down application services, so we asked, 'Why not offload the file services from the server?'" he recalls. "In 1993, we released our first product—a network storage appliance, now called a filer. The message we received was loud and clear: By 1997, we have over 5000 installed units and revenues of $200 million."

Srinivasan claims that the value of offloading just the file service functionality from general-purpose server operating systems is self-evident, "There are something like 30 million lines of code in [Microsoft Windows] NT Server 5.0. There is no necessity that a server be that fat. The concept we follow is offloading server functionality for simplicity and increased efficiency. You don't need a full server [operating system] to perform many functions. Many people have come to the same conclusion, but may not realize it. For example, you don't hear people talking about NT scalability anymore. The issue hasn't gone away, people just buy another server and dedicate the box to one or more functions."[14]

Network Appliance designers have chosen to implement a specialized microkernel operating system on their products to deliver not only efficiency and performance, but also support for a proprietary file management system (see below) that enables the storage and retrieval of files originating in heterogeneous (UNIX and NT) environments.

A number of other NAS vendors have followed Network Appliance's example and also use specialized microkernels optimized for storage services. Nearly all vendors embracing this approach make a similar case. Since file services constitute only a small fraction of the code used in a general-purpose operating system, NAS devices based on a general-purpose OS are no more efficient, and often as cumbersome to maintain as, the traditional server-with-captive-storage platforms they seek to replace.[15]

Among the vendors choosing to use specialized NAS operating systems, only a few—like Network Appliance—develop their own micro kernels from the ground up.[16] Most opt to use third party NAS OS development environments, such as Realm Information Technologies Universal Server[17] or CrosStor Software's (formerly Programmed Logic Corporation) StackOS.[18] These modular development environments are used to create custom file service and network connectivity solutions that, in turn, are often implemented using third party, real-time operating system (RTOS) products. This approach yields the benefits of faster time to market and lower development costs, especially in vendor IT environments that lack the prerequisite skills and knowledge for OS development.

ANATOMY OF A NAS OPERATING SYSTEM

While the developmental approach to NAS operating systems varies from vendor to vendor, most implementations follow the general functional design depicted in Figure 7–4. The three functional subsets of a NAS operating system, as depicted in the diagram, are the host node, the network node and the storage/file system node.

The host node of a typical NAS OS implementation provides most of the rudimentary kernel functionality outlined above. In addition, vendors often assert that the host node provides the remote management capabilities of their NAS products. For example, many NAS devices feature Simple Network Management Protocol (SNMP) support. Host node functionality in the NAS OS enables the device to generate an SNMP-compliant management information base (MIB). SNMP MIBs contain operational status information about the device. Using the MIB, the NAS device can be monitored for proper operation from any SNMP-compliant network or system management console.

Other products have embraced web-based management approaches. In these cases, host node functionality is provided to enable the NAS de-

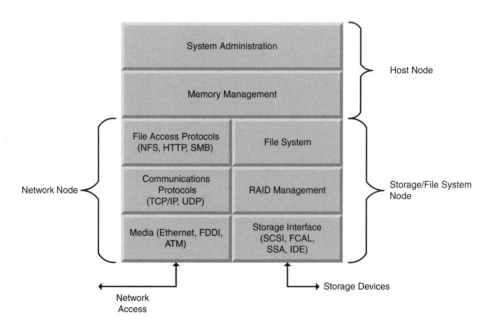

Figure 7–4   Anatomy of a NAS Operating System.

vice to generate its own web page, which can be accessed using a standard web browser and used to configure, administer, and troubleshoot problems on the NAS device.

While some vendors include file management systems in their host node descriptions, Figure 7–4 depicts this functionality as part of the storage/file system node. The storage/file system node of the NAS kernel typically includes:

- A file system used by the NAS OS for storing and retrieving files
- RAID software used to establish a RAID-level configuration among installed disk devices
- Device drivers and interfaces (SCSI, Fibre Channel, IDE, SSA, etc.) for the disk drives used by the platform

Additionally, some products feature "storage management" functionality in the storage/file system node. This functionality may include backup and restore support, hierarchical storage management support, volume management support, and similar functions that can be accessed and operated using the product's management software tool or web browser interface.

HOMOGENEOUS NAS FILE SYSTEMS

File systems constitute a major discriminator among the different NAS devices marketed today. Many workgroup-class NAS devices are designed for use in a homogeneous network environment. This means that they store all files in a manner that makes them available for use *exclusively* by either NT (or other Microsoft Windows variants) or UNIX systems in a network (but not both).

Technically, a NAS device's file system has two components: the local file system and a network file access protocol used to enable remote access for end users to stored files. The most common network file access protocol is the Network File System (NFS) from Sun Microsystems, and many NAS devices support NFS. However, the growth of Windows NT has encouraged the use of the Common Internet File System (CIFS) in many NAS devices, as well.

Sun introduced NFS in 1985. Since then, it has become a *de facto* standard protocol,[19] used by over ten million systems worldwide. NAS devices that use UNIX or UNIX-derivative OS kernels and file systems typically support NFS as a mechanism to enable users to access files and directories located on the NAS disk or array.

NFS constitutes a distributed file system that enables users or processes accessing the NAS device to treat NAS-based files and directories as if they were local to the end station. For example, users can employ standard operating system commands to create, remove, read, write, and set file attributes for NAS-based files and directories in an NFS-based NAS product.

Like NFS-enabled general-purpose servers, NAS devices that use NFS provide access to their resident file system through a client-server relationship with end stations. The NAS device acts as a server and "exports" all or part of its file system for use on the network. End stations or processes that use (or "mount") the server's resources are clients. Once a client mounts a file system that a NAS server exports, the client can access the NAS-resident files.

NFS servers are typically UNIX-based systems, but client implementations are available for virtually every modern computing platform—from desktops to supercomputers—regardless of their native operating system. NFS achieves platform independence by its use of Remote Procedure Call (RPC) protocol primitives built on top of an eXternal Data Representation (XDR) protocol.

RPC is a library of procedures that allow one process (the client process) to direct another process (the server process) to execute procedure calls as if the client process had executed the calls in its own memory address space. Because the client and server are separate, they need not exist on the same physical system.

When NFS-accessed files are shared between heterogenous platforms, an eXternal Data Representation (XDR) protocol provides a standard way of representing data. XDR resolves the differences in the byte orders, structural alignment, and data representations used by the NAS server and the end station client.

Originally, the User Datagram Protocol (UDP) was the preferred transport mechanism for sending and receiving NFS commands and files through a network. Today, TCP/IP is typically used.

In addition to NFS, another network file access protocol popular with NAS device manufacturers is the Common Internet File System (CIFS). CIFS is a public (or open) variation of the Server Message Block (SMB) protocol developed and used by Microsoft in its networks since the mid-1980s. CIFS (sometimes called SMB) is often the preferred protocol for NAS devices targeted to homogeneous, Windows-based networking enviroments.

Given SMB's proprietary architecture and design, it was not as widely supported on heterogeneous client systems as was NFS. However, since the early 1990s, Microsoft has been expending considerable effort to encourage support for the protocol on non-Windows systems. In 1992, SMB was ratified as an X/Open specification.[20] By mid-1996, SMB was expanded and renamed CIFS and Microsoft began to promote CIFS as an open standard for use on the Internet.[21]

The main difference between CIFS and NFS is that the latter is a stateless protocol. Stateless means there is no record of previous interactions in an NFS operation and each interaction request has to be handled based entirely on information that comes with it. This impacts a number of NFS operations, including file access. The NFS protocol emphasizes error recovery over file locking. File locking requires the maintenance of state information (e.g., the file is in use and cannot be accessed and written to by another client at the same time). By contrast, error recovery is simplified by a stateless protocol—with NFS, clients are oblivious to server reboots, provided a connection is restored promptly.[22]

A CIFS file server is not stateless. The Windows networking heritage of the protocol shows through in the emphasis that CIFS places on file locking over error recovery. PC application software relies on strict locking, which, in turn, requires an active, uninterrupted connection. Applications executing on PC clients react to an CIFS server in exactly the same manner as they do to local disk drives: A down server is no different a condition than an unresponsive disk drive. Therefore, PC clients must be warned—and allowed time—to gracefully disengage (i.e., save files, exit applications, and so on) before server shutdowns or reboots.[23]

There are many more specific differences between CIFS and NFS that need not be discussed here. Suffice it to say that many NAS device vendors, perceiving the increasingly widespread deployment of Windows95, Windows98, Windows NT, and Windows 2000 clients and servers, have seen market advantages in defining their microkernels to support the CIFS network file system protocol.

Support for CIFS or NFS is typically a function of the NAS operating system's network node. This node also provides support for the network protocol, such as TCP/IP, that underlies file access protocols, and for LAN media interfaces such as ethernet, FDDI, and ATM.

ENHANCING FILE SYSTEMS AND MULTIPROTOCOL FILE ACCESS

While most workgroup-class NAS devices are targeted to homogeneous network environments, some products endeavor to meet the needs of a heterogeneous environments by sharing physical storage between UNIX and NT systems. As with many RAID array products, these NAS devices provide the means to partition disk arrays according to file system. This approach is roughly equivalent to setting up separate NAS devices to provide file services for separate networks of homogeneous systems. Observers argue that such an approach is inherently flawed. It perpetuates an arrangement of separate storage servers for distinct sets of UNIX and PC clients that is costly to maintain. Moreover, it impairs the development of applications that use both UNIX and NT based data.

An alternative is to implement both NFS and CIFS file access protocols on a partitioned NAS device to facilitate cross-platform file sharing. This approach, too, is fraught with limitations.

For one, both NFS and CIFS are constrained by the inherent architectural assumptions of their hereditary file systems (the UNIX File System in the case of NFS; the Windows file system for CIFS) from delivering seamless cross-platform file services.

Says Dave Hitz, Founder and Director of System Architecture for Network Appliance,

> At the top level, the issue is one of semantics. UNIX and NT file systems have different semantics. An example is UNIX case-sensitive filenames. Another difference is the permissions model. In UNIX, file permissions are identified by owner and group. NT has Access Control Lists (ACLs) that are much fancier. It is a lot easier to set up a NAS device for UNIX access only or NT access only. It takes a lot of serious effort to set one up to handle cross-platform access.[24]

In some cases, Hitz adds, there is no equivalent information to exchange between platforms. For example, the UNIX File System (UFS) does not store a timestamp for a file, indicating when it was created. That means that the CIFS protocol cannot retrieve that information and present it on a PC client.

Unsurprisingly, Hitz notes, the NFS protocol doesn't offer mechanisms for data access beyond the capabilities of UFS. NFS was developed to extend UFS across networks. Similarly, the CIFS protocol extends a PC-oriented file system to remote clients. In both of these cases, the remote file access protocol implementation is described as "native" to the operating system context in which it originated.

Hitz says that another approach to sharing heterogeneous file systems on a NAS device is to use an emulated solution like SAMBA.

> SAMBA is an advanced server that uses SMB or CIFS to access files on a UNIX server. It compensates for differences in file sematics and tries

to make up for the differences between the Windows client's requirements and the capabilities of the server's local UNIX file system. It does this by building a database on a file-by-file basis of the UNIX file system so it looks more like the PC file system.

For example, the server must offer case-insensitive file name lookup for PC clients. For older PC clients, the server must also generate DOS-style "8.3" file names (up to eight characters, plus up to three characters for an optional suffix). An "8.3" file name is not inherently included in UFS, so the CIFS emulation application must store it elsewhere. Similarly, UFS does not provide case-insensitive file name lookup; the CIFS server emulation application must do this for itself.[25]

Hitz says that NAS devices that employ emulation methods—mapping server data to meet client file system requirements—pay a penalty in terms of increased processing overhead and reduced performance. Such emulations are also never complete, he notes, referring to the difficulty in resolving locking concepts in CIFS with those in NFS, "Emulation makes file locking impossible. NT uses physical locks—imagine a locked door. UNIX file systems use advisory locks—imagine a door with a "Please Knock" sign on the handle. You can't resolve this dissonance with an emulated solution."

The solution, according to Hitz, is to use a native file system on the NAS device implemented at the microkernel level for improved performance. That is the thinking behind Network Appliance's Write Anywhere File Layout (WAFL) file system (see Figure 7–5).

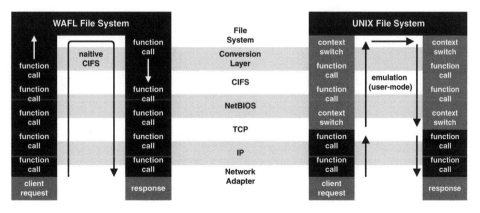

Figure 7–5   Native File System (WAFL) vs. Emulation Application. (*Source:* Network Appliance, Santa Clara, CA.)

Says Hitz, the WAFL file system is designed specifically for extensible file service and implements NFS, CIFS, and HTTP file access protocols natively. Using kernel-level calls, the WAFL file system provides all semantic conversions more efficiently than emulated approaches, which are executed at the user application level. Moreover, the file system delivers kernel-based security and file locking enforcement mechanisms that are stronger than emulators can deliver.

A KLUDGE AT BEST

Anton Murphy, Director of Business Computing with Storage Computer Corporation, observes that cross-platform file sharing—whether within a NAS device or on a stand-alone intelligent storage array—will never be an easy issue to resolve.[26] He emphasizes that the increased intelligence in storage platforms is enabling the more efficient sharing of storage resources in heterogeneous open systems environments. Technologies such as the vendor's own Virtual Storage Architecture can deliver a vast amount of scalable storage that can be allocated on a logical volume basis to both NT and UNIX hosts, Murphy observes. Plus, with increasingly intelligent on-board processors and embedded server technologies, platforms can arbitrate access to data more effectively, applying file locks and performing other functions that can derive the greatest benefits from network-based file access protocols.

However, Murphy concedes that all of these capabilities have moved storage no closer to a "data-sharing nirvana." He agrees with a number of other industry insiders that true data sharing will not happen until the industry can rid itself of the kludges and workarounds necessitated by the inconsistencies in heterogeneous operating systems and file systems.

Innovations like the WAFL file system provide "data storage transparency," says Network Appliance's Cheena Srinivansan. "It eliminates the need to partition and manage storage as separate volumes."[27]

WAFL may constitute a highly efficient technology for heterogeneous data storage and access control, but it is not true data sharing. In the final analysis, says Scott Drummond, Data Sharing Brand Manager with IBM's Data Sharing Competency Center in San Jose, CA, what will be needed is a universal file system.[28]

"How do you get to true data sharing in file systems when they have been created as part of completely different operating systems and are jealously protected by their vendors, Microsoft, Sun Microsystems, or any number of other OS vendors?" Drummond asks. "None of our research at

IBM has gone much beyond the analysis of the problem. No one would be willing to pay what it would cost to implement a universal file system that runs on all platforms. It will still be a problem five years from now."

INTEGRATING NAS WITH THE ENTERPRISE STORAGE INFRASTRUCTURE

Data sharing aside, Network-Attached Storage devices are delivering a storage architecture that complements the efforts of large storage array designers and SAN pioneers in many respects. Like SANs and intelligent array products, NAS devices centralize storage onto fewer platforms, off-loading I/O functions from general purpose servers and enhancing ease of administration and management.

While early reactions to NAS devices were mixed and some ob-servers were troubled by their tendency to decentralize rather than recen-tralize storage, most of these concerns have been put to rest. In early 1999, NAS vendor, Network Appliance, announced a partnership with SAN fabric switch manufacturer, Brocade Communications Systems, aimed at developing storage networking architectures integrating the benefits of both storage area networks (SAN) and network-attached storage (NAS) environments. The companies share an interest in creating "a single, high performance storage solution for managing and sharing enterprise data over an integrated SAN and NAS architecture, using common protocols for data access (see Figure 7–6)."[29]

Such an integration would be a step toward improving the scalability of NAS storage, while setting the stage for enterprise-wide storage infra-structure management via a back-end Storage Area Network.

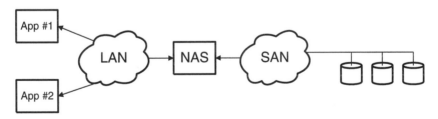

Figure 7–6   A SAN/NAS Shared Architecture. (*Source:* Network Appliance, Santa Clara, CA.)

ENDNOTES

1. Interview with Pat McGarrah, Director of Technology Programs, Quantum Corporation, Milpitas, CA, 1998.
2. The 1.5 terabyte limit is a matter of some disagreement. According to Kevin Phaup, Group Program Manager for Windows NT at Microsoft Corporation, "We no longer use a 32-bit file system. At Compaq's Test Labs, we recently tested a 2.8 terabyte file operating across 340-plus disks treated as a single volume. NT's maximum file size is (2^54-1) bytes and maximum volume size is in the neighborhood of 16 terabytes now and the number of volumes is limited only by the amount of memory in the host system. I presume Sun Microsystems has also changed its 32-bit file system to get around these restrictions." Interview with Kevin Phaup, Microsoft Corporation, Redmond, WA, 1999.
3. *Ibid.* McGarrah observes that the decision hasn't been finalized that Fibre Channel-Arbitrated Loop is the best interface for a switched fabric, "NGIO from Intel is one possibility. It is their replacement for the PCI bus, which does not support hot plugging or a 64-bit operating system. NGIO will allow you to get the RAID controller off the motherboard and to use special storage buses for I/O processing. They are talking about extending the I/O bus using transceivers that are a cross between Fibre Channel and Gigabit Ethernet. The NGIO data frame is designed for networking storage. The first few bytes of the frame can be used to route the frame, enabling the construction of cheap, $5 switches."
4. *Ibid.* McGarrah concedes that there are some workarounds to some of the issues he cites with respect to SANs. Within RAID arrays themselves, SCSI, rather than Fibre Channel-Arbitrated Loop, can be used as a bus and Fibre Channel can be used to connect the cabinet to the SAN, "I have no problems with mixed specifications."
5. Interview with Tom LaHive, Senior Analyst for Server Storage and RAID, Dataquest Corporation, Westborough, MA, 1998.
6. Brian O'Connell and Michael Alexander, "Storage Networks to the Rescue!," ACCESS Magazine, June 1998.
7. Director of the Enterprise Group for Microtest, Inc., Chris Gray, claims that his company originated the concept of the thin server in the early 1990s when the firm delivered a network-attached CD-ROM tower. Says Gray, "We stumbled onto thin server first. We understood that a CD-ROM tower was a single function device that didn't require an owner's manual to operate—kind of like a toaster. In 1993, we released a product that attached to a network with RJ45 and looked like a part of a selected Novell server. Later, we used an NCP emulation on top of IPX to look like a Novell server ourselves to PCs on the LAN. This was the beginning of appliance networking. We have just begun shipping our latest product, the DiscPort™ Virtual Tower, which looks like a server on the net, and has a hard disk that takes an image off a

CD-ROM title for faster response to user requests." Interview with Chris Gray, Microtest, Inc., Phoenix, AZ, 1998.

8. From a Dataquest server category definition quoted in "The Thin Server Landscape," a Creative Design Solutions white paper, Creative Design Solutions, Santa Clara, CA, 1998.

9. According to Carnegie Mellon University, file service is the single largest contributor to server performance degradation. Even under light file service loads, server processors can spend up to 25 percent of their cycles processing I/O requests. This percentage scales upwards rapidly as simultaneous requests increase, dramatically impacting processor and disk subsystem. These findings are presented in "File Server Benchmark Study," a Creative Design Solutions white paper, Creative Design Solutions, Santa Clara, CA, 1998.

10. Interview with James Staten, Senior Analyst, Dataquest, San Jose, CA, 1999.

11. *Ibid.*

12. "Auspex 4Front™ NS2000 System Architecture: Network-Attached Storage for a New Millenium," Auspex Technical Report 24, Auspex Systems, Inc., Santa Clara, CA, 1999.

13. Interview with Cheena Srinivasan, Director of Enterprise Marketing, Network Appliance, Inc., Santa Clara, CA, 1998.

14. *Ibid.*

15. "LynxxNSS™ Network Storage Servers: Architectural Approach and Design," Philip Kao, Product Marketing Manager, Artecon, Inc., Carlsbad, CA, 1998.

16. One Carnegie Mellon University study observes that, while virtually all storage vendors would like to offer NAS products, "The problem for these vendors is the huge cost associated with developing this software. Companies, like Network Appliance, that have done this have placed most of their investments into the software while using commodity hardware. Programmed Logic (PLC) has significantly reduced the storage software development cost by providing an embedded storage management environment (StackOS) that allows its suite of mission-critical storage management products to be run with RTOSs." "An Embedded Storage Management Environment—Programmed Logic," Computer Science Department, Carnegie Mellon University, date unknown.

17. Writing in Dataquest's Client/Server Virtual Views, Issue 15 April 10, 1998, James Staten observes, "REALM has a unique position in the thin-server market as the only vendor currently marketing a complete thin-server-optimized operating environment. While many thin-server vendors are using freeware or traditional operating environments and optimizing them themselves, this may not prove a viable option for many companies because of lack of expertise, time to market, or other issues. REALM allows a company to concentrate on its hardware design and [user interface] without having to design the operating environment or core services. Dataquest expects REALM's environment to be attractive to newcomers to the thin-server market as well as some existing

players looking for some of the features and services REALM delivers. The company's recent move to eliminate per-seat licensing and move to a modular pricing plan should increase the appeal of the Universal environment, as it will allow thin servers to be deployed in a wider range of environments with varying usage models. Dataquest recommends clients investigate REALM's offerings." REALM Information Technologies LLC is located in Atlanta, GA, and can be accessed via the World Wide Web at www.realminfo.com

18. CrosStor Software, which was founded as Programmed Logic Corporation in 1990 by former Bell Labs engineers, provides NAS, SAN, and storage software for OEMS in open systems and embedded markets. Its storage-centric operating system and core file management technology provide network appliances, commercial operating systems and embedded systems with mission-critical storage capabilities. The company's initial mission, to develop storage management and data management products for the UNIX operating system and related open-system technologies, evolved over time to one of supporting the growing need of OEMs to develop dedicated, network-attached storage (NAS) systems. At the same time, embedded manufacturers, selling special-purpose systems that run over real-time operating systems (RTOSs), were demanding high-performance file systems. In 1997, as a direct response to these needs, CrosStor introduced StackOS, its framework for providing storage-centric operating system capability over a thin operating system. CrosStor's product line includes CrosStor NAS, the industry's most advanced, storage-centric operating system for the development of network-attached storage appliances. CrosStor NAS plugs and plays over a commercial or custom RTOS and supports various configurations, from single-disk to multiterabyte filers. It supports CIFS, NFS, and HTTP protocols and lets OEMs create a single appliance that supports Microsoft Windows and UNIX files that can optionally be stored in a single, unified directory. CrosStor's CIFS capability can be enhanced to operate over fibre channel, to create a high-speed protocol for heterogeneous file sharing in SAN environments. CrosStor is headquartered in South Plainfield, NJ, can be contacted via its Web site at www.crosstor.com.

19. There are currently four Requests for Comment associated with NFS on file with the Internet Engineering Task Force (IETF), which maintain order on protocols and information technology affecting on the Internet. RFC's currently related to the NFS protocol are:

- RFC 1094—NFS: Network File System Protocol Specification
- RFC 1057—RPC: Remote Procedure Call Specification Version 2 [supersedes RFC 1050]
- RFC 1014—XDR: External Data Representation Standard
- RFC 1813—NFS Version 3 Protocol Specification

20. Published as XO-92a and XO-92b.

21. Says the Microsoft web site, "Microsoft is making sure that CIFS technology is open, published, and widely available for all computer users. Microsoft has submitted the CIFS 1.0 protocol specification to the Internet Engineering Task Force (IETF) as an Internet-Draft document and is working with interested parties for CIFS to be published as an Informational RFC. CIFS (SMB) has been an Open Group (formerly X/Open) standard for PC and UNIX interoperability since 1992 (X/Open CAE Specification C209)."

22. Andy Watson, "Multiprotocol Data Access: NFS, CIFS and HTTP," Network Appliance Technical Report 3014, Revision 2, July 1998, Network Appliance Inc., Santa Clara, CA.

23. *Ibid.*

24. Interview with Dave Hitz, Founder and Director of Systems Architecture, Network Appliance, Santa Clara, CA, 1998.

25. "Multiprotocol Data Access," *op. cit.*

26. Interview with Anton Murphy, Director of Business Computing, Storage Computer Corporation, Nashua, NH, 1998.

27. Interview with Cheena Srinivasan, Director of Enterprise Marketing, Network Appliance, Inc., op. cit.

28. Interview with Scott Drummond, Data Sharing Brand Manager, IBM Data Sharing Competency Center, San Jose, CA, 1998.

29. "Network Appliance and Brocade Partner to Establish Interoperability Between SAN- and NAS-Based Storage Networking Architectures. NetApp Also Announces Agreement to OEM BROCADE's SilkWorm® Fibre Channel Fabric Switch," Press Release, Network Appliance, Santa Clara, CA, January 25, 1999.

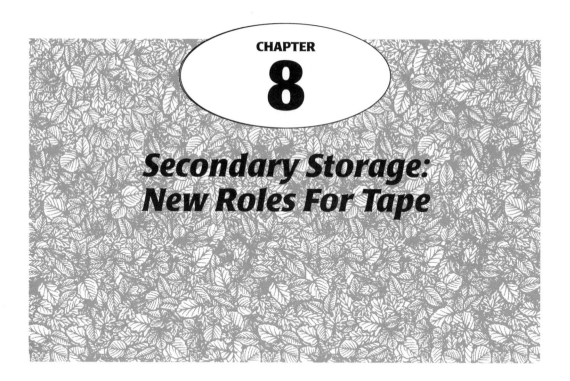

CHAPTER
8

Secondary Storage: New Roles For Tape

In the spring of 1997, while the attention of most IT professionals turned to the potential impact of the El Nino effect on U.S. weather patterns, TeraStor Corporation developers announced plans to ship a revolutionary product that would "take the removable storage media industry by storm." The description of the product, dubbed a "tape killer" by media pundits, contained enough *Star Trek*-quality techno-speak to make industry watchers take note.

TeraStor developers were integrating two technologies: a Solid Immersion Lens (SIL) from Stanford University and fixed-distance, flying read–write head technology developed by Digital Equipment Corporation and later acquired by Quantum Corporation. The result was a near-field recording (NFR) removable media drive.

In operation, the SIL is used to focus a narrow beam of laser light on a magnetic media platter. The laser heats the surface of the media, enabling extremely small magnetic bit cell sizes for data storage. In so doing, the NFR innovation realizes dramatic improvements in storage capacities on magnetic disk media. Also, since the NFR drive is designed like a hard disk drive, it offers faster read–write access capabilities than do tape or magneto-optical drive products.

Figure 8–1 depicts the differences between NFR, magnetic disk, and MO drive read–write heads. The NFR is a hybrid of existing magneto-optical and magnetic hard disk-style read–write head technologies and, according to TeraStor, achieves the highest areal densities possible with current technology. Table 8–1 provides a further comparison of both the media and the drive technologies.

Marketing, like meteorology, is rarely an exact science. The storm forecasted by TeraStor failed to materialize within the expected time-frame. While the company demonstrated functional 10 GB and 20 GB capacity devices per plan in 1998, delays and technical difficulties postponed introduction of the drives to the marketplace. As this book goes to print, no NFR products have shipped from TeraStor.

Despite the delays, NFR has all the earmarks of a technology on the verge of happening. Most significantly, on September 15, 1997, an announcement was made by TeraStor and Quantum Corporation that the companies would jointly develop NFR removable disk technology. Quantum, whose DLTtape format leads the mid-range tape market, made an equity investment in TeraStor early on and licensed its patents to the company for critical component technologies in exchange for the rights to develop, manufacture, and sell its own line of products based on TeraStor specifications.

Additionally, alliances have been made with manufacturers of storage media, including Maxell Corporation, TOSOH, and Imation Corporation, to ensure multiple sources for the storage cartridges that will be used with the removable disk system. Mitsumi Electric Company LTD has been tapped to manufacture the NFR drive itself on an exclusive basis.

TeraStor's Near-Field Recording	Conventional Magneto-Optical	Conventional Hard Disk Magnetic Recording

- <6m Flying Height
- Near-Field Recording
- Plastic Substrate
- Recording Layer Top of Substrate
- Releative Areal Density = 10x

- <1mm Spacing
- Far-Field Recording
- Recording Layer Under Substrate
- Relative Areal Density = 1x

- <2m Flying Height
- Magnetic Field Recording
- Alum/Glass Substrate
- Recording Layer Top of Substrate
- Relative Areal Density = 1x

Figure 8–1   NFR, MO, and Magnetic Read–Write Heads Compared. (*Source:* TeraStor Corporation, San Jose, CA.)

Table 8-1   Technology Comparison Table

Characteristic	Magnetic Hard Disk	Magneto-Optical	Near-Field
MEDIA			
Substrate	Aluminum/Glass	Glass/Plastic	Plastic
Recording Surface	Top	Bottom	Top
Tracks Defined by	Servo Track Writer (STW)	Stamped	Stamped or STW
DRIVE			
Write–Read Technology	Magnetic Field	Far-Field	Near-Field
Writing Process	Coil Switching	Constant Coil (2 Pass)	Coil Switching
Writing Limit	Induction/Gap Flying Height	Objective Lens	Solid Immersion Lens (SIL)
Reading Process	Inductive, MR	Kerr Effect	Kerr Effect
Head Spacing Servo Required	No	Yes	No
Read Channel	PRML	PWM	PRML
Direct Overwrite	Yes	No	Yes
Known Density Limits	Super Paramagnetic Limit	Laser Wavelength Low NA	Orders of Magnitude Beyond Known Limits of Winchester & MO
Major Capacity Enabler and Limiter	Flux sensor Gap Flying Height	Objective Lens Numerical Aperture (NA)	Solid Immersion Lens (SIL)

Source: TeraStor Corporation, San Jose, CA.

Despite this impressive gathering of resources, with delays in product shipment, the original enthusiasm for NFR in the trade press and analyst community has cooled. At this point, NFR is generally relegated to the "niche technology" category by industry observers. For example, Bob Amatruda, Senior Analyst for Tape and Removable Storage at International Data Corporation, observes that rotating media and random access characteristics of NFR "might deliver some advantages in certain applications." However, the analyst adds, the price per gigabyte characteristics of NFR will probably not make the technology a threat to tape.

> The sweet spot for backup and storage products aimed at the back end system [or mid-range] market is 20GB. TeraStor promises a drive with this capacity in 1999. It will have to compete with DLTtape and numerous 4 mm and 8 mm tape products that play well there. In order to compete, the price point for removable NFR media will need to be competitive with tape media, which is falling below $30 per cartridge now for 4 mm.[1]

Using the traditional model of tape backup as a guide, Armatruda may well be correct in his assessment of the future of NFR. Tape, which is the original storage media for computing technology, was supplanted by disk technology as the "primary storage media" (i.e., media for online data storage) for performance reasons in the early 1960s. Since then, tape has found a role as the secondary (i.e., backup or archival) storage media of choice in mainframe, mid-range, and desktop computing environments. In that traditional role of backup and recovery, tape capacity and cost per gigabyte, rather than performance, has provided the discriminator between different products.

However, there are some signs that this is changing. Midpoint loading tape, intelligent tape, and disk-buffered or virtual tape products are already in circulation, or are being prepared for market, that seek to reintroduce performance as a product discriminator. Against this backdrop, alternative removable media such as NFR may find a business case.

THE MARKET FOR TAPE

The tape market is treated by most analysts as three submarkets: the high-end or enterprise/mainframe market; the open systems, network, or mid-range market; and the low-end or desktop market. As suggested in Figure 8–2, different tape products have been developed to meet the typical storage requirements of each market—primarily in terms of capacity, tape durability, scalability, and price.

Using tape media as a guide, the differences in these three markets can be better defined. This delineation is not absolute, however, owing to the periodic repositioning of tape technologies by vendors to capitalize on whatever market is showing signs of growth at any given time.

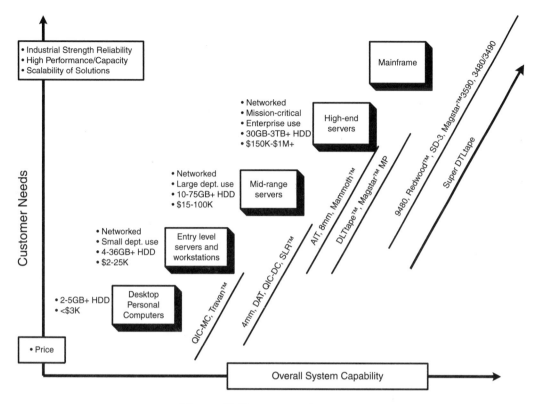

Figure 8–2   Tapes and Markets.

TAPE IN THE LARGE SYSTEMS MARKET

IBM 3480, 3490, 3490E, and Magstar™ 3590 tape cartridges, as well as Storage Technology's Redwood™ SD-3, and an assortment of 19 mm products from companies such as Ampex, are tape media alternatives common to the high-end, enterprise systems/mainframe space. Most products in this market segment feature a cartridge format, which emerged in the 1970s in response to complaints that reel-to-reel tape was too unwieldy to handle and store.

According to one industry watcher, "It is not an exaggeration to say that sales of 3480/90 media have by now exceeded a billion units. But, other than for replacement, sales of new drives [in the high-end market] have probably passed their peak."[2]

Magstar is the latest model in IBM's half-inch, single-hub cartridge line, which comprises the 3480, 3490, and 3490e. The product boasts a capacity of 10 GB per cartridge, and IBM offers numerous Magstar subsystems that feature both ESCON and SCSI connectivity, signaling the positioning of the media for use with applications on both IBM mainframes and mid-range systems. Current Magstar tape libraries from IBM and other vendors can hold thousands of cartridges.

Magstar 3590 is not to be confused with IBM's Magstar MultiPurpose, or MP, tape, which is aimed directly at mid-range systems and special applications. While Magstar MP shares the linear recording method of the original Magstar (data is written to parallel tracks along the length of the tape, much like an audio cassette recorder,[3] see Figure 8–3), MP is completely different in form factor and design from the 3590. Magstar MP uses a 5 GB cassette-style cartridge rather than a single-hub unit, and it uses 8 mm tape rather than half-inch.

The Magstar MP cartridge was especially designed for picking in a robotic library, according to IBM. Sometimes referred to as a high availability or fast access product, Magstar MP is designed begin its operation at the middle of the tape, rather than the beginning, which, the vendor claims, cuts access time in half.

As a fast-access medium, Magstar MP is being positioned as a solution for more than backup and archive applications. According to a report by Strategic Research, high-availability tape products, like Magstar MP, may take on the role of near online storage—traditionally the domain of magneto-optical drives and jukeboxes. The cost per megabyte of storage for high-availability tape begins at $0.05 to $0.08, while optical jukeboxes cost more than twice that amount. This cost difference, says the analyst, is significant when a company is purchasing hundreds of gigabytes of storage.[4]

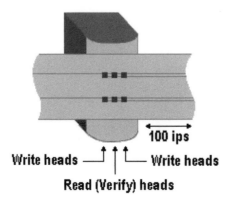

Figure 8–3   Linear Recording Method.

Magstar 3590, too, has become an integral part an IBM offering ultimately aimed at a near online storage role. The Magstar Virtual Tape Server (VTS), introduced in 1997, featured a combination of a Magstar 3590 tape subsystem and a disk array "buffer" intended to "reduce tape operation costs through transparent, effective use of tape resources, and by reducing the number of tape cartridges, tape drives, and automation systems required." (A VTS uses a disk buffer to hold data intended for tape storage until a sufficient quantity of data is present to fill the tape completely, thereby maximizing tape utilization and reducing cost in environments that use a lot of tape.) In early 1999, IBM added an UltraSCSI interface to the its Magstar VTS, enabling its use in the mid-range space.[5]

According to Frank Elliot, Vice President of Marketing and Strategy with IBM's Storage Systems Division,

> Tape has a lot of runway other than archive and backup. Look at our Web Cache Manager for e-business. It is basically a tape library and serial disk array in a black enclosure. The disk caches web pages, and the tape stores less frequently accessed pages. There is a continual update as in hierarchical storage management, but it is an example of how tape can be applied to a business problem other than archive.[6]

This view is echoed by Mike Harrison, Director of Marketing for IBM's Disk Storage Systems Division,

> The fact is, there is a big change going on with tape. In the past, VTS was strictly an archive device, but think about the magnitude of data and access requirements out there. Tape's historical market, backup and recovery, is growing into a much bigger market. Fast-access tape and the virtualization of storage has the potential to find new applications for tape technology in the transactional environment. Over time, we might want to change the product image of VTS and other tape products. But, right now, even within the limits of VTS, you can do other things with it.[7]

One of IBM's chief competitors in the mainframe space is Storage Technology (StorageTek). StorageTek's established Redwood™ media consists of a half-inch, single-hub cartridge that is similar in some respects to IBM's 3480/3490 formats. However, StorageTek has designed Redwood to use helical scan recording, rather than linear recording. Helical scan is a method for reading and writing data to tape using a rotating head/drum assembly, much like the recording mechanism in a video cassette recorder (see Figure 8–4).

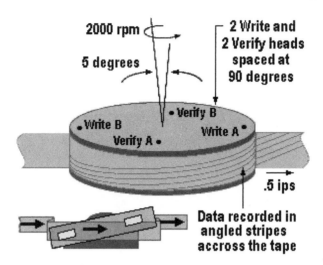

Figure 8–4   Helical Scan Recording Method.

According to StorageTek engineers, helical scan recording enables Redwood to take full advantage of the half-inch tape width, resulting in storage capacities more than sixty times greater than 36-track linear recording technology. Higher capacity results from writing data to the tape in tracks that are at an angle across the width of the tape. Doing so creates a large number of short tracks positioned close together, giving a net result of higher recording densities.

Redwood offers up to 50 GB of storage per cartridge, an 11.25 MB/s transfer rate (uncompressed) and 3:1 ICRC compression, for capacities up to 150 GB. StorageTek has designed the media for use in a range of products including the Redwood SD-3 drive, which supports 10, 25, and 50 GB cartridges, and StorageTek's Powderhorn™ automated tape library system, which can hold a mix of both Redwood and IBM 3480/3490 cartridges.

In 1998, an enhanced version of the Redwood media, the RedWood SD-3 VolSafe cartridge, was introduced that "satisfies U.S. government requirements in applications where data must be protected from overwrite or modification." VolSafe, in effect, became the first tape-based Write Once Read Many (WORM) product in the industry, enhancing its positioning as an alternative to optical WORM drives.[8]

Also in late 1998, StorageTek began shipping a new cartridge, the 9840, co-designed by Imation to be form-factor compatible with older IBM 3480 cartridges (and also the 10,000 tape robots currently installed by

StorageTek throughout the world). The new, half-inch, metal particle tape, with a native capacity of 20 GB, is recorded in longitudinal serpentine mode at a rate of 10 MB/s.

Unlike 3480 cartridges, the 9840 features a dual hub architecture. However, the tape remains inside the cartridge of the 9840, and the read–write head approaches the media rather than the inverse. Better access times are achieved, because there is no need to unload the tape in order to wind it onto an exterior axis.

StorageTek's answer to Magstar MP, the 9840 is also a midpoint loading tape. The tape will automatically wind to its midpoint upon loading and features an 18-second seek time from midpoint to either end. The cost for 9840 is about the same as IBM Magstar media. As with comparable IBM offerings, the 9840 tape drive is equipped with an Ultra SCSI or ESCON interface.

TAPE PRODUCTS CROWD THE MID-RANGE

The interest of IBM and StorageTek in delivering products to the mid-range market should come as no surprise. A January 1999 finding by International Data Corporation (IDC) indicated that mid-range is the growth segment of a $3.3 billion tape drive market.[9] Of the numerous, competing tape technologies in the mid-range space, Quantum Corporation's Digital Linear Tape (DLT) is the leader, with a 30 percent market share and shipments valued at $983 million in 1998, according to IDC.

DLT: KING OF THE MOUNTAIN

Digital Linear Tape originated in the mid-1980s when Digital Equipment Corporation (DEC) developed it as a half-inch tape backup solution for the MicroVAX. The technology was acquired by Quantum Corporation in 1994, and the company now licenses DLT to other tape drive and library manufacturers.

DLT is considered by many to be an adaptation of much older reel-to-reel magnetic recording technology. In operation, the single hub in the DLTtape cartridge serves as one "reel" and the tape drive serves as the other. The DLTtape path is shown in Figure 8–5.

The DLT drive's head guide assembly (HGA) is patented. It consists of a boomerang-shaped aluminum plate with six large bearing-mounted

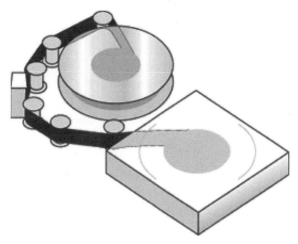

Figure 8–5 The DLTtape Path.
(*Source:* Quantum Corporation,
Milpitas, CA.)

rollers. Upon loading, tape moves from the cartridge, across the read–write head, then onto the take-up reel within the tape drive.

Everything about the design of the DLT drive centers on reducing wear and tear on the media itself and on the drive head (see Figure 8–6). Dual, computer-controlled motors precisely control the tensioning of the tape across the head to ensure optimal levels of contact, acceleration, deceleration, and read–write operation.[10] The HGA rollers do not pull or

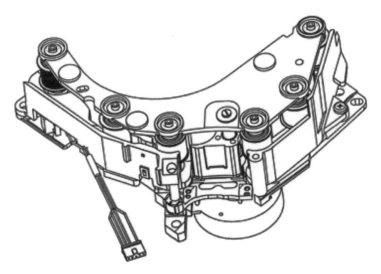

Figure 8–6 The Head Guide Assembly. (*Source:* Quantum Corporation, Milpitas, CA.)

pinch the tape, nor are the wrap angles around the guide controllers too severe. The magnetic side of the tape media never contacts the guides. The end result of this attention to detail is one of the longest head life statistics for any tape drive in the industry: about 30,000 hours. By contrast, 8 mm helical scan tape drives have a head life of approximately 2000 hours, which is considered adequate in an occasional-use, workstation setting.

The current DLTtape system family includes the DLT 2000XT, DLT 4000, and DLT 7000. The 2000XT is targeted to small or departmental mid-range and high-end desktop computer systems. The 4000 supports the same computing platforms, but with additional capacity. The DLT 7000 extends storage support for workgroup networking, enterprise computing, corporate intranets, and the Internet, with increased data transfer rate and capacity as summarized in Table 8–2.

In 1998, Quantum announced that it was extending the DLT product family to include a new generation of products called "Super DLTtape™." Drives are to begin shipping in 1999 and feature between 100 to 500 GB of uncompressed storage capacity and 10 to 40 MB/s transfer rates. They will be downwardly compatible with earlier drives and will be able to read cartridges recorded on DLT 2000, 4000, and 7000 drives.

DLT drives use half-inch metal particle (MP) tape, wider than most other tape products that have evolved from desktop systems into the mid-

Table 8–2   DLTtape Family

	DLTtape System 2000XT	**DLTtape System 4000**	**DLTtape System 7000**
Capacity (GB, native)	15	20	35
Data Rate (MB/second, native)	1.25	1.5	5.0
Bit Density (Kb/i)	62.5	82.5	86.0
Track Density (tpi)	256	256	416
Media Type	MP-1	MP-2	MP-2
Media Length	1800 feet	1800 feet	1800 feet
Recording Channels	2	2	4
Data Compression	Yes	Yes	Yes
Interface	SCSI-2	SCSI-2/Fast	SCSI-2/ Fast Wide

Source: Quantum Corporation, Milpitas, CA.

range space. DLT was the first tape technology to feature double-coated digital tape media, combining solid and liquid lubricants to reduce friction and to enable self-cleaning by the tape.[11] The uniform particle shape, dense binding system, smooth coating surface, and specially selected base film in the tape media enables DLT technology to take advantage of short wavelength recording schemes that bolster read compatibility.

Data recording occurs in a serpentine pattern on parallel tracks that are grouped into pairs on two channel drives and quads on four channel drives. Data recording is bidirectional: Once a set of tracks have been recorded in a forward pass through the entire length of the tape, the tape reverses and the next set of tracks is recorded in the opposite direction. High recording density is achieved by angling the data pattern on adjacent tracks using a technique called Symmetric Phase Recording (SPR) (see Figure 8–7).

SPR enables channel-independent data organization, allowing the DLTtape drive to place data and error correction checking blocks on any of channel pair or quad written by the drive. In the case of a bad block, the drive rewrites on the next available channel. This provides efficient write error handling and allows the unit to write data while a channel is temporarily inoperable or unavailable.

Tape technologies incorporate error detection and correction algorithms to prevent data loss. High-density tape technologies, such as DLT and others aimed at the mid-range market, record more data onto smaller segments of tape and depend more heavily on their error detection and correction schemes to be able to recover recorded data. DLT's error detection and correction system includes parity, multilayers of cyclical redundancy code (CRC), error detection code (EDC), and a multilevel,

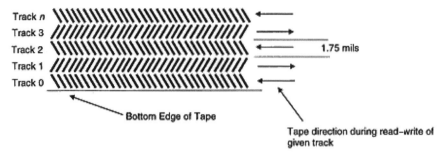

Figure 8–7   SPR Recording. (*Source:* Quantum Corporation, Milpitas, CA.)

interleaved Reed–Solomon error correction code (ECC) to ensure that data is being reproduced correctly, even under adverse conditions.

According to Quantum, a DLT7000 tape drive can recover all of the user data recorded on a single track within a channel up to six consecutive inches in length in the event of tape damage. The drive can recover all data stored on a tape segment up to one and one-half inches long that has been damaged across all four tracks of a channel.[12]

DLT boasts a balanced approach to speed and throughput that makes it appropriate to a broad range of applications. Some competitors attack DLT's data transfer rate, which is by no means the fastest in the industry, ignoring that the fastest tape drive doesn't always deliver the highest throughput. Overall tape throughput depends on a number of factors, including the difference between the tape system data transfer rate and the host system data rate. If the transfer rate of a tape drive is faster than the host data rate, the tape must stop and reposition frequently, degrading performance. DLT technology addresses this with an adaptive cache buffering feature. Using adaptive cache buffering, the drive monitors the host system and dynamically adjusts buffering and data transfer to match the host data rate. In this way, head repositioning is reduced and throughput is optimized.

DLT also provides an effective method for decreasing file access time that makes it appropriate to applications that require frequent file searches, such as HSM. A file mark index is written to the logical endpoint of a DLTtape, which lists the tape segment address of each file on the tape. The drive uses this list when performing seeks by first stepping to the appropriate track containing the requested file data then streaming to the location in the tape where the data is stored. This process delivers DLT's file access speed of 45 seconds on a 20-gigabyte capacity tape.

Super DLTtape™ will build on the capabilities of standard DLT, but will add "an order of magnitude increase over DLTtape capacity and transfer rate." Native capacity improvements of 100 GB to 500 GB per tape, and native transfer rates of 10 MB/s to 40 MB/s, will be delivered through the application of four enabling technologies to the tape product family.

New drives will feature a pivoting optical servo, combining high density magnetic read–write data recording with laser servo guidance, that Quantum says will enable an order of magnitude track count increase over current DLTtapes. Additionally, the new drives will use new magneto-resistive (MR) cluster read–write heads familiar from the hard disk world. The third innovation in the new Super DLT drives is the integration of an advanced Partial Response Maximum Likelihood (PRML) channel, co-developed by Quantum and Lucent Technologies, which enables higher recording densities and more reliable reads for greater capacity and performance. Finally, the new drives will use Advanced Metal Power (AMP) media that includes optical guiding tracks to enable the pivoting optical servo mechanism.[13]

KNOCKING DLT OFF THE TOP OF THE HILL

Quantum's current installed base in the mid-range tape field has even its competitors referring to the technology as a *de facto* industry standard. According to one industry insider, DLT is not necessarily the best, the fastest, the most pedigreed, or the most reliable tape technology, but it enjoys a combination of price and brand recognition that leaves competitors salivating.

There is no dearth of competitors offering vastly different approaches to tape media and drive design—and that doesn't include vendors of new "tape killer" technologies such as NFR. "Everyone," observes Zophar Sante, Senior Product Marketing Manager for Tandberg Data ASA, "is working to knock DLT off the top of the hill."[14]

Sante works with the Norwegian-headquartered Tandberg Data, which markets its own tape technology, Scalable Linear Recording (SLR), but also announced recently a deal with Quantum Corporation to sell DLT-based products.[15] He says that SLR is a descendent of the Quarter Inch Cartridge (QIC) standard established by 3M Company in 1972.

Tandberg's SLR (and competing technologies that build on QIC format tape such as Travan from 3M-spinoff, Imation) represent an "invasion" of the mid-range space by technologies originally developed for the desktop market. Before examining the specifics of these technologies, it may be advantageous to briefly review the QIC standards.

QIC TAPE AND ITS DESCENDENTS

In the early 1970s, incompatibilities between the PC tape drive products of numerous vendors—both between vendors and within their own product families—led to a standards–development initiative that formed the Quarter Inch Committee. While only partly successful in achieving actual compatibility goals, the committee did standardize the form factors of early tape cartridges, and references to QIC standards became a product capability shorthand when selecting tape units for PCs.

QIC cartridges resemble audio tape cassettes, with two reels inside, one holding a spool of tape and the other used for take-up. The reels are driven by a belt built into the cartridge. A metal rod, known as a capstan, projects from the drive motor and pinches the tape against a rubber drive wheel, actuating the spooling and despooling of the tape from one reel to the other.

The QIC format employs a linear (or longitudinal) recording technique in which data is written to parallel tracks that run along the length of the tape. The number of tracks on the media and the overall length of tape spun onto the reels by the manufacturer determine the native capacity of the tape. To this day, QIC tapes are available in two varieties: the DC600 cartridge and DC2000 minicartridge.

Most QIC tape drives feature a composite read–write head consisting of a single write head arranged between two read heads. This configuration permits the drive to verify writes on the fly when a tape runs in either direction across the head. As write verification occurs, a memory buffer on the disk controller (or in some configurations, the portion of system memory that is allocated for use as a buffer) is flushed and new data is acquired from the system memory. If errors are found, the segment is rewritten on the next length of tape.

Early QIC standards used data encoding methods for tape that were popular with the hard disk drives of the day, such as Modified Frequency Modulation (MFM) or Run Length Limited (RLL). During backups, both directory information and data are sent to the tape drive controller, and data is written to tape using a header preface containing directory listing information for the file, followed by the data of the file itself. Some controllers feature error correction and append an error correction code at the conclusion of the data write. Other drives use special software that adds the code directly to file data prior to recording.

In recording mode, the tape capstan actuates the tape so that it moves over the stationary read–write heads at about 100 inches per second. Data is written one track at a time with the simplest configuration, though some vendors added stacked additional read–write heads to improve data transfer speeds.

The operation of the QIC drive is serpentine, and data is recorded in blocks of 512 or 1024 bytes—32 per segment—along a track. With most QIC drives, 8 of the 32 blocks are reserved for error correction code, and each block contains a cyclic redundancy check (CRC) at its end to provide further error recovery protection. A special directory track, or the beginning of track 0, contains a complete directory of backed-up files.

By the 1990s, QIC standards were clearly unable to keep pace with the rapid changes in hard disk technology and capacity. Sony Corporation

Table 8–3   QIC Formats and Capacities

	Tracks	0.25 in Width	Longer Tape	0.315 in Width
QIC-80	28/36	from 80 MB	to 400 MB	to 500 MB
QIC-3010	40/50	340 MB	–	420 MB
QIC-3020	40/50	670 MB	–	840 MB
QIC-3080	60/72	1.2 GB	1.6 GB	2 GB
QIC-3095	72	–	4 GB	2 GB

managed to convince the QIC Committee about the need for longer and wider tapes, setting the stage for increased capacities. Some vendors took the increased capacity tape as the basis for developing entirely new tape formats. Table 8–3 lists some of the common QIC tape formats and their native capacities as of the mid 1990s.

Early QIC tape standards (the committee generated more than 120) embraced a hodgepodge of formats, distinguished in part by their use of parallel tape tracks. Most segregated the tape media into between twenty and fifty parallel tracks. The Travan format, which has evolved as a new stand-alone format using QIC media, uses between seventy-two and 144 tracks.

TRAVAN

The Travan specification represents an effort by 3M (now Imation) and others in the tape industry to "prop up" the QIC standard by offering newer, higher-capacity formats that feature a degree of downward compatibility with earlier QIC formats. Figure 8–8 depicts Imation's view of the future for the Travan standard.

"Travan Technology is now moving very nicely into the low-cost server market," says International Data Corporation analyst Bob Amatruda. "If you compare OEM drive pricing of Travan NS20 (a "network system" Travan product) as a percentage of system cost of servers, it comes out at about half the price of (4 mm tape) DDS-3. Travan NS20 stacks up very, very competitively."[16]

Server manufacturers and integrators offering Travan Technology include IBM, Hewlett-Packard, Acer, Toshiba, Data General, Micron, NCR, Unisys, Hitachi, and Intergraph, with additional announcements antici-

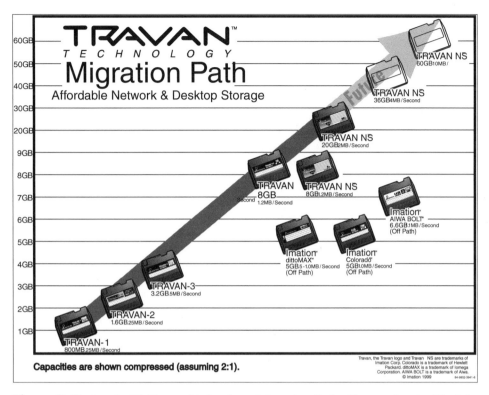

Figure 8–8   Imation™ Travan Technology Migration Path. (Source: Imation™, Oakdale, MN. Corp. © 1999)

pated in the coming months. Travan Technology drive partners include Tecmar Technologies Inc., Seagate Technology Inc., Hewlett-Packard, Aiwa America and Tandberg Data.

SCALABLE LINEAR RECORDING (SLR)

In addition to developing Travan-based (and now DLT-based) drive products, Tandberg Data has added its own innovations to the QIC standards in order to create yet another DC6000 cartridge-based drive format: Scalable Linear Recording. The entire family of SLR format products from the vendor use a dual-reel, linear recording design like the earlier QIC drives, but the media is midpoint loading and accessed through a small door by a head assembly that moves to the tape for reading and writing.

A key difference in the Tandberg Data design from other small server products is its use of an embedded servo system, MR multichannel heads that deliver increased transfer rates, support advanced encoding methods, and provide the basis for ongoing capacity improvements. According to Tandberg's Sante, an SLR100 model will be added in 1999 to the vendor's already extensive product line that delivers 100 GB capacity (with 2:1 compression) and 5 MB/s data transfer rate.[17]

Tandberg's quest to move its products into the mid-range market includes its licensing in 1998 of Overland Data, Inc.'s Variable Rate Randomizer (VR[2 ™]), an advanced data encoding technology that enables the application of PRML to linear tape formats, "yielding instant capacity improvements of up to 100 percent."[18] The primary barrier to implementing PRML on linear tape platforms in the past, according to Overland, has been overcoming instantaneous speed variations (ISV) that occur in host to tape data transfers. The vendor has surmounted this problem by developing a variable-rate encoding technique with a nondeterministic randomizer, which it now implements on a chip and licenses to drive technology manufacturers.[19]

At the time of the Tandberg Data VR[2] announcement, Fara Yale, Director and Principal Analyst at Dataquest, said that adding VR[2] technology to its SLR drives would effectively buy Tandberg a place the mid-range space. "If Tandberg can deliver on the promises of VR[2] technology, it will allow the company to move its future tape drives further upscale, creating a new competitive picture for the company. SLR products will move up in performance and capacity to compete in the mid-range server marketplace."[20]

If the "price to play" in the mid-range is a PRML-enabling chip, other vendors of tape products in the slow-growth, low-end segment of the tape market might follow the Tandberg example, industry observers speculated after the Tandberg/Overland deal. Not surprisingly, Imation announced a similar arrangement with Overland Data in early 1999 to benefit its own Travan product line.[21]

4 MM AND 8 MM CONTENDERS

In addition to QIC-derivative tape technologies, various 4 mm and 8 mm format tape formats also crowd the list of potential contenders for the DLTtape crown in mid-range. Most of these use helical, rather than linear, scanning methods. Helical scanning was adapted from 8 mm home videotape technology introduced in the mid-1980s. As the StorageTek's Redwood suggests, such recording methods enable high-capacity storage by writing data to angled tracks across the width of the tape.

DIGITAL DATA STORAGE (DDS)

Most 4 mm offerings are based on Digital Audio Tape (DAT) media introduced in the mid-1990s as an audio recording media capable of storing CD-quality sound. Sony and Hewlett-Packard joined in creating a standard for the use of the 4 mm tape cartridge in data storage in 1998.[22] Called the DDS (Digital Data Storage) standard, the technology is now in its third generation (DDS-3).[23]

DDS uses a helical scan recording system in which the tape is pulled from a two-reel cartridge and wrapped halfway around a cylindrical drum containing two sets of consecutively arranged read and write heads. As in QIC tapes, the read heads verify the data written by the write heads (see Figure 8–9).

The tape moves much more slowly, about 1 in/s, through this system than does a linear QIC tape. However, as data is recorded in diagonal tracks across the width of the tape, the effective recording speed is equal to 150 in/s.

Each track contains about 128 KB of data, plus error correction code (ECC). A read head verifies the operation of its corresponding write head. If errors are detected, the data is rewritten, otherwise the controller buffer is flushed and ready for writing the next segment. A second write head writes

Figure 8–9 Tape Track in a Helical Scan Recording System.

data at a 40 degree angle to the first. The first and second writes overlap, but they are magnetically encoded (e.g., have different polarities), so information is only read by the corresponding read head. This "helix" pattern, combined with compression technologies developed for DDS, enables 4 mm DDS systems to achieve very high data densities. As with QIC formats, most DSS drives write a directory of files in a partition at the front of the tape, or in a file on the hard disk.

Hewlett-Packard currently chairs the DDS Manufacturers Group—an association that includes competitive vendors such as Sony, Seagate, and Aiwa. HP was also the first to deliver a product based on DDS-3, the latest generation of the DDS technology standard. Table 8–4 identifies the evolution of the DDS standard in terms of capacity and data transfer rate (DTR).

The original DDS format exchanged the DAT continuous data streaming format for a computer data storage format defining a sequence of fixed-capacity groups on a tape. Limited to about 2 GB in capacity, it required two hours of sustained data transfer (typically at about 183 KB/s) to fill a tape.

DDS-2 enabled data transfers to occur in SCSI-2 burst mode and doubled the density of DDS media, while maintaining full DDS functionality and backward compatibility. As an interim improvement to DDS-2, DDS-DC was established to include a data-compression standard.[24]

The latest DDS format evolution, DDS-3, derives its high capacity from the addition of Partial Response Maximum Likelihood (PRML) technology, used to separate recorded data from background noise, and the embedding of timing information along recording tracks. According to HP, using the edge of the tape as a reference point, the drive is able to measure the time it takes to reach the first timing mark. "This is important because, if the timing is too early, the tape speed is increased to center the head on the track, and if it is too late, the tape speed is decreased."[25] In short, this method of time tracking enables both greater format efficiency and more precise head/track alignments.

Table 8–4   DDS Format Evolution

Standard	Capacity	Maximum DTR
DDS	2 GB	55 KB/s
DDS-1	2/4 GB	0.55/1.1 MB/s
DDS-2	4/8 GB	0.55/1.1 MB/s
DDS-3	12/24 GB	1.1/2.2 MB/s

These improvements to DDS position the technology to meet the needs of the low to middle segment of the mid-range tape market. The cost for DDS drives is generally double that of Travan-based products, and the dependence of the technology on SCSI as a drive interface is a further cost multiplier. Drives of each generation of DDS typically support downward read compatibility with tapes recorded in earlier generations.

Just as DDS builds on 4 mm digital audio tape technology, 8 mm tape formats derive their heritage from 8 mm digital videotape. The two share in common the use of helical scan technology for tape reading and writing. However, within the 8 mm data storage market, two distinct technologies have emerged that utilize different data compression algorithms and drive technologies. Exabyte Corporation sponsors Mammoth technology, which uses standard 8 mm tape cassettes. Seagate and Sony have developed both a distinctive cartridge design and a proprietary format known as Advanced Intelligent Tape (AIT).

MAMMOTH

If any episode in the tape industry could be deemed worthy of a Hollywood motion picture, it might be the Exabyte Mammoth story. Mammoth is regarded by former Exabyte management and many industry observers as the technology that should have dominated the mid-range market. Instead, two years of delays in developing drives to support the new tape format opened a window of opportunity that was exploited by DLTtape.

In an *InformationWeek* interview with Steve Georgis, the Director of Technology for Exabyte could not help sounding like Marlon Brando as Terry Malloy in the 1954 film, "On The Waterfront," exclaiming how Mammoth could have been a contender.[26] Says Georgis,

> Our sin was that we set expectations too high. We announced in 1993 that we would ship Mammoth by the end of 1994; it didn't come out until March 1996, so we opened the door for Quantum. . . . Our old drives were based on consumer technology. We realized early on that in order to provide the high reliability needed, we would have to veer away from that [tape mechanism] and develop our own firmware and mechanics. To grow that technology internally was complex. To make that technology simple made it even tougher.

The original intent of Exabyte was to deliver a common standard storage solution that would span from desktop to data center. The company backed away from this strategy in 1998, according to Georgis, "We tried to span all markets, but that didn't work. We closed out our desktop division in December. We are now clearly focused on application servers and mid-range backup. We have two primary goals: Against DLT we want to offer better performance at half the cost; against 4 mm and AIT [Sony's Advanced Intelligent Tape standard] we want to offer the best reliability. Finally, everything we do will be backwards-compatible to Mammoth I."[27]

Accomplishing these goals will first require successful delivery of Mammoth 2, which is scheduled for 1999, and also a very successful campaign to change OEM perceptions of Mammoth and Exabyte (see Figure 8–10). The latter is referenced by one Strategic Research Corporation analyst exploring the subject:

> As I circulate through the industry and ask the OEMs of tape drives what they think of Mammoth's new migration path, the usual answer is "I don't believe it. Why is this?" They say, "Because Mammoth was one year late." History says this comment is not pointed at Exabyte, per se, but an appreciation for how hard it is to take such large steps.[28]

From a hardware standpoint, Mammoth represents a departure from retooled camcorder-based designs that characterized early 8 mm tape backup products. As with DLT drives, the mechanical deck has been designed to reduce tape wear and tension variation, thereby extending tape life. Exabyte designs its product around a solid aluminum deck to maintain tight tolerances while protecting internal elements from dust and contamination and directing heat away from the tape path. The vendor

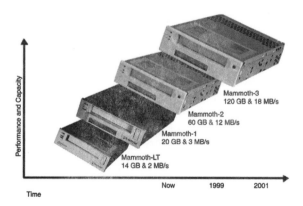

Figure 8–10   The Exabyte Mammoth Road Map. (*Source:* Exabyte Corporation, Boulder, CO.)

also eliminated the capstan from its design as capstans and pinch rollers exert the most wear on tape. This innovation enables the use of advanced metal evaporated (AME) tape and other highly sensitive tape media anticipated for the future.

AME is a data-grade tape, featuring anticorrosive characteristics and a thirty-year archival rating. Its smooth surface helps to substantiate Exabyte's claims that the head life on its drives is 35,000 hours—among the best in the industry.

Seven application specific integrated circuits (ASICs) are implemented on Mammoth drives to enable self-calibration and error reporting. A single processor is used and provides a servo function.

Mammoth supports up to 64 variable-length partitions. A partition is a segment of tape that is used as an entity unto itself. Data within a predefined partition can be erased and new data written in its place. This feature will become more valuable as media capacity continues to grow, allowing Mammoth to support such applications as multimedia and video servers.[29] Mammoth also uses a two-level, Reed-Solomon ECC scheme executed in hardware. ECC corrects errors on the fly by rewriting the blocks within the same track.

Exabyte must wage a "two-front war" to compete with other technologies such as DLT and AIT. The company's marketing literature positions Mammoth as a superior alternative to DLT by referencing DLT's "less reliable" single hub design, DLT's higher price for "comparable performance," and DLT's 40 percent slower data transfer rate in restore operations.[30] The literature then turns to Advanced Information Technology (AIT), a competing 8 mm format, and insists that: AIT drives have more parts, hence higher rates of failure than Mammoth drives; AIT drives use consumer-grade helical scan components that deliver greater wear to tape media; and AIT is optimized for desktop and small server systems while Mammoth is clearly a mid-range product with a clear development path.[31]

ADVANCED INFORMATION TECHNOLOGY (AIT)

The latter assertion does not agree with every independent assessment made of Mammoth and AIT. A 1998 test lab report published in *InfoWorld* found that both Mammoth and AIT share slow speeds (3 MB/s) and that file access times in Mammoth drives (55 seconds) are twice that of AIT drives. The reason cited for the faster performance of AIT is the 16 KB of permanent memory, called the memory in cassette (MIC), that is incorporated into AIT media.

AIT uses a memory chip to store directory file location information for all data recorded on its media. AIT media is also midpoint loading, which enables quick loads and shorter seek times when compared to Mammoth. On the other hand, AIT cartridges are more expensive than, and incompatible with, all other 8 mm cartridges on the market.[32]

AIT has the distinction of being the first "multisourced" tape standard in the industry. The technology borrows from media provided by Sony Corporation, disk drive controller technology from Seagate Corporation, and a hardware-based data-compression scheme called adaptive lossless data compression (ALDC) from IBM. Current drives support advanced metal evaporated (AME) media, as does Exabyte, and AIT drive manufacturers associate AME tape with longer read–write head life, as does Exabyte. (However, Exabyte also refers to its overall drive design as a contributor to extended head life and reduced wear.)

The MIC feature is a key component of the overall performance of the overall technology. According to Seagate, the MIC consists of a 16-Kbit erasable electrical programmable read-only memory (EEPROM) chip that is mounted within the data cartridge and includes a five-pin contact connector. When the data cartridge is inserted into an AIT drive, a mating connector within the drive contacts the MIC connector and data is read directly from the MIC (see Figure 8–11).

The MIC stores all of the information normally found on the first segments of tapes used in other technologies, including indices to mark where data files are located on the tape. Additional data fields have been added that allow application software to write information to the MIC that is separate from the tape format, enabling "smart searching" and seek speeds up to 150 times the normal read–write speed of the drive (see Figure 8–12).

Drive firmware estimates how far to fast-forward or rewind the tape based on MIC data, so an AIT drive does not need to read individual address ID markers as the tape is moving. As the target zone is approached, the motors slow to 75 times the read–write speed to pick up the ID markers for fine-positioning. This scheme also allows for the application software to command the drive to fast-forward to the next available partition and wait for a write or read command to begin.[33]

Seagate says that the MIC enables not only faster access to data, but also improved detection and analysis of media degradation, and better data set management through the use of user-defined volume and partition information. Up to 256 partitions can be created on a single tape.

AIT-1 technology provides a native storage capacity of 25 GB with 3 MB/s transfer speeds. The addition of hardware-based data compres-

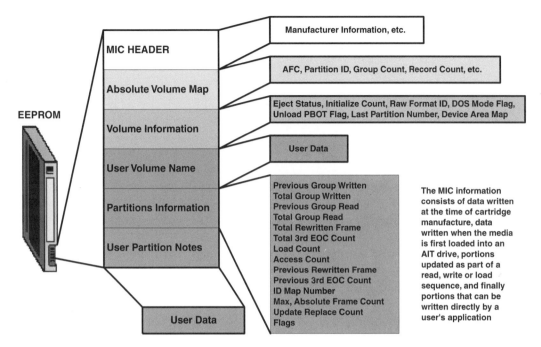

Figure 8–11   AIT Tape Cartridge and MIC. (*Source:* Seagate Technology, Scotts Valley, CA.)

Access to tape is improved

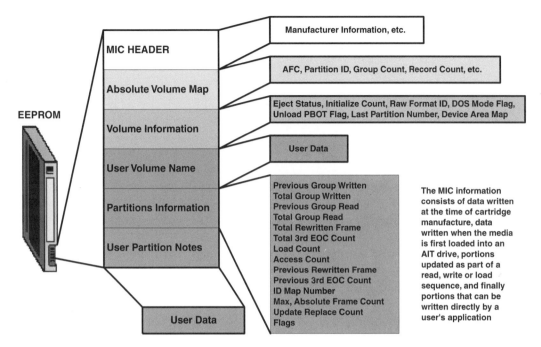

Figure 8–12   AIT MIC-Assisted Seek. (*Source:* Seagate Technology, Scotts Valley, CA.)

sion technology enables the packaging of data as densely as possible in the media provided.

In 1998, Sony announced a second generation of AIT technology, terming it (appropriately enough) AIT-2. The new technology doubles the native capacity per tape to 50 GB (100 GB with compression) and will deliver a 6 MB/sec sustained native transfer rate (12 MB/sec with compression). The new technology will be fully backward-compatible with AIT-1, according to John Woelbern, senior marketing manager of tape streamer products for Sony Electronics Computer Components and Peripherals Group, who further committed the company to "maximizing capacity and speed every two years while keeping the price competitive (see Figure 8–13)."[34]

Sony reportedly achieves the doubled capacity and improved performance features by implementing new technologies for recording heads, channel coding, media formulation, and mechanism design, as well as by implementing its own LSI chips.

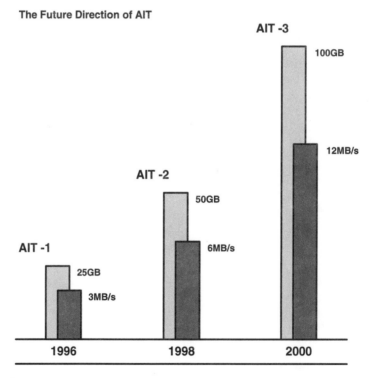

Figure 8–13   The AIT Migration Path. (*Source:* Sony Electronics, San Jose, CA.)

AIT-2 drives incorporate Sony-patented hyper metal laminate heads, which provide higher signal output than conventional heads, thereby allowing the AIT recording density to increase by 50 percent. Higher recording frequency, together with the longer tape and high drum speeds, provide a doubling of both capacity and data transfer rates.

In addition, the Trellis Coded Partial Response (TCPR), developed by Sony, delivers "optimal coding for a helical scan high-density recording format. TCPR strengthens the tapes characteristics against noise and ensures data reliability."

The MIC also changes with AIT-2. The new MIC consists of a 64 Kbit memory chip "incorporates a remote-sensing, noncontact head, which extends the head life." Improvements in advanced metal evaporated (AME) tape technology, including its patented diamond-like carbon (DLC), are also cited as contributing to greater reliability and better recording densities.

NEW PLAYERS ENTER THE MID-RANGE

AIT, Mammoth, DSS, Travan, and SLR, as well as Magstar, Magstar MP, Redwood, and 9840, all represent competing technologies in the midrange secondary storage space currently dominated by Quantum with DLTtape. To this list may be added several new players, whose first products are not scheduled to ship until the end of 1999 or the first months of the new millennium. These include yet-to-be-released offerings from the linear tape-open (LTO) initiative, called Accelis and Ultrium, and the VXA format from Ecrix Corporation.

LINEAR TAPE-OPEN (LTO)

The LTO initiative is guided by a triad of companies—IBM, Seagate Technology, and Hewlett-Packard—who have pooled several "best-of-breed" technologies to define implementations that may be licensed by tape and tape system manufacturers.[35] The companies are building on the multisource concept introduced with AIT technology and seek to create two tape formats that are interchangeable between the drives of multiple vendors. Neither of the two specifications will work with currently deployed drives, though form factor similarities contained in the specifications hint at the intention of the vendors to replace older drives and to use new drives with older libraries and subsystems.

LTO is a linear serpentine technology that "enables a higher number of concurrent channels." The roadmap calls for eight channels with first-generation products and future versions delivering up to sixteen channels. To accomplish this objective, specifications call for the use of state-of-the-art servo and head technologies.

LTO also strives at the realization of 100 Mb/in² —an areal density greater than any available with tape formats on the market at the time of the LTO announcement in 1998. This will be accomplished through the application of "a robust logical format including lock step recording across multiple data tracks protected by a true cross-product Error Correction Code (ECC)." Other features of the specification include an improved data compression algorithm, a new RLL code, dynamic rewrite of data written onto defective areas of the type, dynamic discontinuation of writing on unreliable regions of tape, and the use of LTO Cartridge Memory (LTO-CM) to allow old data to be easily disregarded and new write operations to be precisely triggered. With the new format, recording units will be indexed precisely via the longitudinal position encoded into the servo bands, permitting rapid searching and simplified error recovery.[36]

According to Sharon Stone, Product Line Manager for LTO at IBM, the initiative is designed to bring to market cartridges that are interchangeable among different tape systems from different vendors—a function that has proven problematic with the myriad tape formats on the market today. She notes that "interoperable" is not an adjective to be applied to LTO specification-based devices, "Interoperability issues continue to exist at the level of the operating system. LTO will not address this issue."

She further reports that the Ultrium specification has garnered considerable interest from media manufacturers and drive-maker Fujitsu Limited,[37] while the Accelis specification has not. Ultrium has roughly the same form factor characteristics as Quantum's DLTtape. It uses a single-reel design and targets ultra-high capacity backup, restore and archive applications, delivering up to 200 GB of capacity and data transfer rates of 10 to 20 MB/s (20 to 40 MB/s compressed).

Accelis appears to build on the form factor commonly associated with IBM's Magstar MP. It is a dual-reel tape designed for use with applications requiring fast access times (under 10 seconds) and is expected to deliver 10 to 20 MB/s data transfers on a 25 GB capacity cartridge in its first iteration.

It is worth noting that on the same day that IBM jointly released information about the LTO initiative (datelined Silicon Valley, CA), it also issued a second press release (datelined San Jose, CA) reaffirming its commitment to existing non-LTO tape products in its own product family. The second release stated that the "building blocks"—including Adaptive

Lossless Data Compression, Timing-Based Track Servo, high-efficiency error correction code, midpoint tape loading, a self-enclosed tape path cartridge design, and the ability to use magneto-resistive heads—that it was contributing to LTO are also being applied to its Magstar products. IBM also reaffirmed that both the 3590 and Magstar MP continue to be IBM's near-online products for "today and in the future."[38]

The LTO roadmap, provided in Table 8–5, represents an ambitious model for growing the two tape formats championed by the LTO group. Interestingly, many of the enhancements identified for the drives, including the use of PRML recording methods and metal particle media, transitioning to thin film over time, are already part of the development plans for existing formats, including DLTtape. This fact has both encouraged industry observers to give credence to the initiative and caused many to ask the question, "Why do we need two additional formats?"

Seagate's "Tech Tips," a web site containing advice and resources for value-added resellers, instructs VARs to direct sales of the Accelis to customers "needing online or near-line data inquiry and retrieval of large data-

Table 8–5   The LTO Roadmap

ACCELIS TAPE CAPACITIES

	Generation 1	Generation 2*	Generation 3*	Generation 4*
Native Capacity	25 GB	50 GB	100 GB	200 GB
Native Transfer Rate	10–20 MB/s	20–40 MB/s	40–80 MB/s	80–160 MB/s
Recording Method	RLL 1,7	PRML	PRML	PRML
Media	MP	MP	MP	Thin film
Access Time	<10 sec	<8 sec	<7 sec	<7 sec

ULTRIUM TAPE CAPACITIES

	Generation 1	Generation 2*	Generation 3*	Generation 4*
Native Capacity	100 GB	200 GB	400 GB	800 GB
Native Transfer Rate	10–20 MB/sec	20–40 MB/sec	40–80 MB/sec	80–160 MB/sec
Recording Method	RLL 1,7	PRML	PRML	PRML
Media	MP	MP	MP	Thin film

* Hewlett-Packard, IBM, and Seagate reserve the right to change the information in this migration path without notice.

Source: Seagate Technology, Removable Storage Solutions, Costa Mesa, CA.

bases, libraries, or data 'warehouses.' In other words, if your customer spends as much time reading data from tape as writing to it, then Accelis is the tape to recommend." Ultrium, according to the site, should appeal to customers "using tape in a high-capacity automated backup systems. If your customer expects to write data to tape frequently, but does not retrieve that data very often, then Ultrium is the format to recommend."[39]

Not surprisingly, Quantum Corporation and other entrenched vendors of existing tape formats stress the absence of compatibility in the two proposed LTO formats with tape popular formats that are already in use. Exabyte's Steve Georgis responds to the potential threat posed by LTO with a simple response, "Show me." He notes that all components and technologies in the Mammoth product family was designed or is owned by Exabyte directly.

> Since we control all our technology, we can take this and innovate as the market is ready to grow. We are ready to leverage our design; the other products have to be engineered from scratch. [The LTO initiative is trying to create] a multivendor industry standard. It is difficult enough to make tape drives interchangeable; to make vendors come together is even tougher. The question is this: Why does the marketplace need another tape standard?[40]

The view of the analyst community is more neutral than vendors of products based on competing standards. While several analysts felt that the late 1998 licensing of Ultrium by Fujitsu lent credibility to LTO, Farid Neema, president of market research company Peripheral Concepts Inc., observes only that "The next nine to twelve months will be significant. It will be a pretty confusing period to everyone. Everyone will wonder if all these standards will remain."

Says Neema, "It really depends on how much investment an enterprise has in its current tape backup operations. For mid- and small-sized enterprises, compatibility may not be that critical. But some managers are very concerned with compatibility. They want the assurance that they won't have to do anything [special] in order to get legacy data."[41]

ECRIX AND VXA

Equal parts enthusiasm and ambivalence have also greeted a new tape format proposed by Ecrix Corporation in 1998. Co-founded by Juan Rodriguez and Kelly Beavers—two tape industry veterans with past credits that include management stints at IBM, Storage Technology Corporation, and Exabyte Corporation—Ecrix's claims of a "breakthrough technology" were given more attention than might be afforded to other start-ups.

The offering from Ecrix is known as VXA Architecture, which may be better defined by its three component elements: discrete packet format (DPF), variable speed operation (VSO), and overscan operation (OSO).

DPF is the foundation for VXA technology and its data format. With DPF, data can be arranged on a tape so that it can be read while the tape moves in either direction. Long data strings are segmented into small data packets before being recorded. Packets contains 64 bytes of user data each, plus error correction code, cyclical redundancy check code, a synchronization marker, and address information; 387 packets comprise a track on a VXA tape. These are recorded and read through a buffer array that assigns each packet has a unique address. In this way, the VXA architecture can use any packet to reassemble all of the packets in their original string order.

VXA uses four read heads to access media. Data is read by all heads and stored to a buffer segment, prior to reassembly in order, and transmission to the requestor. If packets are found to contain errors, additional read head passages collect missing packets on the next pass and add them to the data string before forwarding to the host.

Chances of a recording error are reduced by means of a four level ECC is applied to the process in two phases. First, each packet uses a Reed-Solomon ECC to correct small write errors. Then, as the packets are collected in the buffer segment, a three-dimensional (X-axis, Y-axis, and diagonal) Reed-Solomon ECC scheme is applied. Ecrix says that the second ECC operation yields a bit error rate of 1×10^{-17}, affording tremendous error recovery capability.

VSO is Ecrix's technology for matching tape speed to host speed, enabling the reduction or elimination of tape "back-hitching." When the data transfer ends, a VXA drive slows down to enter a "Ready Mode." The drive can restart within 25 ms of its entry into that state.

VXA's OverScan Operation consists of a method for reading tape tracks that have become misaligned with the tape path and recording head—a typical tape wear-related problem with many current tape technologies. OSO provides the technology for VXA's four read heads to overscan the recorded area of the tape (e.g., scan an area greater than 100 percent), ensuring that every packet that can be read will be by at least one of the four heads. This is the mainstay of Ecrix's claim that their format produces truly interchangeable tape. No two drives have the same track geometry. Even small differences can introduce interchangeability obstacles that are not a problem for OSO technology (see Figure 8–14).

Details of the form factor and speeds of VXA technology drives are few in coming as of this writing. One analyst claims to have information that the

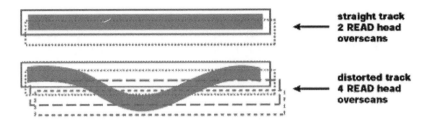

Overscanning guarantees that every packet will be read no matter how a track is aligned
to the head; if a packet is missed by one of the heads, then it is read by the other.

Figure 8–14   VXA OverScan Operation. (*Source:* Ecrix Corporation,
Boulder, CO. www.vxatape.com)

first generation VXA drives will provide 33 GB capacity and transfer rates of
3 MB/s, roughly equivalent in performance to DDS-3 drives. The drives will
use advanced metal evaporated (AME) media with a width of 8 mm, and
share an industry-standard 5.25-inch half-height form factor.[42]

Dataquest analyst, Fara Yale, believes that Ecrix will face enormous
challenges entering the market with yet another tape format. It will confront
an entrenched set of market leaders with established technologies and reseller channels. Ecrix maintains that "conventional streaming tape devices
haven't kept pace with industry price and performance expectations" and
that "their complex mechanics and state-of-the-art electrical components
allow for capacity and transfer rate improvements, but at unrealistic prices."

Writes Yale, "While Dataquest does not rejoice in the introduction of
yet another tape format, we do believe that VXA technology, and Ecrix's
claims of reliability, low-price, and guaranteed data interchange will
prove to be intriguing enough to stimulate resellers and OEMs to take a
close look at the Ecrix products."[43]

INTO THE RACK

Tape formats serve as the fundamental building blocks of automation solutions designed to meet specific storage requirements. The requirements,
themselves, are dictated by the application to which tape technology is
being applied. Traditional applications include backup and restore, hierarchical storage management and archive. Of these, backup is by far the
most common.

In a backup application scenario, tape is deployed to serve as a
repository for the data stored on hard disk or disk arrays. Typically, the
capacity of the disk array exceeds the capacity of a single tape (regardless

of format). To reduce costs, unattended operation of the disk-to-tape transfer is preferred. For this reason in particular, automated tape systems have come into wide use in mid-range and enterprise IT environments.

The list of vendors marketing automated tape systems is far to extensive to cover here. However, most products fit within three high-level categories: stackers, autoloaders, and libraries. Stackers typically consist of a single tape drive and a mechanism for automatically exchanging and loading a stack of tape cartridges. Autoloaders are discriminated from stackers by their ability to load specific tapes on demand. Libraries typically feature the same functional capability as autoloaders but have a much more sophisticated method of operation, including robotic arms, multiple tape drives, a large complement of tape cartridges, and controller electronics and software that enable them to respond to multiple service requests issued by heterogeneous host systems. Bar code readers are often integral to automated tape libraries (ATLs), which use them to identify tape volumes for loading.

In an automation environment, the access and data transfer speeds of tape drives themselves is compounded by the speed of the automation elements. How long a robot arm takes to pick and load a tape, for example, is a multiplier of the latency encountered when reading or writing tape data. ATLs offering multiple, concurrent tape accesses may alleviate latency and shorten the amount of time required to write backup data to tape.

ATLs, and other tape automation solutions, may also alleviate some of the tedium and cost associated with tape management. The purported cost-efficiency of automated tape management—the ability it affords to offload such tasks as tape rotation, manual disaster recovery backup, and inventory management—is cited by many vendors as a return on investment rationale for product acquisitions. Moreover, the multiported capabilities of higher-end ATLs give them the ability to handle a greater volume of data transfers in a shorter period of time. This, in turn, means that backups can be accomplished within the shrinking "backup windows" afforded in busy operating environments.

The value of an automated tape solution is in direct proportion to the direct and indirect costs that the solution offsets and the added capability that the solution delivers that could not be delivered in any other way. The vast array of automated tape offerings are testimony to this fact: Solutions are available to fit virtually any budget or requirements set. Moreover, vendors are becoming more flexible in deployment alternatives.

In the past, ATLs were strictly mainframe peripherals—mainly because of their expense. To share the ATL with an open systems platform required a channel extension (see previous chapter) solution that enabled SCSI, as well as ESCON, connections to the library. Today, many ATLs are delivered with SCSI and Fibre Channel connectivity, as well as drivers for most major operating systems.

Moreover, as the speeds of the building blocks of tape platforms—the tape drives themselves—increase, tape is becoming more viable for use as a near online medium for data storage. This fact has been seized upon by StorageTek, IBM, and Sutmyn Storage, the leaders of a trend toward delivering virtual tape system products.

Virtual tape systems are tape library products with a disk buffer. The concept is not new. VTS was considered years ago as a technology with the potential to reduce the cost of tape by filling each tape to its brim with stored data. At the time, the problem was the cost of the disk buffer. A VTS uses a disk array to temporarily store data until a sufficient amount is available to fill a tape completely. The cost of disk array buffer needed to be offset in tape media savings—a difficult proposition to envision given the relative cost of tape and disk ten to twenty years ago.

With the dramatic decrease in hard disk prices, combined with dramatic increases in disk storage capacity, the old logic no longer applies. Companies like Quantum are discovering that they are actually losing money on hard disk sales. To replace these revenues, they need to combine their disk products with their tape products and produce combined products that capitalize on strengths.[44]

Just as the cost issues associated with VTS have been stood on their head, so has the value proposition for the technology. Virtual tape (as cited above) is an enabling technology for hierarchical storage management. The disk buffer, if sufficiently sized, can store for a time the data that is relegated to tape by HSM software. Statistically, the frequency with which properly migrated data is requested for demigration by end users or applications declines over time. In the short term, storing the migrated data in a disk array provides more expeditious demigration if the data is requested.

Thus, rather than deriving its value from a cost reduction (i.e., using tape media to capacity), the real value of VTS may derive from the capability that it adds (i.e., HSM enablement).

Sizing the disk buffer size for a VTS is still more art than science. One vendor recommends a disk buffer that is adequate to satisfy 100 percent of tape writes and between 70 to 80 percent of tape reads, observing that the absence of such capacities can result in long request queues that can degrade VTS performance. Data compression, backend network bandwidth (the bandwidth in connections between the disk buffer and the tape system), and ATL robotics operating speeds, must also be calculated to design a queue optimized system.[45]

Network bandwidth and connectivity—the SAN or LAN interconnecting the VTS with host platforms and end users—must also be carefully weighed when evaluating a VTS solution for a given IT environment. Taking a storage infrastructure viewpoint, HSM (and also backup and archive) applications entail significant data movements that need to be accommodated through a well-considered strategy.

BACK TO NFR

As the preceding discussion suggests, secondary storage is not simply a matter of capacity. Nor is it solely a matter of price or brand loyalty. The selection of a secondary storage platform depends in large part on the application that the storage is required to support. The characterization of near-field recording drives as a niche technology ignores the fact that all secondary storage platforms are niche technologies, if they are selected wisely and from a storage infrastructure perspective.

It would be wrong to assume that any one technology can effectively replace another in all circumstances. A well-reasoned case study from StorageTek, for example, provides an excellent illustration of how, under a certain set of conditions, tape can provide a more suitable archival storage medium than optical disk.[46]

TeraStor's claims to being a "tape-killer" technology have faded with time, as most marketing rhetoric does. However, the value proposition posed by a removable, rotational, random-access storage media with the performance characteristics of a hard disk and the resiliency of a MO disk is significant. The potential application for such technology in multimedia file backup, for example, is tremendous.

IBM's Frank Elliot observes that we live at a time when everything is being digitized, "A company in Tokyo came to us a short time ago seeking advice on the best way to digitize and store 75 years of radio broadcast recordings."

Perhaps for every type of data to be stored, there is a unique storage technology solution if we are willing to look hard enough for one.

ENDNOTES

1. Quoted in Jon William Toigo, "NFR Storage: From Hurricane to Drizzle," *Solutions Integrator,* October 15, 1998.
2. Hal Glatzer, "The Tale of Tape: Magnetic Technologies for Secondary Storage," *EMedia Professional,* October 1997.
3. Technically, Magstar and Magstar MP media use a serpentine linear recording method. Serpentine refers to a bidirectional recording scheme—the

recording of one track in a forward direction is followed by recording the next track in a reverse direction.

4. "Back to Tape," A Strategic Profile, Strategic Research Corporation, Santa Barbara, CA, June 1997.

5. "IBM Opens up Magstar Virtual Tape Server to the Enterprise: Industry's Leading Virtual Tape Solution Delivers Third Round of Powerful Performance and Capacity Improvements; SAN Solutions Here," Press Release, IBM, San Jose, CA, February 17, 1999.

6. Interview with Frank Elliot, Vice President of Marketing and Strategy, Storage Systems Division, IBM, San Jose, CA, 1998.

7. Interview with Mike Harrison, Director of Marketing, IBM Disk Storage Systems, Boulder, CO, 1998.

8. "StorageTek Sets Industry Precedent; Delivers First Tape Technology To Meet Sec Requirements For Electronic Records Storage: StorageTek VolSafe is the Industry's First WORM (Write Once, Read Many) Tape-Based Storage Solution; Provides Cost-Effective, Scalable Alternative to Optical WORM," Press Release, Storage Technology Corporation, Louisville, CO, July 8, 1998.

9. "Worldwide Tape Storage Market Posts Healthy Revenue Gain in 1998 But Units Drop According to IDC," Press Release, International Data Corporation, Framingham, MA, January 19, 1999.

10. "The DLTtape™ System: Tape Drive and Cartridge Designed Together to Optimize Data Integrity," Quantum White Paper, Quantum Corporation, Milpitas, CA, 1998.

11. "About DLTtape System Products," Quantum White Paper, Quantum Corporation, Milpitas, CA, 1998.

12. "DLT™ Markets and Technologies," Quantum White Paper, Quantum Corporation, Milpitas, CA, 1998.

13. Strategic Briefing, "Super DLTtape™ Overview," Quantum Corporation, September 1998.

14. Interview with Zophar Sante, Senior Product Marketing Manager, Tandberg Data ASA, Oslo, Norway and Simi Valley, CA, 1999.

15. In a September 9, 1998, press release, "Tandberg Data and Quantum Announce Manufacturing License and Marketing Agreement for DLTtape™ Products: New manufacturing and marketing agreement to facilitate expansion of DLT-tape market by providing multiple sources of products and solutions," Oslo, Norway-based Tandberg announced an agreement with Quantum Corporation, "the worldwide tape-drive revenue leader," that established the company as "an independent second source for DLTtape™ drives, including products under development based on Quantum's Super DLTtape architecture as well as the current DLTtape architecture. As part of the agreement, Tandberg Data intends to market a full spectrum of products—including drives, media and tape-automation products—based on the DLTtape platform, which has become the industry standard for protecting mission-critical enterprise data."

16. "Travan Technology Gaining Momentum in Network Backup Market," Imation Press Release, Imation, Oakdale, MN, August 4, 1998.

17. Interview with Zophar Sante, Tandberg Data ASA, op. cit.
18. "Tandberg Data & Overland Complete Cross Licensing Deal for SLR/MLR Technology and VR^2," Tandberg Data Press Release, Tandberg Data ASA, Oslo, Norway, April 1, 1998.
19. "VR^2 Frequently Asked Questions," Overland Data, Inc., Oakdale, MN, 1998.
20. Yale quoted in "Tandberg Data & Overland Complete Cross Licensing Deal for SLR/MLR Technology and VR^2," Tandberg Data Press Release, Tandberg Data ASA, Oslo, Norway, April 1, 1998.
21. "Imation and Overland to Bring VR^2 Technology to Travan Ns Platform: Travan Technology gains major enhancements in capacity and performance for network storage applications," Overland Data Press Release, Overland Data Inc., Oakdale, MN, March 1, 1999.
22. In the early days of DAT's evolution, DAT devices used one of two proposed low-level formatting standards: DDS, developed jointly by HP and Sony, and Data/DAT, developed by Hitachi. DDS offered more storage capacity and faster sustained transfer rates than Data/DAT. DDS devices also write data sequentially, appending data to the existing information, and they can read data randomly, beginning at any point. Data/DAT drives can overwrite existing data files in place, reducing the inefficiencies of multiple copies of the same file. However, the market appears to have standardized on DDS and a few extensions of DDS. Source: "What do you call this, DAT or DDS?" Bert Vermeulen, *Digital Data Storage (DDS) Manufacturers Group Newsletter*, December 1993.
23. The two key standards driving DDS are the DDS recording standard and the DCLZ compression algorithm standard. Standards bodies governing the DDS recording format are ANSI (ANSI X3B5/91-256—June 26, 1991), International Standards Organization (ISO/IEC JTC 1/SC11 Flexible Magnetic Media for Digital Data Interchange) and the European Computer Manufacturers Association (ECMA-139 Adopted as ECMA standard June 28, 1990 3,81mm Wide Magnetic Tape Cartridge for Information Interchange—Helical Scan Recording—DDS Format). The DCLZ data compression algorithm is standardized as ANSI X3B5/91-124 (2nd Draft, April 1991) and ECMA (June 1991 Data Compression for Information Interchange—Adaptive Coding with Embedded Dictionary—DCLZ Algorithm).
24. "The Technology Behind 4-MM DAT Drives," *Byte Magazine*, March 1995.
25. "A Guide to DDS-3," Hewlett-Packard, 1998.
26. "Exabyte Has Mammoth Task Ahead—Steve Georgis, director of technology, Exabyte," *Internet Week*, May 4, 1998.
27. *Ibid.*
28. "Is the Migration Path for 'Mammoth' Credible?" Strategic Profile, Strategic Research Corporation, Santa Barbara, CA, 1998.
29. Mike Holland, "Current Technology and Field Experience Create New Generation of 8 mm Drives," Director of Drives, Exabyte Corporation, *Computer Technology Review*, no date provided.
30. "3 Big Reasons Exabyte Mammoth Is Superior to DLT," Exabyte Marketing Materials, Exabyte Corporation, Boulder, CO, 1998.

31. "3 Big Reasons Why Exabyte Mammoth Is Better than AIT," Exabyte Marketing Materials, Exabyte Corporation, Boulder, CO, 1998.

32. "If the Tape Technology Fits Your Needs, Implement It," *InfoWorld,* 1998.

33. "AIT Technology: The Midrange and Enterprise-Server Backup Solution," Seagate Technology White Paper, Seagate Technology, Scotts Valley, CA, 1998.

34. "Sony Drives the Future of Tape Technology with Next-Generation Advanced Intelligent Tape (AIT) Sony Doubles Speed and Capacity of AIT Format Right on Time," Qualstar Corporation Press Release, Qualstar Corporation, Canoga Park, CA, May 4, 1998.

35. "HP, IBM, and Seagate Introduce Linear Tape-Open (LTO) Technology for Licensing to Storage Manufacturers," IBM Press Release, IBM, Silicon Valley, CA, April 7, 1998.

36. "Technology White Paper: Linear Tape-Open (LTO) Technology," April 1998, Hewlett-Packard, Seagate Technology and IBM.

37. "Linear Tape-Open (LTO) Technology Continues Licensee Momentum with Signing of Fujitsu and Quantegy—Second LTO Licensee Meeting Witnesses Broadening Industry Participation," LTO Press Release, LTO, Silicon Valley, CA, October 21, 1998.

38. "IBM to Play Key Role in Making New Linear Tape-Open (LTO) Technology Available for Licensing," IBM Press Release, IBM, San Jose, CA, 1998.

39. See reseller.seagate.com/Selling/Techtips/index.html.

40. "Exabyte Has Mammoth Task Ahead—Steve Georgis, Director of Technology, Exabyte," *Internet Week,* op. cit.

41. Chuck Moozakis, "Competing Tape Formats Take Off," *Internet Week,* November 9, 1998.

42. Fara Yale, "Ecrix Unveils Its New Tape Technology," Dataquest Alert, October 29, 1998.

43. *Ibid.*

44. Ted Smalley Bowen, "Quantum Outlines Ambitious Storage Plans," *InfoWorld Electric,* March 1, 1999.

45. Deb Saret, "How a 'Virtual Tape' System Can Work for You," *Storage Management Solutions,* January 1998.

45. See "Archival Storage Solutions for PACS," Tim Chunn, Medical Systems Application Manager, StorageTek White Paper, Storage Technology Corporation, Louisville, CO, 1998.

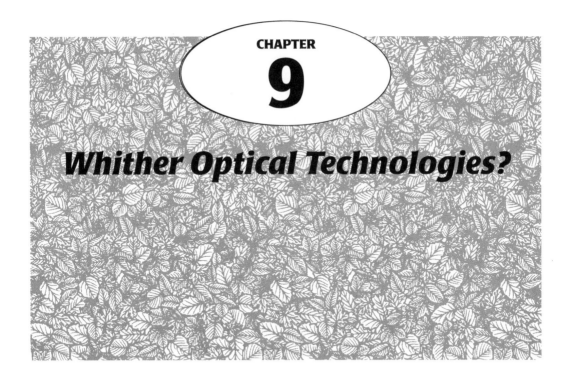

CHAPTER

9

Whither Optical Technologies?

Despite the "format wars" that seem to characterize the mid-range segment of the tape market, the transfer speeds and storage capacities of tape now appear to be doubling every two to three years. The efficiency of tape systems, too, is increasing, thanks to the improving robotics technology and the use of low-cost disk buffers as data staging areas. To some observers fast tape appears to be encroaching on the market previously serviced by rotational secondary storage media, such as magneto-optical disk.

Peter Way, Marketing Manager with Hewlett-Packard's Optical Jukebox Business Unit, doesn't see it that way.[1] He notes that magneto-optical (MO) disk technology is his exclusive focus. Customers want MO for its reliability and performance, and especially for its capability to deliver long-term storage with high accessibility. VTS and fast tape simply do not play in that market.

MO technology originated as a solution to a problem. Organizations were concerned about the high costs of storing and maintaining paper and microfilm records. Accessing the stored media was cumbersome and labor intensive—and costly. However, migrating archival records to magnetic media entailed other costs, risks, and disadvantages. In some cases, audit and legal requirements prevented the use of magnetic storage media altogether.

MAGNETO-OPTICAL TECHNOLOGY EVOLVES

MO technology appeared in the late 1980s to address the requirements of archival storage. It has evolved over time through four generations of development, Way notes.

Initial MO platters could store 650 MB of data. Over time, disks became double-sided and capacities increased to 1.3 GB, then 2.6 GB. In 1998, a 5.2 GB platter was brought to market. At each step, performance has improved and costs have declined (see Figure 9–1).

Optical disk technology, the umbrella name for a technology family of which MO is a part, includes a broad range of products that use light to

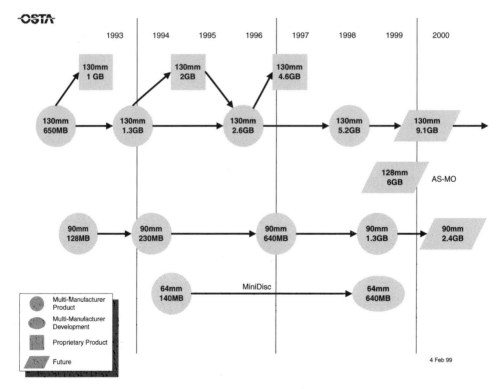

Figure 9–1   Predicted MO Technology Roadmap. (*Source:* Optical Storage Technology Association (OSTA).)

read and write data. CD-ROM, DVD-ROM, and write once read many (WORM) disks cannot be written to by a user, nor can they be erased. Rewritable disk, a category that includes MO, can be rewritten over and over.

Magneto-optical disks, as the name implies, use a combination of magnetic and optical technologies to change the polarity of a magnetic field in the recording medium. The media is both erasable and rewritable.

Data is written to an MO disk using both a laser and a magnet. The laser is pointed to a spot (called a "bit") on the metallic platter and heats it to its Curie point (the temperature at which molecules can be realigned when subjected to a magnetic field). A magnetic write head is then used to change the bit's polarity. This operation requires two write passes.

Reading the MO requires a laser only. The reflected laser light is interpreted as an on or off bit (as in hard disk technology) and binary data is reconstructed. MO disks do not need to be reformatted. Spots can be reheated and remagnetized or demagnetized through the life of the media.

LIMDOW

In 1994, Nikon Corporation invented and patented light intensity modulated direct overwrite (LIMDOW) technology to speed the MO disk write operation. LIMDOW works on the same basic principle as MO drives, but uses magnets built into disk itself instead of a magnetic read–write head to accomplish data writes. With LIMDOW/MO media, data can be written in a single pass, rather than two (see Figure 9–2). Several manufactur-

Figure 9–2   LIMDOW/MO Drive Operation. (*Source:* Nikon Precision Inc., Belmont, CA.)

ers, including Nikon, Fujitsu, Hitachi, Most, Konica, and Sony, have developed increasingly advanced LIMDOW drives.

Not all vendors are sold on LIMDOW. HP, for example, believes that the technology has several drawbacks.[2] For one, adding magnetic strata to MO media increases media costs by about 30 percent, due mainly to complicated manufacturing processes. Increasing the costs for MO media at a time when tape and magnetic disk prices are falling is a step in the wrong direction from a marketing perspective. Moreover, the LIMDOW/MO writing procedure is complex and leaves little margin for error. Since no standards for data interchange exist for LIMDOW/MO, the ability to interchange LIMDOW/MO media between the drives of different vendors is problematic.

HP also notes numerous examples of applications in which LIMDOW/MO might make less sense than conventional MO. The value of LIMDOW/MO's write capabilities is hardly realized in a document image management (DIM) or computer output to laser disk (COLD) application, where reads are far more frequent than writes. These represent two of the most popular applications for MO technology.

Additionally, in enterprise-level deployments, MO disks are typically included in jukeboxes (automated multi-disk MO systems). In this situation, a jukebox is preferred because of the massive storage it offers. Like a VTS, the jukebox may have a large disk drive cache to make frequently requested data more available. Under these circumstances, the time required to swap media generally outweighs the transfer rate performance of the drive.

HP concludes that it is taking a wait-and-see position on LIMDOW/MO and will consider adding the technology to its optical jukebox product family as the technology matures.

PHASE-CHANGE OPTICAL MEDIA

Other rewritable media, such as CD-ReWritable (CD-RW) and DVD-RAM, use phase-change recording. Phase-change involves the use of a laser to transform a section of the media between amorphous (structureless) and microcrystalline (structured) states in order to store bits of data.

Phase-change recording uses changes in media reflectivity to identify binary data. A blank disk is said to be in a crystalline phase. The application of the write laser changes a crystalline spot to an amorphous spot, thereby changing its reflectivity.

Writing is accomplished solely by controlling the intensity of the laser, rather than using the laser in conjunction with a magnet as in magneto-optical (MO) recording. Key to the phase-change recording process are the glass transition temperature and the melting temperature. The glass transition temperature is the temperature at which the media changes to its crystalline state. The melting temperature is the temperature at which crystalline media melt and then cool to the amorphous state. In subsequent writes, the media can be heated back to the glass transition temperature and revitrified to a crystalline state.

Phase change media can be transformed (erased and rewritten) about 100,000 times, while MO media can withstand upwards of one million rewrites (called "cycles").[3] Both MO and CD-RW (and presumably DVD-RAM) media are considered more appropriate for vital records storage than magnetic media because they are not subject to damage by magnetic fields.

MEDIA SELECTION CRITERIA

Magneto-optical disks have several advantages over CD-RW, DVD-RAM, and magnetic disk media. For one, very high data densities can be achieved through the use of short-wave lasers that enable a smaller spot size and more spots per square inch.

In addition to capacity, MO disks also deliver greater reliability and resilience than do conventional hard disk drives. This derives from several attributes of MO disk drive technology. For example, the head fly height of a MO disk drive is typically greater than the head fly height in a magnetic disk drive. With a magnetic disk, the greater the areal density, the closer the head needs to fly to the platter to detect all magnetic bit signatures. With MO disk read–write operations are performed using a laser, which can be operated from a greater distance.

As another safeguard against media damage, the read–write head of an MO disk drive rides in a track. This precludes the possibility of a disk crash.

According to Way, MO disks and jukeboxes provide an excellent, enterprise-class platform for document image management and computer output to laser disk applications. Forthcoming DVD-RAM disks, towers, and jukeboxes, he believes, will be better suited to the small business/small office environment because of their reliance on "consumer-grade" components and media. CD-RW and DVD recordables, says Way, remain primarily desktop technologies (see Figure 9–3). This view is based on the

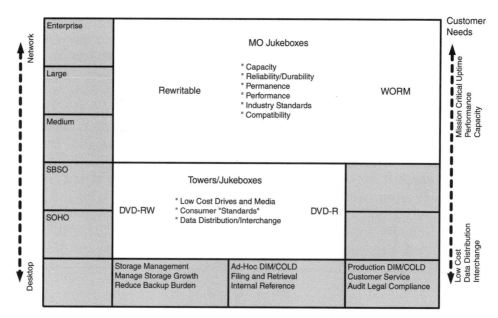

Figure 9–3   Near Online Storage Positioning. (*Source:* Hewlett-Packard, Greenley, CO.)

performance characteristics of each technology, their data storage capacities, and the demands of the market segments where they are used.[4]

DVD FORMATS PROLIFERATE

DVD-RAM standards are not yet finalized, and several competing formats are vying to become the industry standard. Current contenders include:

- **DVD-Recordable (DVD-R):** DVD-R is a record-once, writable DVD format backed by Pioneer. DVD-R drives are currently offered by Pioneer and its resellers and can record once to organic dye-based DVD-Recordable media. This technology is roughly analogous to CD-R and is mainly used as a means to author and test DVD titles. Current technology features a 4.7 GB capacity and the next generation (in early 2000) is expected to feature an incremental write capability.
- **DVD-RW (DVD-Rewritable):** DVD-RW is the rewritable version of DVD-R—the "other" rewritable format endorsed by the DVD Forum.

The first media and drives are expected in late 1999. Prototypes of the 4.7 GB rewritable technology have already been demonstrated by Ricoh, Pioneer, Sony, and Yamaha. DVD-RW uses a phase-change recording, like CD-RW. DVD-R and DVD-RW should be compatible for playback in DVD-ROM drives.

- **DVD-Random Access Memory (DVD-RAM):** DVD-RAM finds favor among Toshiba, Hitachi, and Panasonic, all of whom make internal and external SCSI- and IDE-compatible DVD-RAM drives for PCs and workstations today. DVD-RAM is a phase-change recording media that can be either single-sided in a removable cartridge, or double-sided in a permanent cartridge. DVD-RAM capacity is 2.6 GB per platter side (all DVDs are 120 mm in diameter, the same as CDs, but store four to six times more data than a CD) and media can be read currently only on DVD-RAM drives and on one DVD-ROM drive from Panasonic. DVD-RAM media is characterized by 24 recording zones divided into sectors by preembossed physical pits.

- **DVD-ReWritable (DVD+RW):** DVD+RW is a proposed rewritable format backed by Sony, Philips, Hewlett-Packard, Ricoh, and Yamaha. The 3.0 GB phase-change media uses groove-only recording like CD-RW and can be used as a sequential storage media or as a random-access storage device. Philips, Sony, and Hewlett-Packard have all indicated that they will ship drives by mid-1999. A 4.7 GB capacity is promised.

Despite the plethora of competing standards, industry watchers believe that the DVD-RAM format should resolve itself by the end of year 2000. Many vendors are already readying DVD towers and jukeboxes for late 1999 and early 2000 delivery.

The strength of DVD is high-capacity, optical storage at a comparatively low price. Most industry watchers agree with HP's Peter Way that DVD will emerge as the standard storage and interchange medium for the desktop and for low-end network applications.

SEEING THE FUTURE OF OPTICAL CLEARLY

Admittedly, the above is a rather brief treatment of the optical storage picture. While optical technologies provide specific advantages in particular storage scenarios, their use continues to be aimed primarily at archival rather than online storage applications.

Optical technology must be included within the context of a book on storage management, however, for two reasons. First, optical storage provides one of the few examples of a truly cross-platform file-sharing product. File systems for optical disk storage have been worked out between vendors and standardized, then provided to operating system manufacturers of all stripes. Optical disk drivers and related software can be installed on virtually any type of open system (and many not-so-open ones) and used to access the data stored on the media.

Universal file access is no mean accomplishment, although, in the case of optical storage, it probably reflects the tendency of most server and operating system makers to regard optical storage as too rarefied a technology to threaten core product values or profits. Efforts to develop common file systems for magnetic media have not fared nearly as well.

A second reason for including optical technology in this book is to provide a necessary background for discussing another topic: hierarchical storage management (HSM). With the advent of SANs, HSM is also experiencing a resurgence of interest. Optical technology provides a capability to retain files in near-online storage and in a cross-platform accessible format. As an HSM media, it offers numerous advantages over tape, particularly in applications that can take advantage of its speed and rotational media characteristics.

ENDNOTES

1. Interview with Peter Way, Marketing Manager, Optical Jukebox Business Unit, Hewlett-Packard, Greenley, CO, 1998.
2. "Hewlett-Packard's Position on LIMDOW Recording on Magneto-Optical Disk," Hewlett-Packard Company White Paper, Hewlett-Packard, Greenley, CO, 1998.
3. Charles Newcomer, "Sorting Out Storage Solutions," *Inform,* October 1998.
4. Peter Way, "Competing Technologies for Reference Data Applications," Hewlett-Packard Company White Paper, Hewlett-Packard, Greenley, CO, 1998.

PART 3

STORAGE MANAGEMENT TECHNIQUES

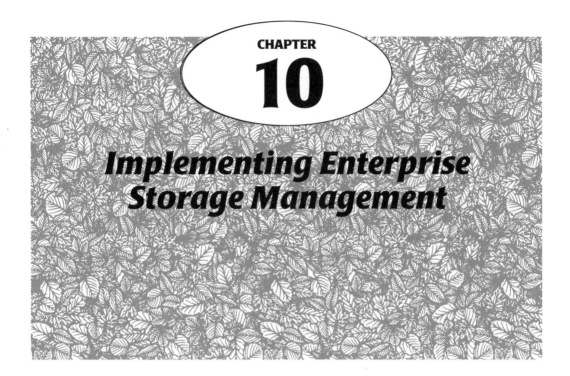

CHAPTER

10

Implementing Enterprise Storage Management

Developing a storage management capability does not occur overnight. Nor does it involve the straightforward deployment of a software package that, once installed, performs all storage management functions on a more-or-less automated basis. Like any project, it proceeds according to a definition of the task and set of objectives.

Storage management, as defined in Chapter One, is the application of procedures and processes to ensure the availability, accessibility, performance and protection of stored data and storage devices. Speaking generically, there are seven objectives in a project aimed at delivering a maintainable storage management capability, as depicted in Figure 10–1.

NEEDS ASSESSMENT PHASE

The project begins with a needs assessment phase, which seeks to examine the current state of storage technology and processes within the distributed environment. This is a prerequisite step that must be performed before storage management policies can be identified. Following is an overview of the primary objective and enabling tasks associated with this phase.

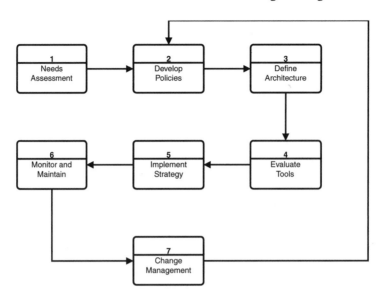

Figure 10-1   Overview of a Storage Management Project.

Assess the current storage environment to discern storage management requirements. Subordinate tasks may include the following:

- Assess current storage resources and inventory storage hardware and management software.
- Determine what is being stored, including age, ownership, size, last use, and frequency of use.
- Identify any mirroring that is in use.
- Identify replicated data sets and how they are maintained, and inventory underlying data movements and how they are supported.
- Identify archival storage practices, their associated data movements and how they are supported.
- Identify backup storage practices, their data movements and how they are supported. Test the restorability of backups.
- Identify any HSM processes that may be in use, their associated data movements and how they are supported.
- Identify any file-sharing solutions that are used, the applications they support, the characteristics of related data movements, and how they are supported.
- Determine what disaster recovery capabilities exist within the organization to safeguard business data from loss. Verify that they have been tested.

- Review current storage acquisition budget and review past spending on storage hardware and software to identify and model trends.
- Identify, based on current and anticipated application development work, what (if any) increase in storage is anticipated in the foreseeable future.
- Review available data on system downtime to determine what percentage can be attributed to storage.
- Review available data (trouble tickets, etc.) to determine application performance issues that might have a storage-related cause.
- Assess network bandwidth demands of current applications as they relate to stored data transfers and determine percentage of network bandwidth associated with data transfers from centralized and distributed storage "repositories."
- Examine secondary storage technologies used in the distributed environment, their missions and their performance levels.

Believe it or not, the above task list may constitute the most frustrating and labor-intensive endeavor of the entire storage management project. These tasks are followed by an analysis of the strengths and weaknesses of current processes for acquiring storage resources, and a critique of current storage deployments on the basis of their availability, reliability, accessibility, scaleability, internal performance, and impact on application and network performance.

POLICY DEVELOPMENT PHASE

From these analyses will emerge a set of requirements that will be used to set the high-level policies guiding storage management activity.[1] Phase two of the project is defined, again generically, by the following objective and subordinate tasks.

Based on present and future requirements, define policies for managing storage.

- Set a policy identifying the types of data that are to be stored on line.
- Set a policy outlining necessary identifying information that should accompany all stored data.

- Set a policy defining the security requirements for stored data and what restrictions will be imposed to prevent unauthorized duplication, write, and read accesses to the contents of shared volumes.
- Set a policy identifying who is responsible for maintaining and managing storage resources (i.e., the storage manager). Identify the specific responsibilities and authority of the storage manager.
- Set a policy on the role of the storage manager in storage acquisition procedures.
- Set a policy defining how storage is to be managed (i.e., the hours of operation of the storage management function, the use of appropriate automation tools, number of personnel, procedures, etc.)
- Set a policy on storage device standards specifying, at a minimum, that they are manageable via some in-band or out-of-band means (see below).
- Set a policy on the maximum acceptable downtime that will be acceptable due to storage-related causes.
- Set a policy on the maximum length of outage that will be tolerated in a post-disaster recovery environment and specify a timeframe for storage recovery.
- Set a policy on hierarchical storage management (if appropriate), specifying the thresholds that will be used to trigger file migration to alternate media, what media will be used, and when migrations will be accomplished.
- Set a policy on hierarchical storage management (if appropriate), specifying acceptable timeframes for demigration of files based on access requests by applications or end users.
- Set a policy on backups, how they will be taken, their frequency, their contents (full, partial, incremental, snapshot), and on the verification of backups.
- Set a policy on virus detection and elimination in active and backup files.
- Set a policy on archival storage, specifying their frequency, storage medium, on- or off-site storage location, retention period, and verification steps.
- Set a policy on volume management, how volumes will be defined, how they will be maintained, and how shared access will be provided.
- Set a policy on capacity planning, how capacity will be reported, and on what basis capacity will be added.

- Set a policy on performance management, specifying storage performance monitoring and reporting requirements.
- Set a policy on data replication, the circumstances under which replication is permissible and the means that may be used to replicate and synchronize replicated data sets.
- Set a policy on mirroring, specifying the percentage of storage capacity that may be used for mirroring, and the percentage of storage capacity that should be reserved at all times for unanticipated growth or temporary storage requirements.
- Set a policy on the types of management tools that are to be obtained and used for the purposes of storage management.
- Set a policy on the responsibility of the storage manager to report on the performance of the storage management, including but not limited to, costs of management, storage uptime, acquisitions and capacities, new technologies, storage-related application performance impact, storage-related downtime, backup performance and status, archive performance and status, HSM performance and status, anticipated acquisitions and their justification.
- Set a policy on the requirements of the storage manager to make reports per the above policy in a paper, electronic, or web-based manner and the frequency of such reports.
- Set a policy on the requirements of the storage manager to maintain current information on new technologies and to propose from time to time pilot or test projects to determine the relevance and contribution that new technologies can make to current storage architecture.

The above are intended as recommendations for policies that will guide the implementation of a storage management framework or architecture and the selection of software products for use in managing it. Management may be in-band or out-of-band, meaning that it may involve the transmission of management information (status, event alarms, etc.) using the same network used to handle data movements themselves (in-band), or they will take some other path that is separate from the normal data path for data movements (out-of-band). In a traditional network management environment, SNMP commands, SCSI Enclosure Services (SES) traffic, and other management traffic is sent, together with data movements, on the primary data network (usually a TCP/IP ethernet). This in-band approach enables managers to access status information from a management station anywhere in the network. However, this strategy also raises two potential problems: (1) if a problem develops in the network, management information is lost; and, (2) management data itself can pose a burden on network bandwidth.

Out-of-band management information network connectivity is designed into many SAN network products (i.e., hubs and switches) and multiported disk array products to surmount these problems. An out-of-band network for management data traffic is particularly important in the case of SANs that utilize a Fibre Channel-Arbitrated Loop topology. In such a topology, management traffic would contend for loop ownership against mission critical application I/O requests.[2]

ARCHITECTURE DEFINITION PHASE

The third phase of the storage management project may occur concurrently with the second and involves the definition of a storage framework or architecture to which storage will ultimately conform. The caveat, ultimately, is introduced only to suggest that rehosting storage must often occur over time and in parallel with existing storage implementations (see phase five below) to prevent disruption of normal application processing. The objective of this phase is clear-cut and an additional breakdown of tasks is not required.

Based on requirements identified in phase one and policies defined in phase two, develop an architecture for storage that uses resources efficiently, provides for managed growth, supports availability and data sharing requirements, supports performance objectives, and protects data from loss or misuse.

This may seem like a herculean effort, but much of the work will have been accomplished in phases one and two to make this objective a bit more straightforward in execution. The project leader will probably need to become more familiar with distributed storage architectures and this book provides a start. Education about SANs as well as less centralized storage architectures may be required. In all likelihood, the future enterprise will continue to feature a mix of technologies and architectures.

Of great importance at this point might be the identification of "dead ends"—installed technologies that will be unable to fit into the storage management vision either because of their lack of support for centralized management or because their capabilities simply do not fit with current requirements. The architecture created in phase three should show a migration path for data stored on these platforms to new platforms that conform to architectural objectives.

The architecture created in phase three is the vision for the future and is not immutable. As with the switched Fibre Channel SANs of today, there will doubtless be many obstacles that still remain to be surmounted before parts of the architecture can be implemented. These should be noted clearly in the narrative accompanying the architectural description and anticipated timeframes for implementation should be provided.

STORAGE MANAGEMENT TOOLS EVALUATION PHASE

Evaluating tools for use in storage management is the fourth phase and the last preparatory phase of the project. The objective of this phase is straightforward:

Using the requirements, policies and architecture set forth in the preceding phases, identify criterion for selecting storage management software products that will provide system, storage and product-level management capabilities.

- This objective borrows from a model use by Hitachi Data Systems, but only in terms of its categories or levels of software requirements (see Figure 10–2).[2] In the HDS example, HDS storage management software products have already been inserted into the product management tier to provide the management of IBM, HDS, EMC, Gad-

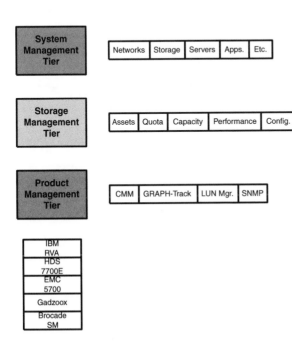

Figure 10–2   HDS Storage Management Model. (*Source:* "Hitachi Storage Central and Storage Area Networks," Hu Yoshida, Hitachi Data Systems, Santa Clara, CA, 1998.) Note: Software and hardware products referenced are for illustration only.

zoox Systems, and Brocade Communications Systems products in a specific SAN example.

A more generic example (see Figure 10–3) would suggest the need for any or all of the following:

• At the system management tier: A software "umbrella framework," used to monitor and/or manage heterogeneous server systems, stand-alone intelligent arrays, NAS storage platforms, SAN network hardware, production networks and production network hardware, applications, and very large databases (VLDBs), might be specified. This product would serve both as the "single view" console for the storage management infrastructure and as the repository for high-level management policies.

• At the storage management tier: Here, a software "suite"—combining integrated products (those sold with the umbrella framework) and point products that represent best-of-breed management tools—might be specified. These tools are used to implement some of the high-level policies of the system management tier, but with a more precise level of detail.

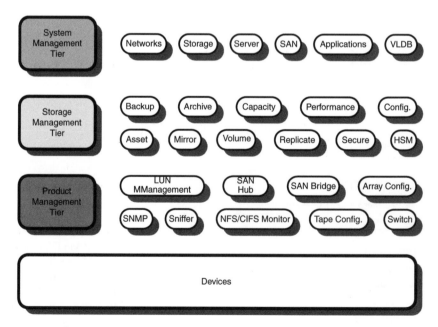

Figure 10–3   Generic Systems Management Software Model.

- Product management tier: These products consist largely of element managers—that is, product-specific software that provides access to the internal configuration of deployed storage and storage networking devices—and protocols such as Simple Network Management Protocol (SNMP). Presumably, some "Sniffer"-like[3] product might be used in both production LANs and in SANs to provide more detailed information about traffic across network segments. Alternatively, in a SAN, such information gathering and reporting capabilities might be added directly to the hub or switch port.

There are many products on the market today that may support systems management tier functions. BMC Patrol, Boole & Babbage Command Post, Tivoli Systems TME and NetView, Computer Associates UnicenterTNG, Hewlett-Packard OpenView, Micromuse Netcool Suite, Cabletron Systems Spectrum, Platinum Technology ProVision, and a number of others deliver monitoring and alarming services typically through the use of SNMP or proprietary agents.

Recently, a major product discriminator has been the application of artificial intelligence, deep mathematics, or neural networking technology to event correlation and response. Most products feature some mechanism that sifts through myriad event messages and delivers filtered, high-level, easy-to-understand information about a significant event to the administrator via a graphical user interface (usually a web browser and/or software client). Some products add policy-based controls to their agents, enabling them to act independently to fix detected problems.

Previously, the primary discriminator between network and systems management framework products was their support for "seamless integration" with element managers. Over time, however, the word "integration" became so meaningless that vendors backed away from it almost entirely.[4]

Still many framework products now feature modular add-ins that enable them to offer some fairly extensive storage, application and database management functionality. Still other frameworks make application, database, or storage management their primary focus. Veritas Software, for example, has been actively buying other companies to add functionality to their own storage-centric framework, Veritas Foundation Suite. The same may be said of Legato Systems, which is busily building out its Networker product family to create a storage framework.

The SAN management framework category remains an open field, but offerings from all major framework vendors are being enhanced as of this writing to incorporate SAN management schemes. Ultimately, this may be facilitated by the work of the Fibre Channel Storage Network Management Working Group, which has been working since 1998 to create tools and mechanisms that "must exist to allow data from multiple SAN components to be correlated and processed in order to facilitate problem isolation."[5] Figure 10–4 depicts the high-level storage area network management architecture proposed by the Working Group. The goal of this architecture is "to provide a common and consistent view of managed resources so that the challenges of SAN management can be addressed."[6]

At a minimum, the selected products should support the enforcement of identified policies, work with the architecture envisioned for the future, and scale to meet future requirements. Other considerations, such as vendor pedigree, may ultimately be less important, given the novelty of SANs and the seminal nature of most products that are being constructed to manage them.

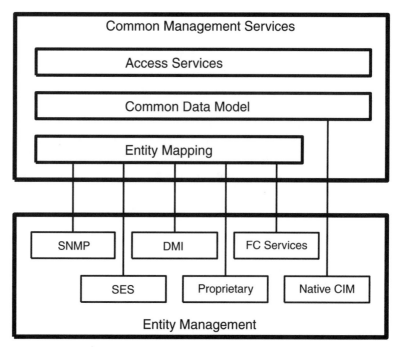

Figure 10–4   Storage Area Network Architecture. (*Source:* Storage Network Management Working Group for Fibre Channel, Fibre Channel Community, Oklahoma City, OK, 1998.)

IMPLEMENTATION AND TESTING PHASE

Phase five of the storage management product involves the implementation and testing of the strategy. The corresponding objective may be stated as follows:

Implement storage management software components to manage existing and evolving storage architecture components, test and verify implementation and design personnel training and documentation to facilitate the proper operation of storage management systems.

Implementation may occur as a series of small steps, rather than in the grandiose fashion of a major system cut-over. This strategy affords testing and training time with minimal disruption to existing operations.

In the model, the entity management services layer corresponds roughly with the device management tier of the generic model offered in Figure 10–3. The common management services layer will serve as a storage management tier, or possibly a systems management tier component, depending on the success of the Working Group in convincing all players in the SAN space to agree upon the use of the Desktop Management Task Force's (DMTF) Common Information Model (CIM) with SAN extensions. The organization is also working on an access service component that will enable management applications to interact with Common Management Services via XML, COM/DCOM, Java™ RMI, or CORBA.

Until a comprehensive storage management framework product is developed (and vendors like Veritas and Legato are getting close to this goal), there will still be opportunities for vendors of point products specializing in specific storage management functions, such as backup/restore, HSM, data replication, and so forth. In addition, the perpetuation of proprietary intelligent storage array products will almost certainly ensure the continuation of element managers developed by the vendors themselves to manage their own products.

Storage managers will need to test various applications to determine the best fit for their environments. Depending on many company-specific variables, the one-stop shop approach of a Computer Associates UnicenterTNG may be preferred over a more piecemeal approach of manually integrating numerous best-of-breed point products. However, this is by no means a certain conclusion for all companies, as many failed efforts to deploy framework products can attest.[7]

Most vendors are delighted to provide their wares on a demonstration basis, and in some cases, to support pilot projects with teams of on-site engineers. If project managers are steeled for the "hard sell," they can derive a great deal of information from the experience.

MONITORING AND MANAGEMENT PHASE

Phase six gets down to the business of using the storage management systems to provide the monitoring, configuration, management, and reporting functions for which they were purchased. The objective for this phase is nearly identical to the definition of storage management itself:

Apply storage management procedures and processes to ensure the availability, accessibility, performance, and protection of stored data and of storage devices themselves.

Phase six represents the ultimate validation of the planning effort. If successful, this project will produce mechanisms for applying the storage management policies defined earlier across a potentially broad array of storage devices and configurations.

CHANGE MANAGEMENT PHASE

Feedback from this phase (which is ongoing) is represented in Figure 10–1 as processing through a seventh phase, labeled simply "Change Management." This is a necessary feedback loop intended to strengthen the storage management capability by bringing policies, procedures, and even architectural components in line with unanticipated realities. Phase seven takes as its objective:

Adjust policies, procedures, architectures, and storage management software deployments to better fit the storage infrastructure.

MODEL VERSUS REALITY

Generic though it may seem, the above project model can be customized readily and adjusted to fit virtually any storage environment. It should be noted, however, that the objectives in this project model are not properly formed. Objectives should have a condition-task-criteria format that enables them to be tested and validated. For example,

> *Given a Fibre Channel switch, a length of multimode fiber-optic cable, an FC-enabled disk drive, and a requirement to create a point-to-point connection, the SAN administrator will make all necessary connections in five minutes in accordance with the Fibre Channel standard.*

For reasons that should be obvious, the condition and criteria portions of the objectives listed here have been omitted. It will be the responsibility of the project manager to fix the conditions by which a storage management capability will be deployed, and it will be the project manager's responsibility to ensure that the effort returns the desired benefit to the organization.

CONTINUED OBSTACLES

The relative simplicity of the project description provided above is not intended to suggest that there is anything simple about developing and implementing a storage management capability. Numerous obstacles persist to effective management.

One major hurdle is a lack of information. It will not be easy collecting all of the information sought in the first phase of the project, and this may be disheartening. The project manager must acknowledge that he or she must depend on the cooperation of system administrators, database administrators, application administrators, and network administrators to collect the information that is needed. This may not always be forthcoming.

The storage management project may be construed as a thinly veiled insult to the system administrator who, for years, has been setting up all storage arrays the same way. No one has complained about it in all that time. Similarly, a network administrator may perceive the information that the project manager is collecting as a signal of yet another encroachment on his or her network management turf. (System management appeared on the scene in the early 1990s, touching off a debate over the relative importance of network and systems management in the grand scheme of the universe. It can sometimes be heard to this day.) Database administrators may see project manager questions as merely irritating or worse—as an opportunity to explain every nuance of RDBMS theory and practice.

These human issues need to be addressed with diplomacy and tact. It also helps to have an organizational meeting with IT management in the room to emphasize the importance of the task and to encourage the full cooperation of everyone involved.

The second obstacle is equally practical. Some vendors are very protective about their products and do not care to have their on-board management features accessed and controlled by third-party software. Mention the word "SAN" to one vendor (who shall be nameless) and its representative will say it invented the technology and has since advanced its products far ahead of anything that SANs could ever hope to provide. Suffice to say that proprietary systems maintain their lock on customers through a combination of warranties, contracts, and complimentary drinks and dinners at expensive restaurants with senior management. If proprietary systems are in use, project managers need to prepare themselves for the hassles associated with integrating proprietary element managers into otherwise "seamless" management solutions.

A final challenge is the availability of personnel to assist in the storage management project. If the experience of system management framework deployments are any example, such a project requires more than one person. Inevitably, the project manager has been more involved in the politics of deployment than the actual fact-finding and strategy formulation.

At least one other resource is involved and that person is typically responsible for ferreting out the technical details, becoming an expert on the subject of system management in the process. The tale has been told many times about the expert "helper" who assists the vendor in the deployment of the management system, attracts the vendor's interest, and is recruited away from the company. In the process, the most knowledgeable resource about the details of the management solution is lost—or can be engaged to consult on a much different pay scale.

Those are some of the pitfalls and traps to avoid as the effort to establish a storage management infrastructure begins to move forward.

ENDNOTES

1. Some policies suggested by "Assessing a Storage Resource," Don Lundell, *Storage Management Solutions,* July 1998.
2. Hu Yoshida, "Hitachi Storage Central and Storage Area Networks," Hitachi Data Systems, Santa Clara, CA, 1998.
3. The Sniffer is now part of the Sniffer Total Network Visibility product from Network Associates, Santa Clara, CA. "The Sniffer Basic Analyzer is a software-based fault and performance management tool that captures data, monitors network traffic and collects key network statistics."
4. Jon William Toigo, "The Next Move in Enterprise Management," *HP Professional,* April 4, 1997.
5. Steven Wilson, Ed., "Managing a Fibre Channel Storage Area Network," White Paper, Fibre Channel Community, Oklahoma City, OK, November 20, 1998.
6. *Ibid.*
7. Jon William Toigo, "Taming the Enterprise Desktop," *Solutions Integrator,* March 1999.

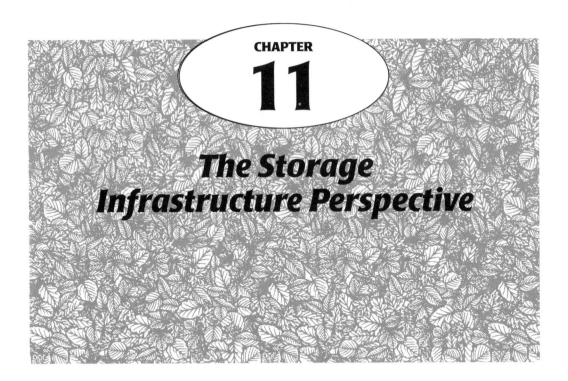

The Storage Infrastructure Perspective

To the casual observer, the term *data storage* suggests a static repository for application and end user–generated information. Its operation is simply and succinctly defined.

Data is created using system processes and temporarily stored in random access memory (RAM)—an expensive, high-performance, and volatile storage media. The data is "saved" by writing it onto the tracks and cylinders of less-expensive, lower-performance, and less-volatile magnetic disk media. The disk media is prepared to receive the data by first being formatted into a storage volume in accordance with the requirements of the server or workstation operating system. As data is recorded on disk, metadata (information about the data) is conveniently filed into a hierarchical file system and represented to the end user in a neatly organized file listing.

Once stored in the static storage repository, the data is said to be "online," meaning that it is accessible to applications and end users. From an operational perspective, this means that the data, in accordance with operating system rules, can be copied back to memory, edited, and saved back to the disk either in place of the retrieved version or as an entirely new file.

Previous chapters have discussed variations on this theme. For example, through the use of RAID software, data may be recorded on a stripe across on an array of disks that are represented as a single logical volume to the operating system. Additionally, data may be replicated on a mirrored disk as it is being written, or checksum information about each block of data may be written to a separate disk or track to protect against data corruption and loss.

Finally, data can be shared among hosts with disparate operating and file systems using special network file system protocols and software. These products allow applications and end users on heterogeneous hosts to see file listings in a manner appropriate to them and to request access to the files. The network access software translates the request, copies the data, places it in the proper format for the requesting system, and delivers it to its requestor.

Considerable effort is being expended today to extend the performance of this static data repository model. For example:

- Vendors are improving the capacities and performance characteristics of disk storage media and interfaces.
- Computer architects are striving to improve processor and bus architectures to facilitate improved I/O throughput.
- Fibre Channel interconnects and Fibre Channel switch fabrics are being introduced to deliver increased speeds in data transfers and greater flexibility in storage platform configurations.
- Software designers are working on methods to remove the impediments to volume "growth" imposed by current operating systems in order to provide scalability without downtime.
- The final frontier of storage—data sharing in heterogeneous computing environments—is being addressed from a number of perspectives by a variety of developers. For example, intelligence is being added to storage array controllers to enable physical storage partitions and "logical volume sharing" among heterogeneous hosts. In other cases, kernel-level file system emulations are being added to intelligent storage systems to handle the conversion of data at machine speeds, expediting file access by heterogeneous hosts while improving security and file integrity. Still other vendors are working to develop universal file systems that can either replace, or work in a complementary fashion with, heterogeneous host operating systems to establish a single, standardized, highly sharable file system for use by all. Operating system vendors show little inclination to adopt

such a universal standard on their own, preferring instead to lobby for the replacement of their competitor's systems with their own products.

In short, the bulk of the work in the storage industry to date has focused on improving the performance and capabilities of the data storage repository itself. This focus derives from the popular conception of a storage repository as a static entity—a natural extension of the modern operating system's treatment of disk storage as a fixed volume peripheral device.

FROM A REPOSITORY TO AN INFRASTRUCTURE VIEW

The word *repository* contributes to the view of static storage. Its etymology, from the Latin *repositorium*, connotes a place where things are deposited for safety and preservation. Storage is conceived as a location where data rests until some application or end user needs it. When this happens, a copy of the data is furnished to the requestor for processing. From this perspective, processing is the dynamic component the equation, driving an ever-increasing storage capacity requirement.

The static view of storage ignores what we currently know about dynamic data movements. For example, many observers argue that much of the 100-percent-per-year-growth that is currently being seen in corporate storage consists of replicated data rather than new data.

There are many reasons to replicate data. Data sets are replicated, in some cases, to enable copies to be placed in closer proximity to end users or applications that need them, improving access time and reducing network backbone traffic. In other cases, data replication occurs to enable such activities as data warehousing and data mining.

According to IBM's Scott Drummond, much of the work of the company's Data Sharing Competency Center is focused less on the enabling of "true data sharing" than on designing processes and technologies for the efficient replication of data and high-speed transport of data copies across distributed storage platforms.[1]

Replication is a part of IBM's definition of data-sharing, albeit a lower level meaning for the term. The company's data sharing web page[2] explains IBM's views on the subject rather eloquently:

> As we look to and for "data-sharing" solutions, we find that not all solutions are created equal. We believe that there are three dimensions to data sharing as it relates to storage solutions.

1. *Storage Sharing:* Two or more like or unlike servers share a single storage system whose capacity has been partitioned for independent use by different servers (see Figure 11–1).
2. *Data Copy Sharing:* Data is replicated for the purpose of sharing or processing on other, like or unlike, servers (see Figure 11–2).
3. *True Data Sharing:* Like or unlike servers can access one unique instance of data while maintaining data integrity (see Figure 11–3).

IBM informs us that, in addition to these archetypes of data sharing, there can also be "blended types of data sharing that vary based upon time, read or writes access or like or unlike server platforms." These blended types include:

- *Point-in-Time or One-at-a-Time Data Sharing:* One platform has full sole read–write access to data for a specific event or time period, releases access, and then another platform has full read–write access to data for a different specific event or time period.
- *Multiplatform Simultaneous Read Access:* More than one platform has read access to the same data at the same time. Because the data does not change, each platform can have unlimited access to the data being shared.
- *Multiplatform Simultaneous Read and Write Access:* In the most complex form of true data sharing, multiple like or unlike platforms have simultaneous read–write access to a single copy of data.

Says Drummond, most customers approach the Data Sharing Competency Center for "data copy sharing"—rather than true data-sharing—solutions.

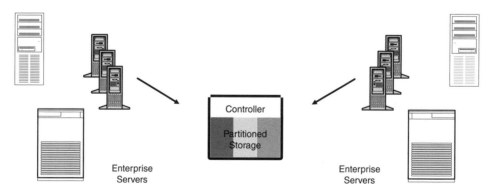

Figure 11–1   Storage Sharing.

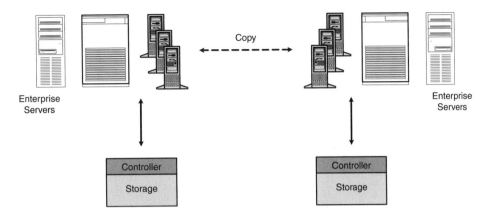

Figure 11–2   Data Copy Sharing.

Frequently, the customer needs a solution that will enable him to migrate new data that is being originated on NT and MVS platforms to UNIX-accessible storage platforms, so that the data can be subjected to secondary analysis (data warehousing). Or, he needs to automate data movements between storage repositories and synchronize the datasets on each storage platform (common in Distributed Computing Environment client/server applications). Or, he needs a solution that will extract data from one storage repository, transform it, and transfer it to another data repository used by a different server (one method for sharing data between heterogeneous hosts). In short, the customers are looking primarily for data copy solutions that deliver data replication at the highest possible speed, using as much automation as possible to contain costs.

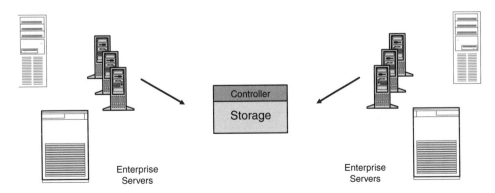

Figure 11–3   True Data Sharing.

A DYNAMIC DATA MOVEMENT EXAMPLE: HSM

From Drummond's description of data replication and data movement, storage begins to look like a much more dynamic and much less static entity. Prior to the appearance of the client/server application and data warehousing requirements that he describes, the dynamic nature of storage was suggested by efforts to deliver hierarchical storage management (HSM) solutions to the distributed computing environment.

HSM was introduced—unsuccessfully for the most part—to the distributed computing environment following the advent of LANs. Proponents sought to use this technology to automate the management of data storage on LAN-based file servers so that dreaded "server disk full" messages and the associated downtime for disk management could be avoided.

HSM is essentially the automatic movement of stored data from hard disks to slower, less-expensive, storage media. HSM hierarchies typically hold that online data should migrate over time to near online (or "near line") media such as optical disk, then to archival or offline media such as magnetic tape. HSM software provides configuration and automation of this process.

In operation, an HSM software process or agent monitors hard disk capacity on a storage platform and activates automatically—either in response to a capacity threshold event or as a scheduled event—to move data from one storage media type to the next. The selection of which data is to be migrated may be based on the age of the data, the date of last access, and/or other criteria specified by the network or system administrator.

With most HSM products, when a file is migrated off the hard disk, it is replaced with a small stub file that indicates where (on what optical disk or tape volume) the original file now resides (see Figure 11–4).

HSM offered a means to deliver and automate in the distributed computing environment the "disk grooming" function typically assigned to an IT storage manager in the mainframe setting. In the glass house setting, HSM was required because of the high cost of disk subsystems. The need to manage storage capacity for maximum cost efficiency was self evident: Failing to do so incurred significant penalties, not only in terms of hardware acquisition costs, but in many practical ways, as well. Planning for new disk subsystems was a complicated process requiring the consideration of many variables, including available environmentally controlled facility and floor space, available power, back plane connectivity, and operating system volume addressability.

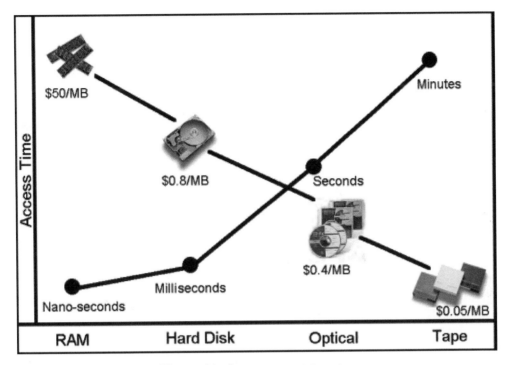

Figure 11-4   HSM Data Migration.

When HSM solutions were developed for the early distributed computing environment, the value proposition was similar to that of the mainframe world. Automated disk grooming functions would save expensive hard disk space by migrating data to lower-cost storage media. In the distributed computing context, however, additional benefits expected from HSM included the elimination of the need for capacity planning and storage management, as well as for personnel who might otherwise be required to manage storage.[3]

Despite these purported benefits, HSM failed to catch on in the distributed environment for a number of reasons. Three important factors were the sharp decline in hard disk prices, dramatic increases in hard disk capacities, and the growing availability of RAID array technology. In short, an abundance of low-cost hard disk storage assuaged concerns that servers would run out of storage. More disk could be added as needed and at an acceptable cost—often lower than the cost of optical disk media and optical or tape subsystems.

Early HSM software products themselves supplied another "nail in the coffin" of distributed HSM. The products were sometimes too efficient about migrating files from online to near- or offline media. Given the comparatively slow speeds of networks until recently, retrieving migrated files from remote tape or optical repositories often entailed lengthy waits. For many years, the lengthy waits to retrieve migrated files from HSM-managed storage hierarchies were rivaled only by the waits involved in restoring files from backups created with early backup/restore software.[4] Those who worked HSM-enhanced environments often felt like the mythical Sisyphus, who was punished in the infernal world by having to roll a huge stone to the top of a hill, only to have it roll down again.

The point of this discussion of HSM is not to argue its utility within a distributed computing context. Rather, HSM and its cousin processes, backup/restore and data archiving, constituted the first "dynamic data movements" within early storage repositories (see Figure 11–5).

Examined from the perspective of data movements, storage is less a static repository than a dynamic infrastructure. Strategies for managing storage (and for creating client/server applications that are "storage-aware") must adopt an infrastructural view of storage if they are to succeed.

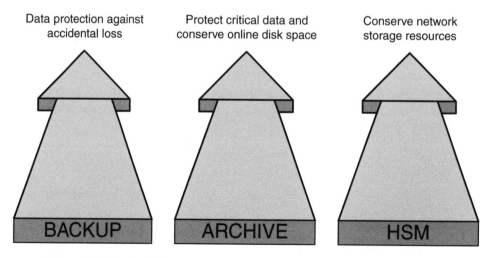

Figure 11–5   Early Dynamic Data Movements Within Storage Repositories.

SAN ARCHITECTURE FORCES STORAGE INFRASTRUCTURE VIEWPOINT

Recently, storage area networks (SANs) have been seized upon as a metaphor for the dynamic storage infrastructure. This is simply a case of an emerging technology and a new storage concept arriving at the forefront of industry attention at the same time. As Dino Balafas, Senior Product Manager for Computer Network Technology observes, SANs are just one more framework for building what he calls a "data sharing infrastructure."[5]

In a white paper on the subject of data sharing, Balafas focuses on the storage infrastructure requirements of a data warehousing application. Taking an infrastructure perspective, he considers three storage frameworks that might meet the data movement requirements entailed in operating the warehouse data repository. His analysis begins with a series of questions pertaining to "data movements" that are designed to identify the hardware and software requirements:

- How far must data move? What are the distances between stored information?
- How scalable is the network fabric for data transfer?
- What are the costs for increasing data movement bandwidth?
- How does the enterprise currently communicate between disparate communication protocols?
- How granular does data access need to be?
- How much free disk space is required for large file transfers?
- What data cleaning or transformations are required?
- How automated can the transfer process be?

STORAGE INFRASTRUCTURE REQUIREMENTS FOR DATA WAREHOUSE APPLICATIONS

Answering the above questions faithfully, according to Balafas, leads to an improved understanding of the storage infrastructure requirements of the data warehouse applications key data movements and helps to establish criteria for evaluating storage framework options for meeting them.

Interestingly, only one question on Balafas's list has to do with the storage capacity requirements of the solution. While a traditional storage perspective would focus on delivering an adequately sized platform to contain the warehouse database, only an infrastructural view of storage makes possible the analysis of the overall storage infrastructure required and provides a basis for assessing options.

In the example provided, three storage frameworks are suggested for managing data movements. The first uses existing LANs (SNA and TCP/IP) to facilitate data movements between mainframe data repositories and open systems storage. Mainframe data is readied for export to the open systems-based storage platform, then is shipped to its destination using a general purpose LAN.

Balafas points out that the drawbacks of this plan center on the use of TCP/IP with mainframes. IP stack processing can impact mainframe performance significantly, he observes. Alternatively, using a mainframe-friendly SNA connection and a TCP/IP-SNA gateway introduces other inefficiencies, such as protocol translation overhead.

The benefits of this framework, however, are that the LAN already exists and new equipment need not be purchased, enabling projects to proceed more quickly.

The drawbacks of the LAN framework for data movement, indicated by the path marked "1" in Figure 11–6, are several. Long-term costs will increase as more mainframe CPU cycles are needed for the movement of data. Furthermore, converting data from mainframe EBCDIC to open systems ASCII for use on the open systems data warehouse storage repository is complicated "by the limited scope of this transport method." Finally, data rates can be very slow, and large data transfers can impact other traffic flows on the network.

Method 2 in Balafas' example utilizes a partitioned disk environment on a large-scale array product. The array product itself provides multiplatform connectivity through its support for direct SCSI, Fibre Channel, and ESCON links to the host systems involved in contributing data to the data warehouse. Data sharing, in this arrangement, is made possible through internal data replication technology provided on the array controller.

This method, too, has its positive and negative attributes. Installation is relatively straightforward with available products on the market, offsetting some of the hardware acquisition cost. Also, the concept behind the solution, partitioning and replication, is simple to understand, so little additional education is required for support personnel. Finally, array controller bandwidth is substituted for network bandwidth as the chief determinant of data throughput.

On the down side, however, method 2 imposes a single-vendor (and often proprietary) solution on the customer. Costs are also generally

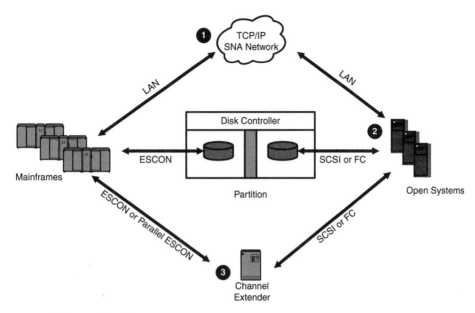

Figure 11–6   Data Movement Framework Alternatives. (*Source:* Computer Network Technology, Minneapolis, MN.)

higher with this solution than with others, Balafas says, owing in part to the specialized hardware and single source nature of the array product. Moreover, most vendors of partitioned disk arrays require the use of flat files for data movement, he observes, which in turn requires the customer to purchase additional storage from the vendor—a cost multiplier.

While faster than LAN-based frameworks (which deliver, according to Balafas, about 2 MB/s throughput), data movements that depend on array controller bandwidth are still quite slow, Balafas estimates about 5 MB/s, resulting in serious delays when transferring larger data files.

Balafas' preferred storage framework, method 3, is one that leverages his company's mainframe channel extension technology, of course. Balafas describes a framework in which mainframe channel extenders are used to facilitate transfers from the backplane of the mainframe directly to the SCSI or Fibre Channel ports of the open systems host's storage platform. A CNT channel extender provides the distance-unlimited ESCON to SCSI or ESCON to Fibre Channel connectivity. Delivering throughput rates of up to 16 MB/s data using a scalable ESCON interface, CNT channel extenders eliminate the protocol conversion and CPU cycle overhead of method 1, the controller bandwidth limitations and single-vendor product costs of method 2, and deliver a much less expensive, higher-performance solution overall.

He concedes that the solution is a complex one, requiring the acquisition, configuration, and maintenance of channel environment maps and new channel extension hardware.

The specifics of the CNT analysis as it pertains to software components of the data warehousing solution are somewhat murky. However, the analysis is interesting because it treats a business application problem from a storage infrastructure point of view. In specifying requirements for an application such as a data warehouse, storage platform and interconnects are paramount. The storage infrastructure must be defined before other aspects of the application are sorted out.

STORAGE-RELATED DATA LAYOUT REQUIREMENTS FOR DATABASES

Most database-driven client/server applications, by their nature, have strong storage infrastructure dependencies and entail some sort of data movements. These need to be understood before the application or database is deployed to ensure that proper support is provided.

ORACLE database management system (DBMS) products, for example, support concurrent accesses by multiple users and processes. For large or very large ORACLE deployments, disk arrays operating RAID 5 level software are often selected as a data repository. RAID 5 provides support for high-speed, random access I/O processing, in addition to providing enhanced reliability and an acceptable price/performance mix.

Ideally, however, a storage platform offering configurable RAID levels would provide the best support for different segments of an ORACLE database. ORACLE segments—such as control files, redo logs, system tablespace, sort segments, rollback segments, data files, and indexes—have very different operating parameters and perform best under different RAID levels, as shown in Table 11–1.

In addition to configurability, performance, and reliability, storage platforms for large ORACLE databases need to provide scalability and a modular design that facilitates upgrades to new or emerging technologies.[6]

However, specifications for storage solutions that stop at the definition of a hardware platform are incomplete. In specifying a large DBMS-based solution, hardware selection would proceed based not only on the selected DBMS product's storage performance and capacity requirements

Table 11-1   Optimal RAID Levels for an ORACLE Database

ORACLE Segment	Optimal RAID Level
Control file	5 or 0+1 (10) or none
Redo logs	0+1 (10)
System tablespace	5
Sort segments	0
Rollback segments	5
Data files including indexes	5

Source: MTI Technology Corporation, Anaheim, CA.

(anticipated database size and growth), but also on its storage infrastructure requirements.

Other questions must be asked to define storage infrastructure requirements. Does the storage platform need to share data among multiple hosts? Does data need to be replicated in several locations within the enterprise? How will cross-platform access to data be provided?

These questions begin to reveal the infrastructure requirements for the storage solution. The answers may have a significant impact on storage product acquisition and the design of the solution overall. For example, the integrator may learn that the selected storage array requires multiple ports for attachment to more than one host (and, in the future, to a SAN switch fabric). Similarly, the data sharing and replication requirements of the solution may require new hardware and software components that entail significant staff training or management costs. These do not reveal themselves without examining the solution from a storage infrastructure perspective.

STORAGE INFRASTRUCTURE REQUIREMENTS FOR MULTIMEDIA APPLICATIONS

Multimedia applications, including digital "nonlinear" editing products used by the audio/video post-production industry, are another example of storage infrastructure-dependent applications. Given the nature of digital video and audio editing, it is no wonder that many of the first implementations of SAN technology have been in the AV field.

In simple terms, a post-production company takes analog audio or video, converts it to a digital form, and edits it by enhancing sound quality, adding special effects, brightening images, and so on. Digitized video or audio, which comprises extremely large data files, is typically recorded on high-capacity, high-speed disk arrays, which then need to be shared among a group of personnel who edit the data concurrently using specialized software tools. Developing a solution that facilitates large data movements, complicated by the need to "stream" data at constant speeds, presents a significant storage infrastructure challenge.

According to Robert Herzan, Vice President of World Wide Sales with integrator Rorke Data, the promise of digital nonlinear editing in a workgroup environment was an unrealized vision until the emergence of SAN technology.[7]

> A/V people have never had the bandwidth for online audio and video editing. They need streaming speeds to accomplish transitions and dissolves in a digital environment and they need the disk capacity to store 20 to 30 hours of digitized video on a storage array so that their technicians could work together on the project. Today, Fibre Channel SANs have made that possible.

Rorke Data's first SAN implementation in early 1998 was a learning experience for the company. They found a video post-production house to serve as a beta test site for a "two-seat SAN implementation." Recalls Herzan,

> The project required a year and a half, with the most important parts of the technology becoming available only in the last six months of the project. We tested the limits of the ANSI Fibre Channel specification. ANSI said that copper networking could go to 30 meters. We found that it was reliable only out to 10 or 15 meters because of noise. To build a storage area network with a greater distance, you need to deploy fiber-optic cable.

Cabling proved the easiest issue to surmount, he notes,

> When we were first deploying the SAN hub product, it was new to market. It had some serious problems when a power shutdown occurred on any device connected in the storage area network. The vendor has since resolved the problem by giving its hub product a more intelligence.

A major obstacle came in the form of volume management software, used to provide file locking and other file management capabilities in the shared storage environment. Rorke says that he tried several products that were initially released to support SAN storage in a clustered environment, "but they were buggy and too cumbersome for a Macintosh-based user."

This led Rorke to co-develop with Charismac, Inc., a developer of disk striping software and utilities, an entirely new file management solution for Macintosh-based SANs. The project was a success and Rorke was launched into a leadership role in the audio-video digital editing integration business.

Rick Picton, Manager of Systems Engineering for MountainGate Imaging Systems, understands the volume management dilemma that Rorke Data integrators confronted in early 1998.[8] MountainGate, also a player in the post-production digital editing market, developed its own CentraVision File System to enable the sharing of SAN-hosted data among heterogeneous operating systems.

Picton says that deploying a digital video editing application requires enormous amounts of scalable storage together with a stable, reliable mechanism for cross-platform file access and locking. In short, a storage infrastructure perspective is an absolute requirement when addressing the requirements of digitial video.

Picton says that a new file system is a prerequisite for SAN success generally, "Current operating systems are not designed for shared access. They rely on buffered cache schemes, which provide high-speed functionality only when you are working with local storage. Cached data cannot be shared, so what worked well with local access works against global or shared access."

Picton also notes that the large files common to digital video and audio editing are not consistent with the design of current general purpose operating systems and their native file systems. These file systems were designed and optimized for numerous, smaller files. Furthermore, the tendency of general purpose file systems to store metadata together with raw data militates against the real-time access required to edit uncompressed digital media files.

In developing the CentraVision File System (CVFS), designers mimicked the ISO 9660 file system, which is implemented using software customized to conform to the operating system requirements of all supported hosts, enabling them to read metadata and raw data stored on CD-ROMs. CVFS was implemented in a similar manner.

CVFS is an operating system component that organizes and maintains the data structure and integrity of the CentraVision Network solution, says Picton. It uses an IP network-based file system manager (FSM) server to manage file access and to coordinate file locking. Client hosts use a CVFS software client and an external file system (XFS) driver that enables them to access the raw data files on shared SAN-based storage and use them in a format that is native to their operating system's capabilities.

Data access is made over a switched Fibre Channel interconnect, while access management is handled over the IP network. "This solution scales well," according to Picton, "because the IP overhead is very small."

Says the engineer, "As the SAN model becomes more prevalent, applications will need to become SAN-aware. Opening and closing files at the block level is a double-edged sword. It needs to be managed carefully."

He notes that Mercury Computer Systems takes a similar approach with its SANergy™ file management product, which was also born in the video editing industry. Mercury developed SANergy to work around problems in volume management software that shipped with early SAN hub and switch products.

Originally, SAN developers set about developing a volume-sharing mechanism for SAN storage. In theory, volume-sharing software would be used to limit write access to SAN storage to one end user or application at a time, while allowing simultaneous read access for multiple users. In practice, the approach played havoc with SAN access. When the host writing to the volume changed, an application needed to be run to reset the ownership of the volume so that another host could access the volume.

Additionally, because of local read caching on those host systems reading a SAN volume, the results of writes made to the volume by its last owner would not display until a "refresh" operation was initiated. Such an operation typically required that the SAN volume be dismounted, then remounted, so that the operating system would delete out-of-date information about the volume.

Approaches like MountainGate's CVFS and Mercury's SANergy endeavor to address the problems of volume sharing by approaching SAN access from a file sharing perspective. SANergy uses an NT operating system extension that redirects file I/O operations over the SAN and directly to shared storage devices.[9]

Windows NT supplies heterogeneous namespace, access control, and security as services. According to Mercury, this allows all existing applications and storage management modules to work without modification under the SANergy system. Metadata coordination is handled over IP via a Meta Data Controller (MDC), and I/O reads and writes take place across high-speed Fibre Channel. Heterogeneous host access is accomplished with Windows NT managing name spaces and security while UNIX and Macintosh hosts read and write data directly from shared NTFS volumes.[10]

Questions persist about the readiness of solutions such as SANergy for enterprise class deployment. In the *Data Communications Magazine* article that accompanied SANergy's recognition as a "Hot Product" in January 1999, the writer concluded that the product's downsides were numerous. Those cited included the fact that the MDC must run under Windows NT, that MDCs cannot fail over to one another, and that "at press time, there was no one who could verify Mercury's SANergy claims."[11]

Nevertheless, SANergy, CVFS, and earlier SAN management products from Rorke Data and Charismac all testify to the importance of a storage infrastructure focus to delivering solutions in the multimedia applications area. Mercury reports that it has enhanced SANergy to

> support concurrent file sharing with full file-level and byte-range locking on Sun Solaris platforms to its existing support for SGI IRIX, Windows NT, and MacOS operating systems. Furthermore, optimizations within SANergy 1.5 expand the range of applications that can benefit from SAN-based data sharing to include small-file/small-I/O operations, in addition to large-file/large-I/O applications such as streaming digital multimedia.[12]

From this and similar announcements by the company, it is clear that it wants to extend its storage infrastructure focus to address other application areas in the distributed computing enterprise.

THE STORAGE INFRASTRUCTURE PERSPECTIVE

To the IT professional, the storage infrastructure perspective enables a more comprehensive analysis of application storage requirements. As the above examples illustrate, there is much more to storage specification than discerning the capacity requirements for program file storage. Every application has its own inherent storage requirements that may include optimal file layouts on storage media, access requirements, data-sharing requirements, periodic large- and small-scale data movements, and data transfer rate dependencies. These requirements, in turn, dictate the kind of storage device that should be used, the degree of storage intelligence required, the bandwidth requirements of data transports, and many other characteristics that go to the dynamic nature of data storage.

The storage infrastructure perspective also yields another important insight into data storage. It reveals the underlying complexity of storage that flies in the face of overly simplified, one-size-fits-all depictions popularized in storage vendor marketing literature. From this perspective, one can clearly see that a SAN, a NAS device, a stand-alone array, or even a captive-storage array product is not a panacea. Repositories provide places to hold data. How they are used, how they are configured, and how they are accessed are all functions of storage management. Without effective storage management even the most expensive and complex storage repository will contribute little to improved application performance.

ENDNOTES

1. Interview with Scott Drummond, Data Sharing Brand Manager, Data Sharing Competency Center, IBM, San Jose, CA, 1998.
2. The home page on the World Wide Web for the IBM Data Sharing Competency Center is located at *http://ssddom01.storage.ibm.com/datasharing/datasharing.nsf.*
3. In this respect, HSM, like most distributed computing solutions, was part of a deception perpetrated by vendors upon cost-conscious businesses seeking to reduce the costs of mainframe-style computing. While few vendors would admit it today, the early sales pitch for distributed computing held that costs would be dramatically lower than mainframe-centric computing and that no administrators or technical support personnel would be required in the decentralized model.
4. To this day, backup software remains the most installed "storage management" component. Arguably, this is because its laborious and time-consuming attributes are offset by a generally perceived need for data backups as a hedge against catastrophic loss. Backups, too, constitute a data movement in a "dynamic" storage repository.
5. "Data Movement for Effective Data Sharing," Computer Network Technology White Paper, Dino Balafas, Senior Product Manager, Computer Network Technology Corporation, Minneapolis, MN, 1998.
6. Edwin E. Lehr and Christopher Schultz, "RAID Technology and Large Databases: Issues in Selection and Implementation," MTI Corporation White Paper, MTI Corporation, Anaheim, CA, 1997.

7. Interview with Robert Herzan, Vice President of World Wide Sales, Rorke Data, Minneapolis, MN, 1998. See also Jon W. Toigo, "Will SANs be Giant Slayers?" *Solutions Integrator*, October 1, 1998.

8. Interview with Rick Picton, Manager of Systems Engineering, MountainGate Imaging Systems Corporation, Reno, NV, 1999.

9. "The Storage Area Network Approach: Volume or File Sharing?" Mercury Product Brief, Mercury Computer Systems, Inc., Chelmsford, MA, 1998.

10. "The SAN Operating System Eliminates File Sharing Bottlenecks," Bruce Beck, Vice President of Sales and Marketing, Shared Storage Business Unit, Mercury Computer Systems, RTC Magazine, October 1998.

11. Mary Jander, "Some SAN Sanity," *Data Communications Magazine,* January 1999.

12. "Mercury Computer Systems Announces SANergy 1.5—Storage Area Network (SAN) Software Extends 'The Power to Share' for the Growing Shared Storage Market," Press Release, Mercury Computer Systems, Inc., Chelmsford, MA, February 9, 1999.

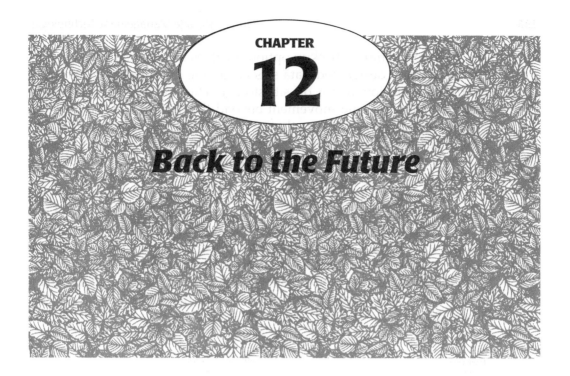

CHAPTER

12

Back to the Future

The marketing literature of many SAN product vendors has contextualized the Fibre Channel-based storage framework rather narrowly. Rather than describing how SANs might enable data warehousing or client-server database applications, vendors have chosen instead to focus on data backup as a generic illustration of SAN benefits.

While one might hope that this choice reflects a renewed interest in disciplined storage management within IT organizations, it is more likely that data backup was selected because it presented the benefits of centralizing storage in a back-end, high-speed network without requiring a lot of explanation about the application itself. Who, after all, does not know what a backup is or why backups need to be performed?

From a storage infrastructure perspective, the enterprise backup application represents a potentially complex series of data movements. Deploying an enterprise-class solution entails more than simply specifying a tape storage platform or a software application. To obtain the best backup solution for a company, numerous approaches and technologies for accomplishing backups need to be examined—all with a storage infrastructure focus.

The most common backup option involves the use of a local tape peripheral to copy designated data sets at routine intervals from hard disk to tape for migration to safe, off-site storage. This one-backup/one-system option entails little data movement beyond the local bus of the host system, but it does represent a costly use of staff time. As the number of systems to be backed up increase, more automation, more data movements, and greater use centralized backup management software products are typically the order of the day.

Within the realm of "enterprise" backup strategies, several options exist for accomplishing backups. Some strategies call for the use of a LAN as a conduit linking groups of workstations and servers to regionalized storage repositories.[1] Other strategies involve the movement of backup data through various storage tiers until it is ultimately hosted on a centralized storage platform or off-site "data vault" that is presumably managed with greater discipline than are lower-tier storage systems (see Figure 12–1).

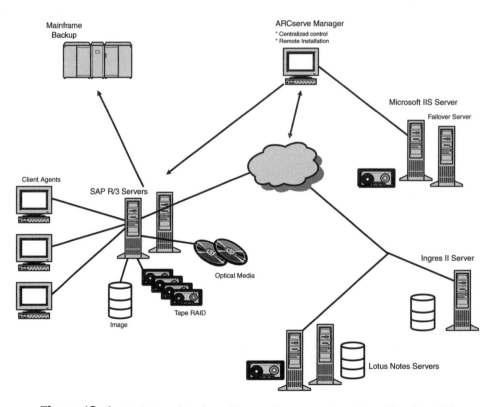

Figure 12–1   Multitiered Backup. (*Source:* Computer Associates, Islandia, NY.)

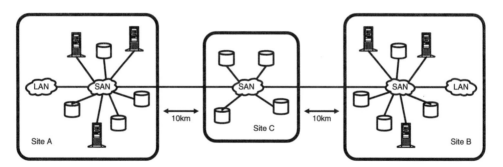

Figure 12–2   SAN-based Backup. (*Source:* Gadzoox Networks, San Jose, CA.)

Enterprise-class storage products, such as Computer Associates' ARCServeIT, Legato Systems' NetWorker, Platinum Technology's NetArchive, IBM/Tivoli Systems' ADSTAR Distributed Storage Manager (ADSM), Hewlett-Packard's OmniBack, Veritas Software's NetBackup, Seagate Software's Backup Exec, and others, offer automated support for, and centralized management of, the processes involved in a LAN-based backup strategy. The primary difference between this approach and the use of a SAN is that data movements through a SAN can be accomplished without impacting production LANs, reserving bandwidth on production networks for "more important" applications (see Figure 12–2).

CONSIDERATIONS FOR SELECTING A BACKUP STRATEGY

From a storage infrastructure viewpoint, many other factors would need to be considered before settling on a backup strategy and framework. Some questions might include:

- Will full volume (entire disk contents) or only incremental (changed files) be backed up? What are the consequences of each approach in terms of data restoral?
- Are heterogeneous file systems being backed up?
- What amounts of data are being backed up? How often?
- What type of media is being used for the backups? Are autoloaders or tape libraries being used?
- What software is being used for backups (see Figure 12–3)?

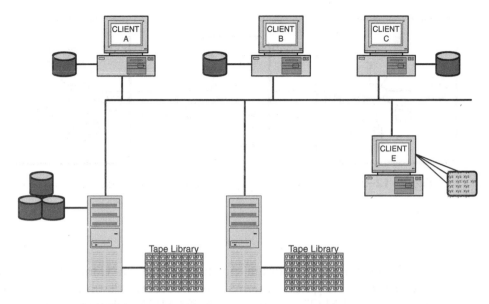

Figure 12–3   Does the Product Support Scheduled and Ad Hoc Full
and Incremental Backups? (*Source:* Platinum Technology, Oakbrook Terrace, IL.)

- Does the backup software provide for "hot" backups of databases
  (e.g., while databases are active) or does it require databases to be
  quiesced?
- Does the backup software provide for active file backup (e.g., backups of application or end user files while in use)?
- Does the backup software enable remote administration of backup
  processes?
- Does the backup software use software agents administered by a
  centralized server, and if so, where is the server located? How large
  are the agents or client processes?
- Are backed up files logged in a database? Where does the database
  reside?
- How are data restorals accomplished? By file? By volume? By system?
- Is a hierarchical storage management system in use? Are HSM file
  stubs included in backups?

REMOTE MIRRORING

While the need for effective backup strategies to ensure business continuity in the wake of a disaster is a given, it is important to take this train of thought one step further before settling on a tape backup strategy.

From a business continuity standpoint, the restore operation is actually the more important aspect of the backup/restore solution. Notes Paul Carrick, Senior Product Manager for Computerm Corporation, companies have become more dependent upon uninterrupted access to information resources than ever before and the impact of access interruptions can be measured tangibly in dollars lost per hour.[2]

Exposure varies from company to company, of course. Some firms estimate the cost of downtime in the thousands of dollars per hour and view a 48- to 72-hour recovery window as "survivable." Others, primarily in the financial sector, stand to lose revenues measured in the tens of millions of dollars per hour during periods of unplanned downtime. To these firms, even a comparatively short-term outage can mean the difference between business continuation and total failure, Carrick says. The bottom line of DR, especially given current vulnerabilities to access interruptions, is simple: Shorten the time to data.

There is a growing realization among many companies that traditional tape-based backup/restore solutions do not meet "time to data" requirements. In a traditional procedure, a company performs a backup of mission-critical data to a tape subsystem. These tapes are then removed from company premises by a tape storage contractor, who loads the media into a truck or van, carts it to an off-site storage facility, logs the media, and if necessary, performs other maintenance activities while the media is in his or her care. On a scheduled basis, the old media is rotated from storage back to the company for reuse as "scratch tape" in performing new backups. This tried and true strategy has the advantage of geographically dispersing information assets so that they are not consumed by a disaster event that affects the company.

However, the drawbacks of this traditional approach to backup are several—especially when viewed from the perspective of "shortening time to data." For one, obtaining tapes from a storage vendor and transporting them to a system recovery facility is a time-consuming process. Many recovery efforts have been delayed when the wrong tape sets were retrieved from storage and a second retrieval was required.

Additional recovery delays may result from the process of sorting and distributing data backups to administrators of multiple host systems.

This practice is increasingly common in mixed mainframe and client/server computing environments.

Finally, the costliest delays can result from the destruction of backup media when a vehicle transporting tape from the off-site storage facility to the recovery site is involved in a traffic accident. This may seem somewhat far-fetched, but, statistically speaking, data is most at risk during its transportation between the storage vendor and company facilities.

The shortcomings of traditional off-site backup methods have been understood for many years. Alternatives, however, were too costly to consider, given risk estimates and anticipated loss exposures. Today, however, a number of converging trends are making the use of these alternative techniques a more attractive proposition for many companies.

One alternative is electronic tape vaulting (ETV). ETV entails the use of a remote tape subsystem, often located at a remote off-site storage or system recovery hot site facility, as a destination for backup data sets generated by a company. Channel extension technology is used to connect the tape system to the I/O channel of the system host via a wide area network link. In effect, the remote tape device is treated as a locally installed tape system.

The benefits of ETV are several. For one, the arrangement eliminates the need to truck tapes to a safe storage facility, load and unload them, and to expose them to additional transportation-related risks.

Secondly, restorals are simplified by making the remote tape unit accessible as a logical subsystem of a new host in a recovery environment. Creating this relationship in advance of an unplanned interruption saves time in a disaster recovery situation. It eliminates the need to perform such manual tasks as loading and organizing tapes on a new tape subsystem and configuring the tape subsystem for use. Restore operations can commence as soon as the host system is operational and the WAN link is established.

Costs for ETV were prohibitively high when the technology was first introduced nearly a decade ago. However, declining WAN costs and order-of-magnitude improvements in network throughput enabled by enhanced data compression techniques in channel extenders themselves have reduced costs considerably, according to Carrick. These factors make ETV a more cost-effective option for remote backup than ever before.

Even electronic tape vaulting may not shorten time to data sufficiently to meet the needs of companies with extremely low tolerances to access interruptions. When this is the case, according to Carrick, another option for expedited restoral is remote mirroring. To better understand remote mirroring, one might consider an example involving a large-scale disk storage array.

Large-scale disk arrays are used by many companies to centralize the storage of terabytes of data on a single storage platform. Vendors of these products argue that deploying such a large and centralized data repository in the controlled environment of a data center "glass house" enables efficient management of storage by disciplined IT personnel, increasing the integrity, security, and availability of the data.

From a disaster recovery perspective, however, this configuration also collects a vital asset—corporate data—into a single location. There, it is subject to loss from a single disaster potential, such as fire, flooding, or a power outage, that might not impact storage that was more decentralized.

Recognizing this, most disk storage vendors also provide utilities for disaster recovery functions, including remote mirroring. Remote mirroring enables the creation of duplicate volumes of data on a physically separate platform. This mirrored data constitutes a data backup in near real-time.

In theory, remote mirroring enables the fast switchover of host systems to a duplicate data store in the event that access to the primary data store is interrupted. The solution is described as "fast" because the data is read directly from a mirrored set of disks rather than having to be copied and reloaded to disk, as with tape. With such a configuration, business can continue in a matter of minutes following an otherwise disastrous interruption of normal information access.

To be effective, of course, such a configuration must manifest two important characteristics: mirroring efficiency and extended distance operation. Mirroring efficiency refers to the impact on normal production systems of mirroring operations. As a rule, a mirroring operation must not introduce latency into normal data read–write operations.

Latency, simply put, is the amount of host CPU "idle time" that accrues while duplicate data is written to a mirrored disk. Latency occurs when CPUs and applications requiring access to the data that is being mirrored cannot access it until copying is completed.

In the past, the "mirror after write"—or synchronous—approach to disk mirroring required that a host CPU's I/O operations be suspended temporarily while duplicate data was being written. This had the consequence of slowing the performance of production systems—an unacceptable outcome.

To address the problem, some disk storage product vendors have worked on strategies to enable concurrent production I/O and mirroring I/O operations. Approaches have included using system or array memory to buffer new read–write operations while mirroring occurs, or adding software intelligence to provide an asynchronous or "semisyn-chronous" operational mode. Semisynchronous mirroring, as implemented by EMC and other array vendors, means that read–write operations are allowed on a controlled basis at the same time as mirror writes occur—that is, additional data can be written before the mirror copying process is complete.

Buffering and semisynchronous mirroring techniques have yielded significant improvements in latency reduction in local mirroring configurations. For disaster recovery purposes, however, mirroring must be able to occur between two disk storage arrays that are physically distant from each other. While local mirroring provides protection against certain disaster potentials, such as an equipment fault in the primary array, it offers no business continuance capability in the event of a "smoke-and-rubble" disaster that consumes the company data center. To enhance survivability, the mirrored array needs to be geographically distant from the primary storage array. Thus, a remote mirroring solution is required.

Efficient remote mirroring has been a goal for storage and channel extension vendors for many years. One challenge to be overcome has been distance-related latency.

The mirroring latency problem alluded to above worsens when the distance between mirrored arrays increases. Increased distance translates to increased travel time, during which I/O processing is suspended in a synchronous mode mirroring environment (see Figure 12–4). The goal of vendors has been to enable remote mirroring over an extended distance without impacting normal I/O operations.

One way to realize this goal is to deploy "surrogate" or multilevel remote mirroring. In this arrangement, shown in Figure 12–5, mirroring operations occur in two distinct phases. In the first phase, the primary disk array is mirrored to a second disk array located in fairly close proximity. In this way, mirroring operations can be conducted expeditiously and will not create latency that impacts production system operations.

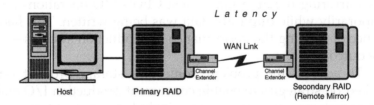

Figure 12–4   Remote Mirroring Incurs Distance-Related Latency.

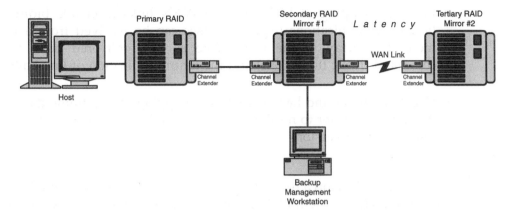

Figure 12–5 Surrogate Mirroring.

To achieve a disaster recovery capability, a second mirroring operation occurs between the mirrored disk array and a third disk array located at an extended distance from the company site—typically at the company's disaster recovery backup facility or hot site. This second mirroring operation is driven by a remote mirroring application that is hosted on a stand-alone PC or workstation connected to the second disk array. It does not involve production hosts, so the distance-related latency created by the remote mirroring operation is irrelevant to normal system operations.

The above scenario depends on channel extension technology in two ways. First, as indicated, channel extension provides the means to extend the host system I/O channel across a wide area network link, enabling a mirrored disk array to be located many hundreds of miles away.

Secondly, modern channel extension technology optimizes the communications link to deliver the greatest possible data throughput over available bandwidth. Some (but not all) channel extension products provide advanced capabilities that contribute to efficient, low-latency, remote mirroring. These advanced capabilities include:

- Hardware architecture optimized for low latency
- Hardware architecture capable of delivering full ESCON throughput across extended distances
- On-channel data compression that compresses larger data blocks for maximum throughput across the extended link
- I/O channel multiplexing to enable the aggregation of multiple host system I/O channels and to handle their traffic across a fewer number of communications links

- Efficient mapping of I/O traffic to WAN links to enable bidirectional communications (e.g., responses can be received from a remote disk array at the same time as new mirrored data and command traffic flows to it) and maximum utilization of link bandwidth

- Highly granular and hardware-based mapping of I/O frame data to ATM cells in order to minimize the overhead associated with frame-to-cell data conversion

In short, to develop a remote mirroring solution that does not add latency to production system I/O operations, a combination of disk mirroring and advanced channel extension functionality are required. Ongoing improvements in both the mirroring functionality offered by storage vendors and the communications-optimization capabilities of channel extension vendors are making remote mirroring possible today.

Electronic tape vaulting and remote disk mirroring are not panaceas. Given their cost characteristics, they may be appropriate in specific applications with extremely "short time to data" recovery requirements. As with any technology solutions, these strategies need to be evaluated carefully on the basis of business-specific factors.

To compare the benefits that may be realized from these strategies, Computerm's Carrick suggests that IT professionals compare the application of each strategy to the restoral of a four-terabyte database in the wake of a disaster. To restore such a database using a conventional backup/restore process, tapes (the correct tapes) must be retrieved from storage, delivered to the recovery location, loaded in proper order and sequence, updated with data that was processed after the last backup, and loaded back to the recovery storage array. This is a multiday process.

With electronic tape vaulting, the transportation components of this procedure are eliminated and, depending on the configuration of the backup process, so too may be the need to restore significant quantities of update information. With many ETV implementations, incremental backups of changed data are made across the WAN connection at frequent intervals to shorten data loss exposure windows. Moving four terabytes of data from the electronic tape vault across an optimized ATM link to a new storage platform at a recovery site requires about 9.3 hours. This assumes the use of channel extension-based data compression and communications optimization technologies to deliver backup data (versus a day or more by truck).

With remote mirroring, the restoral process is virtually instantaneous. Mirrored volumes may be accessed and utilized to support processing from a recovery site. At the same time, each remote volume can be mirrored to a local volume until both are synchronized. Eventually, the local restored volume becomes the primary volume and the remote continues in operation as a mirror.

There are, of course, dollar costs associated with each alternative and each must be evaluated individually. Ultimately, companies may find that a mixture of traditional, ETV, and remote mirroring approaches are appropriate based on the relative criticality of applications and their related data.

Given the falling costs of technology, the growing size of corporate data sets, the expanding capabilities of enabling technologies such as channel extension, and the increasing dollar loss exposures represented by unplanned interruptions in access to corporate data, IT professionals would be well-advised to reinventory their backup/restore solution.

HIERARCHICAL STORAGE MANAGEMENT

Backup solutions are more complex today than ever before. A solution that fits the specific requirements and capabilities of the distributed computing environment can only be developed by approaching the problem from a storage infrastructure perspective.

The same holds true for hierarchical storage management applications, which have lately experienced a resurgence of interest owing, in part, to the announcement of "fast" (midpoint) loading tape systems and "virtual" (disk-buffered) tape systems for the "open systems" market by IBM and other manufacturers. Both of these tape technologies provide methods to reduce the amount of time required to demigrate files (e.g., return them to the file storage where they resided prior to HSM migration) when requested by an application or end user.

Midpoint loading tape improves stored-file access time by beginning its seek operation in the middle of the media. With virtual tape systems, a tape library is fronted by a disk drive array, which serves as a data buffer. Originally designed as a technology for filling tape media to capacity (by writing data to the disk buffer until it contains a sufficient amount of data to fill an entire tape, then writing the data to the tape), this technology is now being positioned as "HSM in a box."

The potential of these technologies to reduce lengthy demigration wait time has sent many backup software vendors on a quest for HSM software modules to "plug into" their existing backup software suites. At least one vendor, Legato Systems, has warned fellow vendors against re-peating the errors of the past.

In the past, the vendor observes, "HSM was thought of as a panacea to all storage management problems, and vendors promised dramatic reduc-tions in total cost of ownership: 'Just install this software and all your stor-age management problems will go away.' After deployment, IS personnel found that they traded in one set of problems for another and business-critical information was not being protected or managed effectively."[3]

Legato worries that vendor oversell will lead to misconceptions about HSM. According to the vendor, HSM should not be deployed as a substitute for backup and archiving or to reduce hardware storage costs. The former rationale is a "common trap that IS personnel fall into." While there is rarely confusion about the distinction between backup and HSM, archive and HSM are often confused, since some IT organizations back older files to tape archives periodically to increase disk space. A true archive is a copy of a file system at a given point in time, not necessarily performed as a disk cleaning measure.

The second misconception, that deploying HSM will save hardware storage costs, does not derive from a problem of semantics, but a practical matter of cost trends. It is difficult to justify that deploying HSM will save storage dollars, the vendor observes, "given the rate at which street prices for storage hardware have been decreasing."

In previous experiences with HSM, says the vendor, many IT depart-ments found that the dynamics of the mainframe data center did not apply to the distributed computing environment. Adopting a storage in-frastructure perspective, Legato cautions that "issues such as heteroge-neous platforms, operating systems, network bandwidth, and varying tape speeds [need to be] considered before deployment" in order to de-rive any measurable benefits from HSM.[4]

Some industry observers claim that the total solution cost for HSM, including software, hardware, and personnel costs, easily approaches $75,000 or more.[5] This number can be much higher if data movements re-quire the upgrading of network infrastructure.

Still, according to Legato and others, this cost may be offset by curb-ing the demand for online storage and by reducing network bandwidth demands for backup. Curbing disk capacity demands are expected to be one result of migrating older files, which are estimated to comprise as much as 80% of data stored on hard disk,[6] to offline or near-line media, thus freeing more space on existing disk storage. Using HSM to cull disk storage volume is also expected to benefit LAN performance by reducing backup traffic. This argument assumes that LANs are used as data transports and also that decreased bandwidth utilization by backup data movements will not be offset by increased bandwidth utilization by HSM data migration and demigration.

Again, before deploying HSM (or any application), its requirements must be assessed from the storage infrastructure perspective. The data movements of the application must be understood and analyzed to arrive at a realistic set of software, hardware, and network requirements and to develop a solution that meets them.

THE IMPACT OF HSM ON STORAGE PLANNING

Richard Munroe, President and Chief Technology Officer for Acorn Software, is concerned about the impact of HSM applications and virtual tape on such important storage management practices as capacity planning. He notes that HSM

> effectively "smears" storage usage in such a way that one can more effectively use the resources one has. Individual tools like virtual tape and HSM are not replacements for storage planning. They can "stretch" the existing storage, but they don't measure up to a well-documented and understood storage capacity and growth plan.[7]

He concludes that

> Storage planning absolutely requires that one understands one's application and its effect on capacity planning, well beyond the counting of megs of memory and gigs of storage and number of drives. One must look at the real world needs for storage in order to develop realistic plans.[8]

Munroe's point is well taken. As the narrative of this book repeatedly asserts, the storage infrastructure has become the centerpiece of modern distributed computing. In application development, adopting a storage-centric view is key to delivering coherent and integrated technology solutions that meet business requirements. Without such a perspective, the best methodologies and application development tools can not deliver solutions that use resources efficiently.

Referring to a "storage infrastructure" may elicit a chuckle or two from developers and integrators who read this book. The term may seem inappropriate when applied to many IT environments. Integrators report that it is not uncommon to enter a customer site and to discover a haphazard collection of storage technologies that have been pieced together on an *ad hoc* basis that lack even the minimum of storage management. In many cases, business-critical storage platforms are rarely (if ever) backed up.

In such an environment, it is essential that vendors, integrators, and developers work together with IT managers, system administrators, and business professionals to encourage a more disciplined approach to storage management. As more demanding applications are deployed, an unmanaged storage infrastructure can only contribute to performance degradation across all production systems and networks.

Unplanned data growth and *ad hoc* storage product acquisitions tend to drive demands for bigger servers and bigger network pipes to handle distributed storage access requirements. This, in turn, drives up the total costs for computing within companies. The good news is that once business managers are made to understand the connection between poor storage management and degraded performance, higher costs, and increased downtime in mission-critical systems, their support for initiatives to build a disciplined storage infrastructure is almost always forthcoming.

ENDNOTES

1. A good general presentation of this strategy can be found in "Optimizing Storage Management Architectures by Distributing Centrally Controlled Storage Devices Wherever They're Needed," Sam Diamond, *Storage Management Solutions*, March 1998.
2. Interview with Paul Carrick, Senior Product Manager, Computerm Corporation, Pittsburgh, PA, 1999.
3. "Hierarchical Storage Management for the Distributed Client/Server Environment," Legato White Paper, Legato Systems, Palo Alto, CA, 1998.
4. *Ibid.*
5. Ranga Rangachari, "Selection Criteria for HSM and Archive Storage Solutions," *Computer Technology Review*, June 1995.
6. *Ibid.*
7. Richard C. Munroe, "Application-Driven Storage Management," *Storage Management Solutions*, January 1999.
8. *Ibid.*

CONCLUSION

PART

4

CONCLUSION

CHAPTER 13

The Holy Grail

The multiple techniques and strategies for enterprise storage management described in the preceding chapters underscore a fundamental point. As of this writing, no single storage architecture is pervasive in the modern corporate enterprise. In its absence, there can be no single, comprehensive, integrated set of software utilities for managing the modern storage infrastructure—at least, not one that meets the custom requirements of all companies.

This may not be the case forever. Several leading vendors, including Sun Microsystems, EMC Corporation, and Compaq Computer Corporation, have articulated visions for the future of storage and storage management that promise a more responsive, more manageable infrastructure in the future.

As of this writing, each vendor is working actively to ensure that its approach will become sufficiently pervasive over time to be viewed as a *de facto* industry standard. As with most competing vendor approaches, each vision statement is criticized by adherents of competing approaches.

Typical charges include that the vision is proprietary or slanted to favor the products of its vendor sponsor. This observation is not without merit. In every case, the vision articulated by the vendor holds that the realization of "storage nirvana" will not occur without the vendor's evolving product line.

In addition to the "lack of openness" argument, the forward-looking storage infrastructure and management initiatives are typically characterized by critics and competitors as "vapor"—full of sound and fury but signifying nothing. Indeed, it is often difficult to discern substance from market speak when reading the press releases and inevitable white papers that accompany media events announcing vendor strategic visions.

One problem that IT professionals confront involves distinguishing between the various visionary perspectives of the vendors. Most use the same words and phrases. For example, nearly all visions refer to a storage "pool"—an almost mystical entity that solves all problems of fixed volume size, heterogeneous access, true data sharing, and myriad other issues. The underlying architecture of the pool is almost always a SAN (a problematic descriptor, since vendor interpretations of the meaning of storage area network vary greatly), which is augmented by yet-to-be-developed software.

Another aspect that raises confusion is the "clubbiness" of each announcement. Each vendor strives to discriminate its initiative from those of its competitors and courts the press, the software development community, CIOs, and IT professionals to become card-carrying members. The inevitable follow-on to a vendor storage vision announcement is a list of "industry leading companies"—almost always the same list of companies—that have already joined the club. Like remoras attaching themselves to sharks, virtually the same set of storage software and SAN switch and hub vendors show up for every announcement party. To the remoras, there is nothing disloyal, heretical, or unethical about the practice. They are embracing all visions until a clear leader emerges.

Finally, virtually all storage vision announcements are heavily laden with references to "standards associations"—mainly to give the impression that each initiative springs from the well of open standards. Most associations cited are not standards groups at all, but marketing organizations that are themselves promoting a particular technology or set of technologies. Where no group with an agreeable charter exists, the visionary vendor substitutes its own creature—announcing both a vision and a standards group in the same press release.

Setting all of the above to one side, it remains important to become familiar with the three major industry initiatives (as of this writing) to realize the Holy Grail of enterprise storage management. While it is premature to predict which initiative (if any) will yield a *de facto* industry standard, it is valuable to examine how vendors see the problems of storage and the steps for their ultimate resolution. To avoid characterizations of this book and its author as advocates of any particular initiative, they are presented in chronological order by date of announcement.

SUN MICROSYSTEMS AND STORE-X

The first to market with a "visionary strategy" was Sun Microsystems, which articulated its Intelligent Storage Network vision in January 1998. Jeff Allen, Vice President of Network Storage, claims that the initiative traces its origins to 1994, when the company announced the first Fibre Channel storage solution in the industry: the SPARC Storage Array.[1] In January 1998, says Allen, the company furthered its leadership role by providing the first Fibre Channel SAN implementation, "loosely defined as a hub-based Fibre Channel-Arbitrated Loop featuring all Fibre Channel storage for direct attachment to Solaris."

In its press release, Sun termed its solution a building block toward the realization of an Intelligent Storage Network architecture that "delivers mainframe-class reliability, availability, and serviceability (RAS), as well as headroom for unlimited growth and multiplatform information sharing." As long-term strategy, Sun promised to eventually support Microsoft Windows NT (which they now do, according to Allen) and advised customers and prospects to "future-proof" their storage hardware acquisitions by purchasing the vendor's current line of Sun™ StorEdge™ products.

"With the Intelligent Storage Network model," the vendor said, "customers will be able to build heterogeneous storage systems with interchangeable building-block components; offer end users anytime/anywhere access to multiplatform information; load data warehouses in a fraction of the time previously required; consolidate storage systems for cost savings; and manage the storage environment from anywhere with a Java™ technology web browser."[2]

To some industry observers, Sun appeared to have come out with its storage infrastructure vision prematurely as interest in the trade press cooled. However, in December 1998, the company revisited the strategy and announced "Project StoreX" shortly after Compaq unveiled its Enterprise Network Storage Architecture (ENSA) and a month after EMC Corporation's announcement of its Enterprise Storage Architecture (see below).

The StoreX announcement articulated the Sun storage vision in more specific terms. Project StoreX was described as "a development platform" that could provide an open way for servers, storage systems, switches, hubs, and software from different manufacturers to work with one another in a SAN framework. The StoreX storage infrastructure, built on "pools" of storage and servers, would make any data available to any user, eliminating the need for point-to-point connections.

Allen provides further clarification of the strategy. First, he notes that the term SAN "is widely misused in the industry. Today, it is a storage interconnect. IP is required for file and volume management. At the end of the day, everyone is asserting that Fibre Channel is the panacea, but the interconnect may be completely different in five years. Companies may be using IP over Fibre Channel."

Allen also disagrees that the intelligence in a SAN will ultimately reside in a Fibre Channel switch, as some vendors suggest. Instead, "controller technology is where the functionality to manage the SAN must reside," he argues.

To these assumptions about the future of storage, he adds, "Disk systems are increasingly optimized for the applications they support. No one design fits all. Streaming video, online transaction processing, data warehousing, etc., all have their own storage requirements. We see hardware suppliers continuing to build their own hardware with their own management interface. Operating system vendors continue to press their own approach for managing storage. Application vendors, such as SAP, Oracle, and others all have their own management interface."

Against this backdrop of diversity, says Allen, Sun is endeavoring to impose policy-based management through its StoreX Project, "StoreX envisions disk bricks—disk arrays with personality modules—[as an evolving paradigm.] StoreX aims at developing an open storage management platform based on Java that can impose policy-based management without touching the proprietary management implementations made by separate hardware and software vendors. StoreX will decide who gets storage first, it will control storage allocation so that more storage resources are made available to an application when resources are low."

For the storage allocation process to be fully automated, Allen contends, the cooperation of all hardware and software vendors in opening their interfaces for access by the StoreX management tool is required. This may be a difficult sell to certain computer makers and storage array vendors, he concedes, but it is a potential boon to SAN switch and hub makers, as well as less recognized storage products vendors. "Right now, Brocade has to write an interface for every vendor's hardware [in order to use them with its Fibre Channel switch]. It would be better to be able to write a single interface to StoreX, which will work with everything."

Sun is working toward the adoption of StoreX by SNIA. Allen chooses not to engage in competitive rhetoric with EMC or Compaq, asserting instead that StoreX could be very useful to these companies in realizing their storage infrastructure visions as well. Says Allen, "Forcing all vendors to write to your product application programming interfaces (APIs) is crazy. Only Java works with everything."

According to the StoreX Project announcement, the vendor envisions a Java-based "universal framework" to be used for the development of "platform-independent management services and interfaces" and "platform-specific data services" such as backup, remote dual copy, data sharing, and remote mirroring.

> Project StoreX provides a migration path to the benefits of Sun's Intelligent Storage Network™ concept. The Intelligent Storage Network removes the physical and logical barriers between devices to create a free flow of information and data services. By simplifying management of data services in heterogeneous environments, Project StoreX transforms the Intelligent Storage Network from vision to reality.[3]

In its StoreX release, Sun also cited an industry alliance forming around its initiative "driven by the critical need for the industry to standardize. The days of proprietary lock-in storage interfaces are over."[4] Early joiners included Oracle, Veritas Software, Seagate Technology, Legato, Vixel, Gadzoox, Creative Design Solutions, Qlogic, StorageTek, Tandberg Data, Fujitsu, ATL Products, Quantum, and Exabyte. Only a few days before, many of these companies were also reported to have signed on to Compaq's ENSA initiative.

COMPAQ'S ENSA

Bob Passmore, Director of Strategic Marketing for Compaq Computer Corporation's Storage Products Division, says that the Enterprise Storage Network Architecture (ENSA) initiative, unveiled in December 1998, derives from customer storage management challenges and experiences.[5] He recites the components of the storage infrastructure challenge almost by rote. He notes,

Companies are doubling the amount of storage they deploy each year. Measured in petabytes, that means that a typical UNIX shop deployed more storage last year than in the past thirty years combined.

The cost per megabyte for storage has declined to a point where a company can deploy an unprecedented amount of storage without breaking its IT budget.

Companies generally do not perceive the hidden cost of storage—that it must be managed, and that management costs increase linearly with the number of gigabytes of storage deployed. According to the best estimates I have seen, a UNIX shop will need to hire a full-time IT staff member for every 200 GB of new storage that is added in order to manage that storage. In an NT shop, a new, full-time equivalent staff resource will be needed for every 70 to 90 GB of storage.

Says Passmore, to reduce storage management costs, a company must either consolidate storage resources and/or deploy some sort of central storage management tool, "With current tools, this may cut storage management costs by half—but not for long."

Confronting increased management costs as storage continues to proliferate, many companies will try to outsource the problem, he predicts:

In essence, they will hire more resources. This strategy may see them through one more year. Ultimately, the management problem will return to the hands of the internal IT organization. Meetings will be scheduled to discuss how to approach the storage management problem. The staff who should attend will be unable to participate, because they will be busy running daily fire drills. In a distributed computing enterprise, every day is characterized by change—in business priorities and directions. These have an immediate impact on the enterprise IT infrastructure.

He summarizes the storage challenge against a backdrop of modern corporate IT operations, citing:

- Increased pressure on storage resources to meet mission-critical, yet constantly changing application requirements
- 1980s distributed architectures struggling to meet year 2000 demands
- 24x7x365 operations for IT organizations with global, Internet-based, end users and zero tolerance for downtime

- Economic futures of entire businesses, and possibly entire nations, riding on a strand of glass fiber connecting nanosecond silicon storage to microsecond mechanical storage

With ENSA, Passmore says, Compaq has worked out the basics of an architecture and an approach "that delivers a value proposition in four key areas."

The first of these areas is Volume Virtualization. Says the director,

> We need to go beyond the current thinking about a volume to embrace the concept of a virtual volume. We can take a RAID 5 array and present it to a server as a volume. Virtualization goes beyond that. Imagine if you can take all storage, regardless of its physical distribution, and virtualize as a part of one very large storage pool. Policy-based management tools can be applied to it easily, and it would only take a small number of people to manage it entirely. Imagine if you could then present this enormous volume to a server—not physically—but as a virtual volume for use with an application. The physical storage is part of the pool. The pool senses the need from the server and presents physical blocks as they are needed by an application.

Volume Virtualization will provide a workaround for the fixed volume size dilemma that confounds current efforts to grow storage without downtime, he observes. In addition to virtual volumes, another value proposition of ENSA is Dynamic Scaling. Passmore describes this function, "A management tool watches the pool as a whole and warns when a high water mark is being approached. As needed, it adds unallocated storage to the pool. Whenever any device plugs into the pool, it is automatically allocated physical blocks of storage from the pool, when finished the blocks are deallocated. No operator intervention is required."

Passmore uses the analogy of a public utility to describe the manner in which dynamic scaling should deliver storage resources to applications, "When you turn on a light, you don't need to call the power company to request a certain number of amps, and you don't need to call the power company to discontinue service when you turn the light off so that you won't be billed for it. Imagine that you can connect to this pool just by plugging in a network cable, and disconnect just as easily. That is dynamic scaling."

The third value proposition of ENSA, according to the director, is Data Replication. Says Passmore,

Certain facts of life stay with us. Every customer needs to do backup, whether he or she likes it or not. Eventually, something will go bump in the night and you will need to restore data from backups. Restore is the real application. But restore applications today have a major drawback. They take a lot of time to do. If you have a four terabyte database, and you spend a lot of money, you may be able to restore it in three or four hours. If you don't have a lot of money, the restore will take days. Companies need instant restore.

Passmore says that instantaneous restoral of data can be accomplished with today's technology, "Let applications quiesce, take a snapshot of the volume, and let the application continue to do its thing. Technically, it is not a copy, though it behaves like one in every sense of the word. At a cost of 5 to 20 percent additional storage, you can copy on write, or copy after write. You can do it every half-hour for finer resolution. When you need to restore, just change the pointer on the volume: instant restore."

He adds that "old-fashioned" backups still have a role to play. He notes that tape copies are required in a case of massive infrastructure failure. However, in most cases of data loss, "you can just replace the damaged hardware or software or database that caused the failure in 99.9 percent of the cases, temporarily attach to the virtual volume containing the replica, and you are back in business."

ENSA's fourth value proposition is Simplified Management. With the virtual storage pool, management is a matter of setting policies and distributing them to storage management servers, says Passmore. Storage management servers are "dedicated servers strategically located around the enterprise and tasked with executing the policies set for storage."

Whether automated or operator-assisted, storage management simply watches the utilization of storage resources to look for bottlenecks. "If a bottleneck is detected," Passmore says, "just move some resources to resolve it."

"Storage is very latency sensitive," he observes, "so the management application needs to be able to identify problems quickly and move resources to correct them quickly." To Passmore, this is storage management infrastructure nirvana—a Holy Grail that he and his fellows at Compaq Computer Corporation are working toward realizing within the next few years. He believes it can happen because it is grounded in very practical reality.

It is all well and good to have a vision, but you can't expect to have everyone throw away everything they have invested money in for the past five years. We break no operating system rules with this idea. The

> virtual volume looks and feels like a local hard drive to the server. We do
> not require that data be centralized into a few large boxes. That is a
> failure-prone, low-performance option. Our infrastructure is distributed.

Moreover, says Passmore, large parts of the technology required are already available today. Not the virtualization of all storage or the copy-after-write snapshots, he concedes,

> But we are able to share physical storage. We are able to present virtual volumes to servers with our storage and clusters extensions to Windows NT. We can do snapshots and project them over a network to a backup server. We have remote mirroring capabilities. And, we have centralized, policy-based management in the form of the Storage-Works Command Console that can be combined with hardware to make a centralized storage management server that can be used to perform backups and restores.

Compaq has taken ENSA initiative as far as it can on its own, Passmore observes. On January 25, 1999, the company announced the formation of an alliance with Emulex, Brocade Communications Systems, Gadzoox Systems, Veritas Software, Legato Systems, Computer Associates, and others, tasked with a mission to break down the final barriers and realize the ENSA vision.

The next step is to tame the SAN. Passmore says that Compaq "piggy-backed" its ENSA vision on the Fibre Channel infrastructure early on. However, he concedes that the interoperability issues in Fibre Channel are nontrivial and will require a cooperative effort among vendors of SAN hardware and software, as well as server vendors, to surmount. With the combined resources and support of the other ENSA partners, he believes that SANs will come into the mainstream at last.

EMC'S ENTERPRISE STORAGE NETWORKS

In November 1998, EMC Corporation announced its storage infrastructure strategy, Enterprise Storage Networks, at a media event staged in New York City. According to Jim Rothnie, EMC's Senior Vice President and Chief Marketing Technical Officer, "Vital elements of true enterprise storage networks include platform-independent storage systems; centralized management software; tested interoperability; robust online storage-to-storage data movement; storage-based security; and data center class support."[6]

EMC marketing literature exclaimed that

> enterprise storage replaces an outdated legacy of deploying storage as
> a computer peripheral with storage devices dedicated to individual
> host computers. That "bad, old way" of handling storage leads to iso-
> lation of data in individual islands, an information archipelago in
> which data is difficult to share, manage, and protect. Enterprise stor-
> age involves deploying storage as a common resource to which a
> broad array of different types of servers can connect. By providing a
> common pool of storage, it serves as an effective focal point for the
> management, protection, and sharing of information.[7]

While EMC's rhetoric was strikingly similar to both Sun's StoreX and
Compaq's ENSA descriptions, vendors of the "open standards approaches" wasted little time in dismissing the EMC approach as proprietary. The ENSA Technical White Paper, released in the month following
the EMC announcement, differentiated itself from the EMC in no uncer-
tain terms.

> ENSA differs significantly from EMC's strategy in several key ways.
> First, ENSA allows storage to be geographically deployed where it is
> needed while retaining a central management scheme, whereas EMC
> strives to consolidate all data into a centralized location and then pro-
> vide it to application servers over a network. Second, ENSA is broadly
> based on Open Standards, while EMC retains subsystems that are
> highly proprietary and restrictive in the storage components they sup-
> port. Another difference is the approach to management and service.
> ENSA is designed to empower the system manager to control and con-
> figure nearly all aspects of his or her subsystem, and Compaq offers
> optional management and maintenance services. EMC continues with
> its historic approach of retaining significant control over the cus-
> tomer's storage pool properties and the storage systems require EMC
> maintenance. While the customers can perform some configuration
> and system manipulation themselves, EMC does not allow nearly the
> flexibility that Compaq provides with ENSA.

Critics of the EMC approach believed that their suspicions about
EMC's proprietary strategy were validated in March 1999, when EMC announced the implementation of its storage infrastructure, consisting entirely of Symmetrix hardware and software.[8] EMC's Rothnie disagrees
adamantly with this assessment.[9]

He notes that there were six components in the March announcement,
constituting "an immediately available solution for companies seeking an

answer today for their storage management issues." The "pieces" included a new Fibre Channel switch product from EMC; new Symmetrix storage products supporting industry-standard Fibre Channel and SCSI intercon-nects; a stated commitment to invest $250 million for interoperability test-ing (of EMC's own configurations); the establishment of a Fibre Alliance consortium "open to all vendors, to establish interoperability standards with respect to storage management;" new software products for moving data more efficiently and securely through a Fibre Channel environment; and, new professional services "designed to help customers learn about Fibre Channel and implement the Enterprise Storage Network."

Says Rothnie, "There are a lot of initiatives around and a lot of 'vi-sioneering.' We set out to do more than start a club. That announcement provided customers with an interoperable SAN solution today that fea-tures security, support, and interoperability. Vision is the least important thing to focus attention on. Reality is what must be judged. That is why we have 35 percent of the market today, while Compaq and Sun have only about 10 percent each." Rothnie says that his customers are looking for a way to

> take dispersed data and get it under control. You could look for a way to centralize storage management, then scatter Symmetrix arrays around the enterprise. But our customers don't want to do this. Our direct sales focus on companies with two to three hundred gigabytes of data and up. They want to be able to manage all of their Symmetrix platforms as one storage pool. Fibre Channel doesn't make storage look like a storage pool, the storage system must be intelligent enough to manage the data. Our Symmetrix Remote Data Facility (SRDF) was recently introduced as a mechanism to allow data to move online and robustly. It will become a key piece of our Enterprise Storage Network infrastructure moving forward.

Rothnie concludes by projecting the future of storage. "Larger com-panies will centralize storage onto fewer, more intelligent, networked platforms. Smaller companies will probably outsource that data storage via the Internet."

OTHER VISIONS

Since early 1999, additional announcements have been made by IBM, Dell Computer Corporation, StorageTek, and 3COM that adopt the same general "visionary" rhetoric popularized by Sun, Compaq, and EMC, combined with strong product tie-ins. (In fact, StorageTek and 3COM Corporation announced an alliance in March 1999, then retracted the announcement the following week owing to a "change of direction at 3COM Corporation.") As of this writing, it would appear that no individual alliance is garnering enough industry-wide support to achieve the level of cooperation that all vendors claim to be seeking. As a consequence, SAN interoperability standards will likely be held hostage to vendor competition until at least one vendor begins delivering a SAN solution to market and gains sufficient share to become a *de facto* industry standard.

During the one-week alliance between 3COM and StorageTek, Joan Wrabetz, Vice President and General Manager for StorageTek's SAN Operations, summarized the varying viewpoints that must be resolved to realize the storage management nirvana.[10] According to Wrabetz, "Some of the architectures that have been discussed thus far adopt a server-centric viewpoint. The SAN is just plumbing, management intelligence resides on a server."

Says Wrabetz, the architectures seem to be designed "not to enable multiple vendor storage solutions, but to protect the interests of server manufacturers such as Sun, Dell, and Compaq."

She believes that server vendors are concerned about the possible loss of "captive storage revenues" if open SANs come to fruition and are doing their best "to protect their primacy," which they have already lost.

Says Wrabetz, "I believe that they will be forced to evolve over time. Switch value-add features will replace some server functions."

A second viewpoint in the industry, according to Wrabetz, is "storage-centric." She refers to vendors of storage disk arrays who seek to embed all control of storage on the disk controller, a solution she regards as "not viable in the long term."

"For there to be an open SAN based on this architecture, there would have to be a homogeneous disk controller for all products," she observes, noting that this is an unlikely development from companies like EMC Corporation. She cites companies with large and diverse storage requirements and insists that scalability is sacrificed when companies deploy large-scale proprietary arrays instead of open SANs.

Wrabetz insists that what is needed is an information-centric viewpoint, "one that is not server or storage centric, but that recognizes that there are roles for intelligence in many places in the SAN—on the disk array controller, the server, and the switch—all accessible by open interfaces. That is what is missing today."

THE QUEST CONTINUES

The quest for the Holy Grail of data storage management continues. Like the quests of the Middle Ages, this one is also characterized by crusaders with mixed objectives ranging from visionary zeal to self-interest. In the meantime, it is up to IT managers and staff to do what they can to create their own storage infrastructures and to derive the benefits that effective storage management can deliver.

For now, the pace of advancement of storage technology is far ahead of the "pain curve" for IT organizations. As the market has demanded more storage, faster storage, and greater storage capacity, vendors have been ready with products to meet the need. While this may be regarded as a good thing, it has also helped to cultivate a *laissez-faire* attitude among many IT professionals, who harbor an unstated belief that the situation will continue indefinitely.

This view, however, is a fallacy. As the unplanned deployment of storage products continues, IT organizations are creating an environment that is prone to both dramatic increases in total cost of ownership and disastrous interruptions of mission-critical business applications.

Inevitably, these companies will be forced to embrace rational storage resource planning. It is better that proactive steps be taken today, than expensive reactive ones tomorrow.

The first step is education.

ENDNOTES

1. Interview with Jeff Allen, VP Marketing, Network Storage, Sun Microsystems, Newark, CA, 1999.
2. "Sun Redefines Storage For The Network Age With The Intelligent Storage Network™: Highly Flexible And Infinitely Scalable New Architecture Enables Multiplatform Devices to Work Together," Palo Alto, CA, January 28, 1998.
3. Sun Microsystems "Project StoreX" Home Page, *http://www.sun.com/storage/storex*, Sun Microsystems, Palo Alto, CA, 1999.
4. "Sun Microsystems Delivers the Industry's First Open Management Platform for the Storage Developer Community: Industry Leaders Oracle, VERITAS Software, Seagate Technology, Quantum and StorageTek Join Sun in Support of Building Open Applications That Reduce the Cost and Complexity of Storage Management," Sun Microsystems Press Release, Sun Microsystems, Palo Alto, CA, December 14, 1998.

5. Interview with Bob Passmore, Director of Strategic Marketing for Compaq Computer Corporation's Storage Products Division, Houston, TX, 1999.

6. "EMC Maps Out Strategy for Heterogeneous Enterprise Storage Networks: Storage Leader Moves Customers Closer to the Vision of a 'Universal Data Tone'," EMC Corporation, Hopkinton, MA, November 3, 1999.

7. "Enterprise Storage Networks: Not All Storage Networks Are Created Equal," EMC Backgrounder, EMC Corporation, Hopkinton, MA, 1999.

8. "EMC Delivers World's First Integrated Enterprise Storage Network Solutions: Building the Infrastructure for a Connected World Through New High-Availability Fibre Channel Switch, Software, Symmetrix Systems and Professional Services," EMC Press Release, EMC Corporation, Hopkinton, MA, March 1, 1999.

9. Interview with Jim Rothnie, Senior Vice President and Chief Marketing Technical Officer, EMC Corporation, Hopkinton, MA, 1999

10. Interview With Joan Wrabetz, Vice President and General Manager for SAN Operations, Storage Technology Corporation, Louisville, CO, 1999.

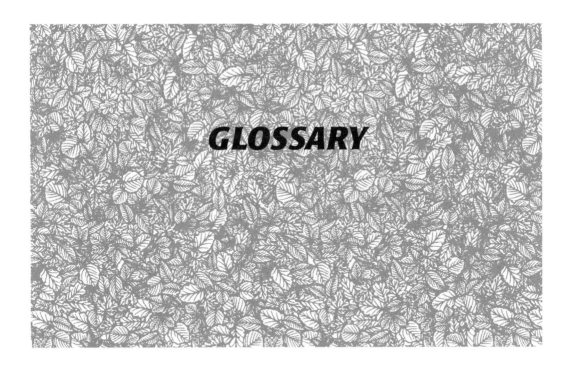

GLOSSARY

ABLATIVE WORM: An optical disk storage technology that uses a laser to permanently alter optical media when writing data. To write, the laser focuses on the disk's metal recording layer with enough heat to create a hole, or pit, in the recording surface.

ACCESS TIME: Of a hard disk, the combined time for seek, head switch, and rotational latency in a read/write operation. Of an optical disk, the time it takes to access a data track and begin transferring data. In an optical jukebox, it's the time it takes to locate a specific disk, insert it in an optical drive, and begin transferring data to the host system. If the disk is already in the drive, then access time is determined by seek time. Otherwise, it's determined by disk swap time, spin-up time, and seek time.

ACCESS: Refers to the process of obtaining data from, or placing data into a disk storage device, register, or RAM (i.e., accessing a memory location).

ACTUATOR ARM: A mechanical device used to carry all read/write heads in a multi-platter disk drive.

ACTUATOR: An electro-mechanical device that moves an object, such as the robotic arm that moves an optical disk within the jukebox, or the device that controls the read/write head on a disk drive.

ADAPTIVE CACHING: Technology that allows the drive to tune the cache (number of segments and segment size) to best suit the system's needs.

ADDRESS MARK: Two byte address at the beginning of both the ID field and the data field of the track format. The first byte is the "A1" data pattern, the second byte is used to specify either an ID field or a data field.

ADDRESS: (physical) A specific location in memory where a unit record, or sector, of data is stored. To return to the same area on the disk, each area is given a unique address consisting of three components: cylinder, sector, and head. *CYLINDER ADDRESSING* is accomplished by assigning numbers to the disk's surface concentric circles (cylinders). The cylinder number specifies the radial address component of the data area. *SECTOR ADDRESSING* is accomplished by numbering the data records (sectors) from an index that defines the reference angular position of the disks. Index records are then counted by reading their *ADDRESS MARKS.* Finally, *HEAD ADDRESSING* is accomplished by vertically numbering the disk surfaces, usually starting with the bottom-most disk data surface. For example, the controller might send the binary equivalent of the decimal number 610150 to instruct the drive to access data at cylinder 610, sector 15, and head 0.

ADJUSTABLE INTERLEAVE: Interleaving permits access to more than one memory module, e.g., if one memory module contains odd-numbered address and another even-numbered address, they can both be accessed simultaneously for storage. If the interleave is adjustable, the user may select which ranges or areas are to be accessed each time.

ADVANCED INTELLIGENT TAPE (AIT): A helical scan technology developed by Sony for tape backup/archive of networks and servers, specifically addressing midrange to high-end backup requirements.

ALLOCATION UNIT: A group of sectors on the disk reserved for specified information. On hard drives for small computer systems, the allocation unit is usually in the form of a block, cluster, or sector. (*See also BLOCK, CLUSTER,* and *SECTOR.*)

ALLOCATION: The process of assigning particular areas of the disk to specific data or instructions. (*See also ALLOCATION UNIT.*)

AMERICAN NATIONAL STANDARDS INSTITUTE (ANSI): A standard-setting, independent organization that develops and publishes manufacturing and design standards for the United States.

AMERICAN STANDARD FOR CODED INFORMATION INTERCHANGE: ASCII

ANSI: *See AMERICAN NATIONAL STANDARDS INSTITUTE.*

APPLICATION PROGRAM: A sequence of programmed instructions that tell the computer how to perform an end use task (i.e., accounting, word processing, or other work for the computer system user). To use a program, it must first be loaded into *MAIN MEMORY* from some *AUXILIARY MEMORY* such as a floppy diskette or hard disk.

ARCHIVAL MANAGEMENT: A storage management solution for cataloging files and moving them to long-term storage, where they can be stored and accessed inexpensively.

ARCHIVE: A copy of reference data or document images that are stored on optical disks, floppies, tape, paper, or microfiche. Typically refers to long-term storage of data for later possible access.

AREAL DENSITY: Bit density (bits per inch, or BPI) multiplied by track density (tracks per inch, or TPI), or bits per square inch of the disk surface. Bit density is measured around a track (circumferential on the disk), and track density is radially measured.

ARRAY: A group of disk drives which have been combined into a common array and appear as a single LSU (Logical Storage Unit). (*See also DISK ARRAY.*)

ASCII: *See AMERICAN STANDARD FOR CODED INFORMATION INTERCHANGE.*

ASPI (ADVANCED SCSI PROGRAMMING INTERFACE): A protocol developed by Adaptec and supported by host adapter OEM's is used by some SCSI application programs to communicate with SCSI adapters.

ASYNCHRONOUS DATA: Data sent usually in parallel mode without a clock pulse. Time intervals between transmitted bits may be of unequal lengths.

ASYNCHRONOUS TRANSFER MODE (ATM): A network architecture that divides messages into fixed-size units (cells) and establishes a switched connection between the originating and receiving stations; enables transmission of various types of data (video, audio, etc.) over the same line without one data type dominating the transmission.

ATA (AT Attachment): This term defines the signal and logical protocol described in X3.221 for IDE (Integrated Drive Electronics) peripherals. (*See also INTERFACE.*)

ATAPI: *See AT ATTACHMENT PACKET INTERFACE.*

AT ATTACHMENT PACKET INTERFACE (ATAPI): A command protocol used for accessing ATA (IDE) peripheral devices. Widely used on CD-ROM and Tape Backup units attached to ATA bus.

AT BUS: An acronym representing Advanced Technology bus. The standard PC compatable peripheral bus to which video cards, I/O cards, internal modem cards and sound cards are added. Also called the ISA bus, it runs at a maximum of 8.33 MHz and has a 16-bit wide data path.

AUTHORING SOFTWARE: A software package that allows a user to create interactive media and multimedia presentations.

AUTOLOADER: A single-drive, tape-based backup device that houses a number of tape cartridges. An autoloader is designed to support routine, automatic backup procedures, using a mechanical arm to sequentially load a new tape for daily backup.

AUTOMATIC BACK UP OF FILES: A technique for providing security against file loss through accidental overwrite. One weakness of this method is that files take up twice the room on a disk.

AUXILIARY MEMORY: Memory other than main memory; generally a mass storage subsystem, it can include disk drives, backup tape drives, controllers, and buffer memory. Typically, *AUXILIARY MEMORY* is non-volatile.

AUXILIARY STORAGE DEVICE: Devices, generally magnetic tape and magnetic disk, on which data can be stored for use by computer programs. Also known as secondary storage.

AVERAGE ACCESS TIME: The average track access time, calculated from the end of the *CONTROLLER* commands to access a drive, to drive "seek complete" time averaged over all possible track locations at the start of *ACCESS*, and over all possible data track *ADDRESSES*.

AVERAGE LATENCY: The average time required for any byte of data stored on a disk to rotate under the disk drive's read/write head. Equal to one half the time required for a single rotation of the platter.

AVERAGE SEEK TIME: The average time it takes for the read/write head to move to a specific location. Calculated by dividing the time it takes to complete a large number of random seeks by the number of seeks performed.

BACKUP DEVICE: Disk or tape drive used with a fixed Winchester disk drive to make copies of files or other data for off line storage, distribution or protection against accidental data deletion from the Winchester drive, or against drive failure.

BACKUP FILE: File copies made on another removable media device (disk, tape, or sometimes a remote hard disk system) and kept to ensure recovery of data lost due to equipment failure, human errors, updates, and disasters.

BACKUP: (1) A duplicate copy of a program, disk, or data files. (2) A procedure for duplicating key data files, often automatically, and storing them in a safe place for the purpose of file recovery.

BACKWARD COMPATIBILITY: A design standard that assures that new software, hardware, devices, and media will be compatible with earlier versions.

BAD BLOCK: A block (usually the size of a sector) that cannot reliably hold data due to a physical flaw or damaged format markings.

BAD TRACK TABLE: A list affixed to the casing of a hard disk drive that states which tracks are flawed and cannot hold data. This list of bad tracks is entered into the low-level formatting program when the drive is formatted at the factory.

BANDWIDTH: The amount of data that can be transmitted via a given communications channel (e.g., between a hard drive and the host PC) in a given unit of time.

BASE CASTING: The rigid structure which holds the mechanical sub-assemblies of a hard disk drive. Together with the top cover, creates an airtight, extremely clean enclosure.

BI-DIRECTIONAL BUS: A bus that may carry information in either direction but not in both simultaneously.

BINARY: A number system like the decimal numbers, but using 2 as its base and having only the two digits 0 (zero) and 1 (one). It is used in computers because digital logic can only determine one of two states —"OFF" and "ON." Digital data is equivalent to a binary number.

BIOS (BASIC INPUT OUTPUT SYSTEM): A program permanently stored in the memory of the computer and is available without an operating system disk. For example it performs the internal self test of the computer and searches for the operating system on the disk drive.

BIT CELL LENGTH: Physical dimension of the bit cell in direction of recording along the disk circumference of a track.

BIT CELL TIME: The time required to pass one bit of information between the controller and the drive. Cell time is the inverse of the drive's data rate.

BIT DENSITY: Expressed as "BPI" (for bits per inch), bit density defines how many bits can be written onto one inch of a track on a disk surface. It is usually specified for "worst case," which is the inner track. Data is the densest in the inner tracks where track circumferences are the smallest.

BIT JITTER: The time difference between the leading edge of read and the center of the data window.

BIT SHIFT: A data recording effect, which results when adjacent 1's written on magnetic disks repel each other. The "worst case" is at the inner cylinder where bits are closest together. *BIT SHIFT* is also called pulse crowding.

BIT: An abbreviation for a binary digit which can be either 0 or 1. A bit is the basic data unit of all digital computers. It is usually part of a data byte or word but bits may be used singly to control or read logic ON/OFF functions. A bit is a single digit in a binary number. Bits are the basic unit of information capacity or a computer storage device. Eight bits equal one byte.

BIT: The smallest unit of data. Consists of a single binary digit that can take the value of 0 or 1.

BLOCK ERROR RATE: The average number of errors that occur (or can occur) while writing or transmitting a block of data.

BLOCK: A group of BYTES handled, stored, and accessed as a logical data unit, such as an individual file record. Typically, one block of data is stored as one physical sector of data on a disk drive. In UNIX workstation environments, the smallest contiguous area that can be allocated for the storage of data. UNIX blocks are generally 8 KB (16 sectors) in size. In DOS environments, the block is referred to as a cluster. (Note: This usage of the term block at the operating system level is different from its meaning in relation to the physical configuration of the hard drive.) (*See also CLUSTER* and *SECTOR*.)

BOOT: Short for bootstrap. Transfer of a disk operating system program from storage on diskette or hard disk drive to computer's working memory.

BPI (Bits per inch): A measure of how densely information is packed on a storage medium. (*See also FCI*.)

BPSI (Bits per square inch): A measure of areal density calculated by multiplying bits per inch (BPI) by tracks per inch (TPI).

BUFFER: A temporary data storage area that compensates for a difference in data transfer rates and/or data processing rates between sender and receiver.

BURST MODE: A temporary, high-speed data transfer mode that can transfer data at significantly higher rates than would normally be achieved with non-burst technology; the maximum throughput a device is capable of transferring data.

BUS: A length of parallel conductors that forms a major interconnection route between the computer system CPU and its peripheral subsystems. Depending on its design, a bus may carry data to and from peripheral's addresses, power, and other related signals.

BUS MASTERING: A method of data transfer which allows data to be moved between a peripheral controller and system memory without interaction with the host CPU or a third party DMA controller. This technique allows the peripheral controller to take control of the system bus, and in the case of EISA, to move data at up to 33MB/s.

BYTE: A sequence of adjacent BINARY digits or BITS considered as a unit, 8 bits in length. One byte is sufficient to define all the alphanumeric characters. There are 8 BITS in 1 BYTE. The storage capacity of a disk drive is commonly measured in MEGABYTES, which is the total number of bits storable, divided by eight million.

CACHE: A temporary storage location, usually Random Access Memory (RAM), for data. In input/output operations, the organization of the cache is important because it enables time-saving functions such as read-ahead.

CACHE HIT: This occurs when the data requested is already in the cache. A cache hit saves the time of getting the data from the rotating disk; the seek, latency, and read times.

CACHE MEMORY: A portion of RAM allocated for storing frequently accessed information from a storage device.

CAM: *See COMMON ACCESS METHOD.*

CAPACITY: Amount of memory (measured in megabytes) which can be stored in a disk drive. Usually given as formatted capacity. (*See FORMAT OPERATION* and *FORMATTED CAPACITY.*)

CARRIAGE ASSEMBLY: Assembly in a hard disk drive which holds read/write heads and roller bearings. It is used to position the heads radially by the actuator, in order to access a track of data.

CD-ROM (Compact Disk Read Only Memory): A read only storage device which retrieves up to 660 Mbytes of information from a removable laser disk similar to an audio compact disk.

CENTRAL PROCESSOR UNIT (CPU): The heart of the computer system that executes programmed instructions. It includes the arithmetic logic unit (ALU) for performing all math and logic operations, a control section for interpreting and executing instructions, fast main memory for temporary (VOLATILE) storage of an application program and its data.

CHANNEL: In regard to disk drives, a channel is an electrical path for the transfer of data and control information between a disk and a disk controller. The Primary and Secondary Hard Drive Port Addresses are an example of two channels.

CHARACTER: An information symbol used to denote a number, letter, symbol, or punctuation mark stored by a computer. In a computer a character can be represented in one (1) byte or eight (8) bits of data. There are 256 different one-byte binary numbers, sufficient for 26 lower case alphas, 26 upper case alphas, 10 decimal digits, control codes, and error checks.

CHIP: An integrated circuit fabricated on a chip of silicon or other semi-conductor material, e.g., a CHIP is an integrated circuit, a microprocessor, memory device, or a digital logic device.

CIFS: *See COMMON INTERNET FILE SYSTEM.*

CLIENT: Typically, a desktop computer hooked up to a network, and designed to work with a more powerful server that runs applications and stores data.

CLIENT/SERVER: An environment that allows interactions between "clients" (typically desktop computers) and "servers" (computers that store data and run software programs). In client-server environments, data may be stored on a remote server rather than a computer's hard disk; applications may be stored on a server and delivered to individual desktop computers as needed. The server acts as a gateway to the network, running administrative software controls and providing access to the network and its resources.

CLOCK RATE: The rate at which bits or words are transferred between internal elements of a computer or to another computer.

CLOSED LOOP: A control system consisting of one or more feedback control loops in which functions of the controlled signals are combined with functions of the command to maintain prescribed relationships between the commands and the controlled signals. This control technique allows the head actuator system to detect and correct off-track errors. The actual head position is monitored and compared to the ideal track position, by reference information either recorded on a dedicated servo surface, or embedded in the inter-sector gaps. A position error is used to produce a correction signal (FEEDBACK) to the actuator to correct the error. (*See TRACK FOLLOWING SERVO.*)

CLUSTER SIZE: Purely an operating system function or term describing the number of sectors that the operating system allocates each time disk space is needed. In DOS environments, the smallest contiguous area that can be allocated for the storage of data. DOS clusters are usually 2 KB (4 sectors) in size.

CLUSTERED SERVERS: The concept of combining multiple host computers together through a private communication line, such as Ethernet backbone, to form a ring of host computers; this ring of host computers act as a single entity, capable of performing multiple complex instructions by distributing the workload across all members of the ring.

CLUSTERED STORAGE: The concept of combining multiple storage servers or intelligent storage devices together to form a redundant ring of storage devices; clustered storage systems typically perform multiple read and write requests through parallel access lines to the requesting computer.

CODE: A set of unambiguous rules specifying the way which digital data is represented physically, as magnetized bits, on a disk drive. One of the objectives of coding is to add timing data for use in data reading. (*See DATA SEPARATOR, MFM,* and *RLL.*)

COERCIVITY: A measurement in units of orsteads of the amount of magnetic energy to switch or "coerce" the flux change (di-pole) in the magnetic recording media.

COMMAND: (1) An instruction sent by the central processor unit (CPU) to a controller for execution. (2) English-like commands entered by users to select computer programs or functions. (3) A CPU command, which is a single instruction such as "add two binary numbers" or "output a byte to the display screen."

COMMAND DESCRIPTOR BLOCK (CDB): SCSI commands are issued from an initiator by transferring a Command Descriptor Block to the target device. For some commands, a parameter list sent during a Data Out phase accompanies the request. A CDB contains an opcode, logical unit number, set of command parameters, and control byte.

COMMAND OVERHEAD: *See OVERHEAD.*

COMMON ACCESS METHOD (CAM): Defines a set of software and hardware interfaces which attempt to standardize an operating system's access to peripheral devices.

COMMON INTERNET FILE SYSTEM (CIFS): A proposed standard protocol that lets programs make requests for files and services on remote computers on the Internet or across any TCP/IP network. CIFS uses the client/server programming model. A client program makes a request of a server program (usually in another computer) for access to a file or to pass a message to a program that runs in the server computer. The server takes the requested action and returns a response. CIFS is a public or open variation of the Server Message Block (SMB) protocol developed and used by Microsoft. The SMB protocol is widely used in today's local area networks for server file access and printing.

COMPACT DISK-READ ONLY MEMORY (CD-ROM): An optical disk recording format in which the optical disk carries pre-recorded data, music, or software. Users cannot add or delete data to a CD-ROM.

COMPACT DISK-RECORDABLE (CD-R). An optical disk recording format that allows data to be written to optical disks. The disks can be recorded just once, but played virtually without limit.

COMPACT DISK-REWRITABLE (CD-RW): An optical disk recording format that allows disks to be recorded and re-recorded, much like floppy disks or audio tapes. The disks can be rewritten up to 10,000 times and played virtually without limit.

COMPUTER OUTPUT TO LASER DISK (COLD): An optical storage technology for transferring computer-based information to an optical disk for near-online storage. Typically used as an alternative to paper or microfiche-based storage of computer-generated reports.

CONSOLE (also called CRT or Terminal): A device from which a computer can be operated; often includes a monitor and keyboard.

CONSTANT ANGULAR VELOCITY (CAV): The technique whereby data recorded with a variable linear density can be read on a disk with a constant velocity. Despite the varying density of data on the disk, the disk's rotational speed remains constant during reads.

CONSTANT LINEAR VELOCITY (CLV): A storage technique that adjusts the speed of a spinning disk so that the large outer tracks (which normally spin faster) are slowed down during writes, and can thus hold more data than the smaller inner tracks. Typically used in CD-ROM, CLV results in a constant data delivery rate.

CONTINUOUS COMPOSITE WORM (CCW): An optical disk storage technology that uses magneto-optical (MO) media to support both rewritable and write-once operations in a single drive. CCW is governed by industry standards that specify multi-layer data protection measures, including procedures for overwrite protection and blank-checking.

CONTROLLER: A controller is a printed circuit board required to interpret data access commands from host computer (via a BUS), and send track seeking, read/write, and other control signals to a disk drive. The computer is free to perform other tasks until the controller signals DATA READY for transfer via the CPU BUS.

CORE: Originally a computer's main memory was made of ferrite rings (CORES) that could be magnetized to contain one bit of data each. *CORE MEMORY* is synonymous with *MAIN MEMORY*. Main memory today is fabricated from *CHIPS*.

COST OF OWNERSHIP: The purchase price of equipment plus the cost of operating this equipment over its projected life span.

CPU: *See CENTRAL PROCESSOR UNIT.*

CRASH: A malfunction in the computer hardware or software, usually causing loss of data. *(See HEAD CRASH.)*

CRC: *See CYCLIC-REDUNDANCY-CHECK.*

CYCLIC-REDUNDANCY-CHECK (CRC): Used to verify data block integrity. In a typical scheme, 2 CRC bytes are added to each user data block. The 2 bytes are computed from the user data, by digital logical chips. The mathematical model is polynomials with binary coefficients. When reading back data, the CRC bytes are read and compared to new CRC bytes computed from the read back block to detect a read error. The read back error check process is mathematically equivalent to dividing the read block, including its CRC, by a binomial polynomial. If the division remainder is zero, the data is error free.

CYLINDER: The cylindrical surface formed by identical track numbers on vertically stacked disks. At any location of the head positioning arm, all tracks under all heads are the cylinder. Cylinder number is one of the three address components required to find a specific *ADDRESS*, the other two being head number and sector number.

DAISY CHAIN: A way of connecting multiple drives to one controller. The controller drive select signal is routed serially through the drives, and is intercepted by the drive whose number matches.

DAT: *See DIGITAL AUDIO TAPE.*

DATA: Information processed by a computer, stored in memory, or fed into a computer.

DATA ACCESS TIME: *See ACCESS TIME.*

DATA ACCESS: When the controller has specified all three components of the sector address to the drive, the ID field of the sector brought under the head by the drive is read and compared with the address of the target sector. A match enables access to the data field of the sector.

DATA ADDRESS: To return to the same area on the disk, each area is given a unique address consisting of the three components: cylinder, head, and sector. *HORIZONTAL:* accomplished by assigning numbers to the concentric circles (cylinders) mapped out by the heads as the positioning arm is stepped radially across the surface, starting with 0 for the outermost circle. By specifying the cylinder number the controller specifies a horizontal or radial address component of the data area. *ROTATIONAL:* once a head and cylinder have been addressed, the desired sector around the selected track of the selected surface is found by counting address marks from the index pulse of the track. Remember that each track starts with an index pulse and each sector starts with an address mark. *VERTICAL:* assume a disk pack with six surfaces, each with its own read/write head, vertical addressing is accomplished by assigning the numbers 00 through XX to the heads, in consecutive order. By specifying the head number, the controller specifies the vertical address component of the data area.

DATA BASE MANAGEMENT SYSTEM (DBMS): Application program used to manage, access, and update files in a data base.

DATA COMPRESSION: An automatic utility that reduces the size of a data file by removing redundant bits of information. An algorithm built into the hardware, firmware, or software handles compression and de-compression.

DATA ENCODING: To use a code such as GCR, MFM, RLL, NZR, etc. to represent characters for memory storage.

DATA FIELD: The portion of a sector used to store the user's DIGITAL data. Other fields in each sector include ID, SYNC, and CRC, which are used to locate the correct data field.

DATA MIGRATION: *See HIERARCHICAL STORAGE MANAGEMENT (HSM).*

DATA SEPARATOR: The circuit that extracts data from timing information on drives that store a combined data and clock signal.

DATA TRACK: Any of the circular tracks magnetized by the recording head during data storage.

DATA TRANSFER: The movement of data from one point to another within a computer system, for example, from an optical disk to a computer's hard disk.

DATA TRANSFER RATE (DTR): Speed at which bits are sent: In a disk storage system, the communication is between CPU and controller, plus controller and the disk drive. Typical units are bits per second (BPS), or bytes per second. I/O transfer rate is the data rate between the drive and the CPU. Internal transfer rate is the rate data is written to/from the disk. (*See TRANSFER RATE.*)

DATA WAREHOUSE: A large centralized database designed to hold and manage a company's information over a long period of time. Data warehouses are often used to mine key data for reference, for example, to detect trends, spot new market opportunities, and monitor business results.

DECREASE THE FLYING HEIGHT: A method for increasing areal density. Since the head core is closer to the media surface, the lines of flux magnetize a smaller area. Thus, more bits can be recorded in a given distance, and higher BPI (bits per inch) is achievable.

DEDICATED SERVO: An older technology in which timing or positioning signals are located on a dedicated platter containing no user data. These signals provide the information the actuator needs to fine-tune the position of the read/write heads. (*See also EMBEDDED SERVO.*)

DEFAULT: A particular value of a variable which is used by a computer unless specifically changed, usually via an entry made through a software program.

DENSITY: Generally, bit recording density. *SEE AREAL, BIT,* and *STORAGE DENSITY.*

DIGITAL: Any system that processes digital binary signals having only the values of a 1 or 0. An example of a non-digital signal is an analog signal which continuously varies, e.g., TV or audio.

DIGITAL AUDIO TAPE (DAT): A storage technology that uses 4mm tape to record data. DAT is similar to an audio tape, but instead of recording data linearly along the length of the tape, data is recorded at an angle. This recording format, called DDS, is the industry standard for all DAT devices.

DIGITAL DATA STORAGE (DDS): A recording format used by all major DAT drive and media manufacturers, and the only recognized industry standard for DAT systems. A number frequently follows the DDS designation to indicate the generation of the standard: for example, DDS-3 represents a third-generation product.

DIGITAL LINEAR TAPE (DLT): A serpentine technology first introduced by Digital Equipment Corporation and later developed by Quantum for tape backup/archive of networks and servers; DLT technology addresses midrange to high-end tape backup requirements.

DIGITAL VIDEO DISK (DVD): A disk that closely resembles a standard CD in size, color, and physical format, but holds about seven times as much data. A typical CD holds about 650 MB of data, whereas today's DVDs hold 4.7 GB, with a target capacity of about 17 GB in the future. A two-hour feature-length movie can fit on a DVD, making it an attractive medium for the entertainment industry as well as PC makers. The current state of DVD technology, allowing play-back but not recording on DVDs. Multiple DVD-RAM and DVD-Rewritable standards exist to support both play-back and recording on DVDs. At this time, no standards have been adopted industry-wide for recordable/rewritable DVD.

DIRECT ACCESS: Generally refers to an *AUXILIARY MEMORY* device, having all data on-line. A tape drive without a tape mounted is not direct access, but a *WINCHESTER DRIVE* is direct access device.

DIRECTORY: A special disk storage area (usually cylinder zero) that is read by a computer operating system to determine the *ADDRESSES* of the data records that form a *DISK FILE.*

DIRECT MEMORY ACCESS (DMA): A means of data transfer between peripheral and host memory without processor intervention. DMA improves speed and efficiency by allowing the system to continue processing even while it is retrieving new data from the drive.

DIRTY CACHE: A cache page in which data has been written or modified but which has not yet been copied to the storage device. Once the data has been copied to disk, the page is said to be clean.

DISK ARRAY (or ARRAY): A linked group of small, independent hard disk drives used to replace larger, single disk drive systems. The most common disk arrays implement *RAID* (redundant array of independent disks) technology. (*See also RAID.*)

DISK CONTROLLER: The chip or circuit that controls the transfer of data between the disk and buffer. (*See also DISK DRIVE CONTROLLER* and *INTERFACE CONTROLLER.*)

DISK DRIVE CONTROLLER: The hard disk drive controller electronics, which include the disk controller and the interface controller. (*See also DISK CONTROLLER* and *INTERFACE CONTROLLER.*)

DISK FILE: A file of user data, e.g. the company employee list, with all NAMEs and information. The data in the file is stored in a set of disk *SECTORS* (records).

DISK OPERATING SYSTEM (DOS): A computer program which continuously runs and mediates between the computer user and the *APPLICATION PROGRAM*, and allows access to disk data by *DISK FILE NAMEs.*

DISK OVERHEAD: *See OVERHEAD.*

DISK PACK: A number of metal disks packaged in a canister for removal from the disk drive. *WINCHESTER DRIVES* do not have disk packs.

DISK STORAGE: Auxiliary memory system containing disk drives.

DISK SWAP: 1. The act of swapping one optical disk for another. To complete a swap, a jukebox autochanger mechanism must remove a disk from the drive, put it away, retrieve a new disk, and insert it in the drive. The drive then spins-up the new disk and the operation is complete. 2. Changing out a defective or malfunctioning hard disk drive.

DISK PLATTER: For rigid disks, a flat, circular aluminum disk substrate, coated on both sides with a magnetic substance (iron oxide or thin film metal media) for non-VOLATILE data storage. The substrate may consist of metal, plastic, or even glass. Surfaces of disks are usually lubricated to minimize wear during drive start-up or power down.

DISKETTE: A floppy disk. A plastic (mylar) substrate, coated with magnetic iron oxide, enclosed in a protective jacket.

DISTRIBUTED COMPUTING ENVIRONMENT (DCE): A set of middleware standards that defines the method of communication between clients and servers in a cross-platform computing environment; enables a client program to initiate a request that can be processed by a program written in a different computer language and housed on a different computer platform.

DISTRIBUTED NETWORK: A network that divides data processing, storage, and other functions into separate units rather than having them all handled by a single computer.

DMA: *See DIRECT MEMORY ACCESS.*

DOCUMENT IMAGE MANAGEMENT (DIM): A storage management solution for converting paper documents, photos, and receipts into an electronic format that can be accessed from a computer.

DOS: *See DISK OPERATING SYSTEM.*

DRIVE GEOMETRY: The functional dimensions of a drive, including the number of heads, cylinders, and sectors per track.

DRIVE: A computer memory device with moving storage MEDIA (disk or tape).

DRIVER: A software component or set of file commands that allow an application to communicate with another application, driver, or hardware device. A driver receives I/O requests from higher levels within the operating system and converts those requests to the protocol required by a specific hardware device.

DROP-IN/DROP-OUT: Types of disk media defects usually caused by a pin-hole in the disk coating. If the coating is interrupted, the magnetic flux between medium and head is zero. A large interruption will induce two extraneous pulses, one at the beginning and one at the end of the pin-hole (2 DROP-INs). A small coating interruption will result in no playback from a recorded bit (a *DROP-OUT*).

DRUM: An early form of rotating magnetic storage, utilizing a rotating cylindrical drum and a multiplicity of heads (one per track). Disks stack more compactly than drums.

DYE POLYMER TECHNOLOGY: An optical disk storage technology that uses a translucent plastic disk and thermal-sensitive dye recording layer to store data. Heat generated by the drive's laser causes the dye to turn translucent where the laser is focused, causing a change in reflectivity that is detected during reads. Used for CD-R.

ECC: *See ERROR CORRECTION CODE.*

EFFECTIVE ACCESS TIME: The actual time it takes to access data. In an optical jukebox, it involves variables such as disk swap time, disk spin-up time, seek time, and transfer rates of the host computer and software application.

EISA: *See EXTENDED INDUSTRY STANDARD ARCHITECTURE.*

ELECTROMAGNETIC INTERFERENCE (EMI): Interference resulting from the presence of electromagnetic fields from electrical and/or electronic devices.

ELECTRO-STATIC DISCHARGE (ESD): A cause of integrated circuit (CHIP) failure. Since the circuitry of CHIPs are microscopic in size, they can be damaged or destroyed by small static discharges. People handling electronic equipment should always ground themselves before touching the equipment. Electronic equipment should always be handled by the chassis or frame. Components, printed circuit board edge connectors should never be touched.

ELEVATOR SORTING: A method of sorting records or cache pages by physical location on disk so that the information may be written to disk with less seek and rotational latency.

EMBEDDED SERVO SYSTEM: Servo data is embedded or superimposed along with data on every cylinder. Timing and positioning signals are interspersed in data tracks. These signals provide the information the actuator needs to fine-tune the position of the read/write heads. (*See also DEDICATED SERVO.*)

ENCODING: The conversion of data into a pattern of On/Off or 1/0 signals prior to writing them to the disk surface. (*See also MFM* and *RLL.*)

ENCRYPTION: A security method in which electronic data is scrambled and decoded using a software algorithm.

ENHANCED IDE (EIDE): The market identity given to a collection of four features that are designed to help meet the future needs of the market. Enhanced IDE features include: High-capacity addressing of ATA hard drives over 528 Mbytes, fast data transfer rates for ATA hard drives (support for PIO mode 3 up to 13.3 Mbytes per sec), Dual ATA host adapters supporting up to 4 hard disk drives per computer system, non-hard disk ATA peripherals (such as CD-ROM).

ENHANCED SMALL DEVICE INTERFACE (EDSI): A set of specifications for the drives. (*See also SCSI.*)

ENTERPRISE NETWORK: A system of network connections that links all of a company's LANs, allowing enterprises to communicate across many geographic locations and sites.

ENTERPRISE STORAGE NETWORK (ESN): According to EMC Corporation, an integrated suite of products and services designed to maximize heterogeneous connectivity and management of enterprise storage devices and servers. ESN, generically, constitutes a dedicated, high-speed network connected to the enterprise's storage systems, enabling files and data to be transferred between storage devices and client mainframes and servers.

EPROM: *See ERASABLE PROGRAMMABLE READ ONLY MEMORY.*

ERASE: To remove previously recorded data from magnetic storage media.

ERASABLE PROGRAMMABLE READ ONLY MEMORY (EPROM): An integrated circuit memory chip that can store programs and data in a non-volatile state. Ultraviolet light is used to erase EPROM, which can then be reprogrammed with new data.

ERROR: *See HARD ERROR and SOFT ERROR.*

ERROR CORRECTION CODE (ECC): An embedded code that allows detection of a mismatch between transmitted and received data in a communications system, or between stored and retrieved data in a storage system. The ECC can correct errors, but within limits.

ERROR DETECTION: A software or firmware algorithm that looks for inconsistencies or errors in a data file as it is being stored. More advanced levels of error detection will not only detect problems, but also correct errors or inconsistencies automatically.

ERROR RATE: The ratio of data that is incorrectly recorded relative to the entire amount of data written.

ESDI: *See ENHANCED SMALL DEVICE INTERFACE.*

ETHERNET: A local area network standard for hardware, communication, and cabling.

EUROPEAN COMPUTER MANUFACTURERS ASSOCIATION (ECMA): An international organization founded in 1961 and dedicated to the standardization of information and communication systems.

EXECUTE: To perform a data processing operation described by an instruction or a program in a computer.

EXTENDED INDUSTRY STANDARD ARCHITECTURE (EISA): An enhanced AT bus architecture designed by nine manufacturers of PC compatibles and announced in September 1988. EISA provides backwards compatibility with existing 8- and 16-bit hardware cards. In addition, EISA supports 32-bit data paths, 33 Mbytes/sec data transfers from Bus Mastering peripheral cards, automatic configuration, and a more sophisticated I/O addressing scheme. (*See also AT and ISA.*)

EXTERNAL DRIVE: A hard disk drive mounted in an enclosure separate from the computer system enclosure. An external drive has its own power supply and fan and is connected to the system by a cable.

FABRIC SWITCH: In this category of storage area network (SAN) switches, any port on any switch can provide (subject to bandwidth availability) full speed access to any other port on the network. The network consists of a fabric of linked switches.

FAILOVER: The transfer of operation from a failed component (e.g., controller, disk drive) to a similar, redundant component to ensure uninterrupted data flow and operability.

FAST ATA: Fast ATA is the market identity given to disk drives that support the high-speed data transfers resulting from implementing the industry standard protocols: Programmed input/output (PIO) mode 3, Multiword direct memory access, read/write multiple sectors per interrupt.

FAST SCSI: The original SCSI specification defined synchronous data transmission speeds of up to 5MHz. By assuming transceivers which provide tighter timing margins, the SCSI-2 standard allows synchronous transfers of up to 10MHz. Devices which utilize these faster timings are called Fast SCSI devices.

FAT (File allocation table): A data table stored on the outer edge of the disk and used by the operating system to determine which sectors are allocated to each file and in what order.

FAULT TOLERANCE: The ability of a system to cope with internal hardware problems (e.g., a disk drive failure) and still continue to operate with minimal impact, such as by bringing a backup system online.

FC-AL: *See FIBRE CHANNEL ARBITRATED LOOP* (FC-AL).

FCI: *See FLUX CHANGES PER INCH.*

FEEDBACK: A closed-loop control system, using the head-to-track positioning signal (from the servo head) to modify the HEAD POSITIONER signal (to correctly position the head on the track).

FETCH: A CPU read operation from *MAIN MEMORY* and its related data transfer operations.

FIBRE CHANNEL: A high-speed, serial, storage/networking interface that offers higher performance, greater capacity and cabling distance, increased system configuration flexibility and scalability, and simplified cabling. One can view Fibre Channel simply as a transport vehicle for the supported command set (usually SCSI commands). In fact, Fibre Channel is unaware of the content of the information being transported. It simply packs data in frames, transports them to the appropriate devices, and provides error checking.

FIBRE CHANNEL ARBITRATED LOOP (FC-AL): One of the possible physical topologies of Fibre Channel. In this topology, the Fibre Channel is connected in a loop with devices all connecting to the loop. It can be thought of as a similar structure to a token ring network. Up to 126 nodes can be connected to the loop.

FIBRE CHANNEL FABRIC: One of the physical topologies of Fibre Channel. In this topology, the addressing of ports on a network of Fibre Channel nodes is made independently of the physical location or address of the target port. Switches are responsible for passing Fibre Channel packets to the target port regardless of which Fibre Channel loop or switch where the port physically resides.

FIBRE CHANNEL LOOP COMMUNITY (FCLC): An international non-profit organization whose members include manufacturers of servers, disk drives, RAID storage systems, switches, hubs, adapter cards, test equipment, cables and connectors, and software solutions.

FIBRE CHANNEL POINT-TO-POINT: One of the physical topologies of Fibre Channel. This topology provides a simple, direct connection be-tween just two nodes, approximating traditional SCSI topology.

FIBRE CHANNEL PORTS: Fibre Channel ports come in a number of types depending on the topology of the Fibre Channel network. N_Ports are simple equipment node ports in a point-to-point connection topology. NL_Ports are node ports connected to an Arbitrated loop. F_Ports are point-to-point ports connected to a fabric. Generally this means that the F_Port is a port on a switch. FL_Ports are ports connecting from one loop to a switch and thus to a fabric. E_Ports are expansion ports used to inter-connect switches together. G_Ports are classified by some switch compa-nies as ports that can be either E_Ports or F_Ports depending on usage.

FIBRE CHANNEL SPECIFICATION: A specification for the Fibre Chan-nel serial interconnect, which may be used as the infrastructure for a SAN. FC-0 is the Physical layer of the Fibre Channel protocol stack. This layer includes the definition of all physical components used in Fibre Channel. FC-1 is the Encode/Decode layer in Fibre Channel specification. It covers the byte encoding and character-level error control. FC-2 is called the Framing Protocol Layer. It incorporates the management of frames, flow control, and CRC generation. It also manages sequences of frames com-prising a transmission, and exchanges between nodes on the Fibre Chan-nel to accomplish commands akin to the SCSI I/O sequence. This layer also provides the management of the three service classes: Class 1, Class 2, and Class 3. FC-3 is called the Common Services Layer and is currently not used. FC-4 is the Protocol Mappings Layer and is the layer that maps protocols such as SCSI and IP to the underlying layer protocols.

FIBRE CHANNEL TOPOLOGY: A number of possible topologies, or methods for interconnecting devices or nodes, have been specified for Fibre Channel. These include point-to-point, Arbitrated Loop, and Fabric topologies. (*See FIBRE CHANNEL POINT-TO-POINT, FIBRE CHANNEL ARBITRATED LOOP, and FIBRE CHANNEL FABRIC.*)

FILE ALLOCATION TABLE (FAT): What the operating system uses to keep track of which clusters are allocated to which files and which are available for use. FAT is usually stored on Track-0.

FILE RECOVERY: The process of using backup files to replace lost files after a power failure, facility damage, virus infection, system crash, or human error.

FIRMWARE: Permanent instructions and data programmed directly into the circuitry of read-only memory for controlling the operation of the computer. Distinct from software, which can be altered by programmers.

FIXED DISK: A disk drive with disks that cannot be removed from the drive by the user.

FLEXTURE: An extremely pliable plastic circuit which connects the accuator assembly electronics to the base casting. The drive may have access times that move the heads from the outer diameter to the inner as low as 20 milliseconds and this flexture rides along.

FLOPPY DISK: A flexible plastic disk coated with magnetic media and packaged in a stiff envelope. Comes in 8-inch, 5-1/4-inch, and various sub-4 inch sizes. *FLOPPY DISKS* generally exhibit slow *ACCESS TIME* and smaller *CAPACITY* compared to *WINCHESTER DRIVES*, but feature removable diskettes.

FLUX CHANGE: Location on the data track, where the direction of magnetization reverses in order to define a 1 or 0 bit.

FLUX CHANGES PER INCH (FCI): Linear recording density defined as the number of flux changes per inch of data track. The number of magnetic field patterns that can be stored on a given area of disk surface, used as a measure of data density. Also known as flux density. Synonymous with FRPI (flux reversals per inch). In MFM recording 1 FCI equals 1 BPI (bit per inch). In RLL encoding schemes, 1 FCI generally equals 1.5 BPI. (*See also BPI.*)

FLUX DENSITY: *See FLUX CHANGES PER INCH.*

FLYING HEIGHT: The distance between the read/write head and the disk surface, created by the cushion of air that results from the velocity of the disk rotation, which keeps the two objects from touching. Smaller flying heights permit denser data storage but require more precise mechanical designs. Also known as fly height.

FOOTPRINT: The amount of floor space that a piece of equipment (e.g., a rackmount enclosure) occupies.

FORMAT: To write a magnetic track pattern onto a disk surface, specifying the locations of the tracks and sectors. This information must exist on a disk before it can store data. The purpose of a format is to record "header" data that organize the tracks into sequential sectors on the disk surfaces. This information is never altered during normal read/write operations. Header information identifies the sector number and also contains the head and cylinder *ADDRESS* in order to detect an *ADDRESS ACCESS* error.

FORMATTED CAPACITY: The amount of space left to store data on a disk after writing the sector headers, boundary definitions, and timing information during a format operation. Actual capacity available to store user data.

FORM FACTOR: The industry standard that defines the physical, external dimensions of a particular device.

FRICTION: Resistance to relative motion between two bodies in contact; e.g., there is sliding friction between head and disk during drive power up/down.

FULL HEIGHT DRIVE: Winchester 5-1/4" drive which fits in the same space as full height mini-floppy drive (called the full-height form factor), which is 3.25 inches high.

G: A G is a unit of force applied to a body at rest equal to the force exerted on it by gravity. Hard disk drive shock specifications are usually called out in Gs. A shock specification of 40 Gs non-operating means that a drive will not suffer any permanent damage if subjected to a 40 G shock. This is roughly equivalent to a drop of the drive to a hard surface from a distance of 1 inch.

GAP: (1) Part of the disk format. Allows mechanical compensations (e.g., spindle motor rotational speed variations) without the last sector on a track overwriting the first sector. (2) An interruption in the permeable material of a read/write head, usually a glass bonding material with high permeability, allowing the flux fields to exit the head structure to write or read data bits in the form of flux changes on the recording media.

GAP LENGTH: Narrowing the head gap length achieves higher bit density because the lines of force magnetize a smaller area where writing data in the form of flux changes on the recording media.

GAP WIDTH: The narrower the gap width, the closer the tracks can be placed. Closer track placement results in higher TPI.

GCR (GROUP CODE ENCODING): Data encoding method.

GIGABYTE (GB): 1 Gigabyte = 1,073,741,824 bytes (or approximately one thousand million bytes).

GUARD BAND: (1) Non-recorded band between adjacent data tracks, (2) For closed loop servo drives, extra servo tracks outside the data band preventing the Carriage Assembly from running into the crash stop.

HALF HEIGHT: A standard drive height of 1.6 inches—the equivalent to half the vertical space of a 5.25-inch drive. (*See also LOW PROFILE.*)

HARD DISK DRIVE: Sometimes called rigid disk drives, or Winchester disk drives. An electromechanical device that can read rigid disks. Though similar to floppy disk drives, the hard disks have higher bit density and multiple read/write surfaces.

HARD ERROR: A data error that persists when the disk is reread, usually caused by defects in the physical surface. Hard errors are caused by imperfections in the disk surface, called media defects. When formatting hard disk drives, hard error locations, if known, should be spared out so that data is not written to these locations. Most drives come with a hard error map listing the locations of any hard errors by head, cylinder, and BFI (bytes from index—or how many bytes from the beginning of the cylinder).

HARD SECTOR MODE: A hardware-controlled convention defining a fixed number of sectors per track in any specified zone.

HARD SECTORED: A term describing a hard drive that determines the starting location of each sector from information in the embedded servo. This method is the most common and is newer and more precise than soft sectored techniques. (*See also SOFT SECTORED.*)

HARDWARE: Computer equipment (as opposed to the computer programs and software).

HARDWARE ARRAY: A group of disk drives which are all members of the same array and share the same logical name or unit number.

HDA: *See HEAD/DISK ASSEMBLY.*

HDA INTERCONNECT: Connects the drive electronics to the mechanical assembly.

HEAD: An electromagnetic device that can write (record), read (playback), or erase data on magnetic media.

HEAD CRASH: A head landing occurs when the disk drive is turned on or off. This function normally does not damage the disk as the disk has a very thin lubricant on it. A head crash occurs when the head and disk damage each other during landing, handling, or because a contaminant particle gets between them. Head crash is a catastrophic failure condition and causes permanent damage and loss of data.

HEAD/DISK ASSEMBLY (HDA): A sealed Winchester assembly including disks, heads, filter, and actuator assembly.

HEAD LANDING AND TAKEOFF: In Winchester drives, the head is in contact with the platter when the drive is not powered. During the power up cycle, the disk begins rotation and an "air bearing" is established as the disk spins up to full RPM (rotations per minute). This air bearing prevents any mechanical contact between head and disk.

HEAD LANDING ZONE: An area of the disk set aside for takeoff and landing of the Winchester heads when the drive is turned on and off.

HEAD POSITIONER: Also known as the *ACTUATOR*, a mechanism that moves the *CARRIAGE ASSEMBLY* to the cylinder being accessed.

HEAD SKEW: *See TRACK SKEW.*

HEAD SLAP: Similar to a head crash but occurs while the drive is turned off. It usually occurs during mishandling or shipping. Head slap can cause permanent damage to a hard disk drive. (*See HEAD CRASH.*)

HELICAL SCAN RECORDING (HSR): Used widely in VHS formats for video recording, the HSR tape recording method writes at an angle across the width of a tape, allowing higher storage densities on half-inch tape.

HELICAL SCAN: A DAT recording method whereby heads record data at an angle rather than in a straight line (linear) which uses the entire width of the tape.

HEXADECIMAL (HEX): A number system based on sixteen, using digits 0 through 9 and letters A through F to represent each digit of the number. (A = 10, B = 11, C = 12, D = 13, E = 14, F = 15.)

HIERARCHICAL FILE SYSTEM (HFS): The file management system in which directories have sub-directories and sub-subdirectories. In MS Windows and Macintosh operating systems, the directories and sub-directories are represented as folders nested within other folders.

HIERARCHICAL STORAGE MANAGEMENT (HSM): A storage system in which new, frequently used data is stored on the fastest, most accessible (and generally more expensive) media (e.g., RAID) and older, less frequently used data is stored on slower (less expensive) media (e.g., tape).

HIGH-LEVEL FORMATTING: Formatting performed by the operating system to create the root directory, file allocation tables, and other basic configurations. (*See also LOW-LEVEL FORMATTING and FAT.*)

HOME PAGE: The main page on a Web site that serves as the primary point of entry to related pages within the site and may have links to other sites as well.

HOME: The reference track of a hard disk, usually the outermost track (track 0), used for recalibration of the actuator.

HOST ADAPTER: A plug-in board that acts as the interface between a computer system bus and the disk drive.

HOST BUS ADAPTER (HBA): A hardware card that resides on the PC bus and provides an interface connection between a SCSI device (such as a hard drive) and the host PC.

HOST-ATTACHED STORAGE: A storage system that is connected directly to the network server; also referred to as server-attached storage.

HOT SPARE: A spare disk drive which, upon failure of a member of a redundant disk array, will automatically be used to replace the failed disk drive.

HOT SWAP: The operation of removing a failed disk drive, which is a member of a redundant array, and replacing it with a good drive.

HUB: A device that splits one network cable into a set of separate cables, each connecting to a different computer; used in a local area network to create a small-scale network by connecting several computers together.

I/O PROCESSOR: Intelligent processor or controller that handles the input/output operations of a computer.

ID FIELD: The address portion of a sector on a formatted hard disk. The ID field is written during the Format operation. It includes the cylinder, head, and sector number of the current sector. This address information is compared by the disk controller with the desired head, cylinder, and sector number before a read or write operation is allowed.

IDE: *See INTEGRATED DRIVE ELECTRONICS.*

IMAGE-BACKUP MODE: Used with streaming tape, image-backup mode records an exact copy of the disk, including unused sectors and bad tracks.

INDEX (PULSE): The Index Pulse is the starting point for each disk track. The index pulse provides initial synchronization for sector addressing on each individual track.

INDEX TIME: The time interval between similar edges of the index pulse, which measures the time for the disk to make one revolution. This information is used by a disk drive to verify correct rotational speed of the media.

INDUSTRY STANDARDS: Rules or guidelines, established by independent consortia, to control the development and manufacture of products and devices in the electronics industry. Industry standards for audio CDs, for example, are what assure consumers that any audio CD will work in any CD player.

INDUSTRY STANDARD ARCHITECTURE (ISA): The standard 16-bit AT bus designed by IBM for the PC/AT system. ISA was the only industry standard bus for PCs until the release of IBM's MCA (MicroChannel Architecture) and EISA (Extended Industry Standard Architecture). (*See also EISA.*)

INFRASTRUCTURE: The physical equipment (computers, cases, racks, cabling, etc.) that comprises a computer system.

INITIALIZATION: *See LOW-LEVEL FORMATTING.*

INITIATOR: A SCSI device that requests another SCSI device (a target) to perform an operation; usually a host computer acts as an initiator and a peripheral device acts as a target.

INPUT: Data entered into the computer to be processed, or User commands or queries.

INPUT/OUTPUT (I/O): The process of entering data into or removing data from a computer system. The reception (read) or transmission (write) of computer signals; the entire connection path between the CPU bus and the disk drives.

INSTITUTE OF ELECTRICAL AND ELECTRONICS ENGINEERS (IEEE): The largest technical society in the world, consisting of engineers, scientists, and students. Articulates standards for computers and communications.

INSTRUCTION: The most basic task that a computer performs. A single instruction involves a single, simple calculation processed by the computer. When working on a computer, many instructions are strung together one after another to complete the larger tasks that the operating system or software directs. (*See also MIPS.*)

INTEGRATED DRIVE ELECTRONICS (IDE): A disk drive interface that incorporates the drive controller into the drive electronics. IDE drives are used in IBM-compatible computers. Also known as ATA.

INTELLIGENT PERIPHERAL: A peripheral device that contains a processor or microprocessor to enable it to interpret and execute commands, thus relieving the computer for other tasks.

INTERCHANGEABILITY: The ability to use one brand or type of storage media in a variety of drives. For example, manufacturers of audio tapes and tape players support industry standards for interchangeability, so any tape will work in any player.

INTERFACE: A connection between hardware devices, applications, or different sections of a computer network. A hardware or software protocol (contained in the electronics of the disk controller and drive) that manages the exchange of data between the drive and the computer. The most common interfaces for small computer systems are ATA (also known as IDE) and SCSI. (*See also AT* and *SCSI.*)

INTERFACE CONNECTOR: Attachment point for the interface ribbon cable: 40 pins for ATA; 50 pins for SCSI Narrow, etc.

INTERFACE CONTROLLER: The chip or circuit that translates computer data and commands into a form suitable for use by the hard drive and controls the transfer of data between the buffer and the host. (*See also DISK CONTROLLER* and *DISK DRIVE CONTROLLER.*)

INTERFACE STANDARD: The interface specifications agreed to by various manufacturers to promote industry-wide interchangeability of products such as disk drives and controllers. An interface standard generally reduces product costs, allows buyers to purchase from more than one source, and allows faster market acceptance of new products. (*See SCSI, ESDI.*)

INTERLEAVE: The arrangement of sectors on a track. (*See also INTERLEAVE FACTOR.*) The interleave value tells the controller where the next logical sector is located in relation to the current sector. For example, an interleave value of one (1) specifies that the next logical sector is physically the next sector on the track. Interleave of two (2) specifies every other physical sector, three (3) every third sector, and so on. Interleaving is used to improve the system throughout based on overhead time of the host software, the disk drive, and the controller. For example, if an *APPLICATION PROGRAM* is processing sequential logical records of a *DISK FILE* in a CPU time of more than one second but less than two, then an interleave factor of 3 will prevent wasting an entire disk revolution between *ACCESSES.*

INTERLEAVE FACTOR: The ratio of physical disk sectors skipped for every sector actually written. The number of sectors that pass beneath the read/write heads before the next sector arrives. For example, a 3:1 interleave factor means that the heads read a sector, then let two pass by before reading another, requiring three full revolutions of the disk to access the complete data track.

INTERNAL DRIVE: A disk drive mounted inside a computer either in a drive bay or on a card installed in an expansion slot.

INTERNATIONAL ORGANIZATION FOR STANDARDIZATION (ISO): A worldwide organization that develops, publishes, and promotes international industrial and technical standards. The term ISO is not an acronym, but a derivative of the Greek word isos, which means "equal."

INTERNET: A worldwide system of linked computer networks.

INTEROPERABILITY: The ability of one computer system to control another, even though the two systems are made by different manufacturers.

INTERRUPT: A signal, usually from a peripheral device to a CPU, to signify that a commanded operation has been completed or cannot be completed.

INTRANET: A computer network, based on Internet technology, that is designed to meet the internal needs for sharing information within a single organization or company.

IOPS (I/Os PER SECOND): A measure of performance for a host-attached storage device or RAID controller.

ISA: *See INDUSTRY STANDARD ARCHITECTURE.*

JBOD: *See JUST A BUNCH OF DISKS.*

JUKEBOX: Also called an optical disk library, a jukebox is a standalone cabinet that holds multiple optical disk drives and cartridges for high-speed, high-capacity storage. It includes a robotic arm to pick an optical cartridge from its storage slot, move it to one of several drives, then return it to the slot when it is no longer needed.

JUST A BUNCH OF DISKS (JBOD): A non-RAID disk array.

KERNEL: The core of an operating system such as Windows 98, Windows NT, Mac OS or Unix; provides basic services for the other parts of the operating system, making it possible for it to run several programs at once (multitasking), read and write files and connect to networks and peripherals.

KILOBYTE (KB): A unit of measure consisting of 1,024 bytes.

LAN: *See LOCAL AREA NETWORK.*

LANDING ZONE: A non-data position on the disk's inner cylinder where the heads can land when the power is off. In a portable computer, the heads also move to the landing zone after a period of inactivity to save power and extend battery life.

LATENCY, ROTATIONAL: The time for the disk to rotate the accessed sector under the head for read or write. On the average, latency is the time for half of a disk revolution.

LEGACY: A computer, system, or software, that was created for a specific purpose but is now outdated; anything left over from a previous version of the hardware or software.

LIBRARY: *See JUKEBOX.*

LIGHT INTENSITY MODULATION DIRECT OVERWRITE (LIM-DOW): An optical recording technology that allows write procedures to be accomplished in one pass of the optical read/write head over the media. LIMDOW accelerates optical performance, but requires somewhat complex and expensive optical media, and involves a more complicated write procedure that leaves less margin for error compared with other optical technologies.

LINEAR TAPE OPEN (LTO): A tape format developed by HP, IBM, and Seagate Technology.

LOCAL AREA NETWORK (LAN): A communications network used to connect computers and other electronic devices within a confined geographical area. For example, a LAN can connect users within a single site, allowing them to share data, exchange e-mail, and share peripherals.

LOGIC: Electronic circuitry that switches on and off ("1" and "0") to perform digital operations.

LOGICAL BLOCK: *See SECTOR.*

LOGICAL FORMAT: Refers to low-level formatting. In relation to DOS-specific format requirements, refers to the translations accomplished by the controller in situations where the hard drive data configurations do not match DOS format limitations.

LOGICAL UNIT NUMBER (LUN): An addressing scheme used to define SCSI devices on a single SCSI bus.

LOOK AHEAD: The process of anticipating events in order to speed up computer operations. For example, a disk drive can use look ahead caching to speed subsequent sequential data requests. When the drive receives a request for data, it reads not only the data requested into the cache buffer but also "looks ahead" and reads data immediately following the requested data into cache until the cache buffer is filled. Once loaded into cache, the information can be accessed almost instantaneously, without the need for additional read operations.

LOOKUP: The action of obtaining and displaying data in a file.

LOW LEVEL FORMAT: The first step in preparing a drive to store information after physical installation is complete. The process sets up the "handshake" between the drive and the controller. In an XT system, the low level format is usually done using DOS's debug utility. In an AT system, AT advanced diagnostics is typically used. Other third party software may also be used to do low level format on both XTs and ATs.

LOW PROFILE: A standard drive height of 1 inch. (*See also HALF HEIGHT.*)

LOW VOLTAGE DIFFERENTIAL (LVD): An Ultra2 SCSI signaling method that increases bus data rates to 80 MB/s, double the fastest SCSI-2 standard (40 MB/s).

LUN: *See LOGICAL UNIT NUMBER.*

MAGAZINE: A removable chamber that holds multiple optical disk cartridges or magnetic tapes, often used for high-volume automated backup.

MAGNETIC MEDIA: A disk or tape with a surface layer containing particles of metal, or metallic oxides that can be magnetized in different directions to represent bits of data, sounds, or other information.

MAGNETIC RECORDING: The use of a head, recording head, recording media (tape or disk), and associated electronic circuitry for storing data or sound or video.

MAGNETO-OPTICAL (MO): An optical disk storage technology that uses a combination of magnet and laser to alter the magnetic flux directions on a disk's recording surface, much like a magnetic hard disk. The laser heats a small point on the disks' recording surface to 150 degrees Celsius. At this temperature, the polarity of the disk's recording surface can be altered with a magnet, causing a change in reflectivity that is detected during reads. MO is the dominant technology for rewritable optical disks, and meets ANSI, ISO, and ECMA industry standards for interchangeable optical disk cartridges.

MAGNETO-RESISTIVE HEAD (MRH): A special read head technology designed to support data acquisition from media with very high recording densities. Based on materials with special magneto-resistive properties, e.g., whose electrical resistance changes in the presence of a magnetic field, read heads incorporating MR material are more sensitive to changes in the strength of magnetic fields, enabling them to read more densely-packed bits stored on tape or disk media. This mechanism cannot be used for writing, so a conventional thin film inductive write head element is deposited alongside the MR stripe.

MAIN MEMORY: Random-access memory used by the CPU for storing program instructions and data currently being processed by those instructions. (*See RANDOM-ACCESS MEMORY.*)

MAINFRAME COMPUTER: A large computer generally found in data processing centers. (*See MINICOMPUTER* and *MICROCOMPUTER.*)

MAMMOTH: A proprietary tape technology of Exabyte Corporation.

MANAGED HUB: This is a technique for providing statistics information about the traffic on a hub. Typically, no actual management of the hub is possible using this interface, but information and notification of failures can be achieved. This interface often uses Simple Network Management Protocol (SNMP) Management Information Bases (MIBs) as a standard protocol for providing this information.

MEAN SWAPS BETWEEN FAILURE (MSBF): A measure of reliability specific to optical jukeboxes, usually determined in benchmark testing. MSBF refers to the average number of disk "swaps" a jukebox and its internal mechanisms can be expected to deliver before maintenance is required. A statistical calculation used to predict the average usefulness of a robotic device (e.g., a tape library) with any interruption of service.

MEAN TIME BETWEEN FAILURE (MTBF): The average time before a failure will occur. This is not a warranty measurement. MTBF is a calculation taking into consideration the MTBF of each component in a system and is the statistical average operation time between the start of a unit's lifetime and its time of a failure. After a product has been in the field for a few years, the MTBF can become a field proven statistic. The higher the MTBF, the more reliable the equipment.

MEAN TIME TO REPAIR (MTTR): A measure of the complexity of design in electronic equipment. Highly modular designs—i.e., those that use interchangeable, hot-swappable components—typically have a low MTTR since failed components can be replaced with functioning components.

MEAN TIME until DATA LOSS (MTDL): The average time from startup until a component failure causes a permanent loss of user data in a disk array. The concept is similar to MTBF, but takes into account the possibility that RAID redundancy can protect against loss due to single component failures.

MEDIA: A physical storage medium. Includes optical disks, CDs, magnetic tapes, hard disks, and other technologies used to store computer-based information. The magnetic layers of a disk or tape. (*See DISK/PLATTER.*)

MEGABYTE (MB): A megabyte is 106 or 1,000,000 bytes. One megabyte can store more than one million characters.

MEMORY: Any device or storage system capable of storing and retrieving information.

MFM (Multiple frequency modulation): A method of encoding analog signals into magnetic pulses or bits.

MICROCOMPUTER: A computer whose central processor unit (CPU) is manufactured as a chip or a small number of chips. Personal computers are examples of microcomputers.

MICROINCH: One-millionth of an inch.

MICROSECOND: One-millionth of a second.

MILLISECOND: One-thousandth of a second.

MICROSOFT WINDOWS NT: An operating system developed by Microsoft for high-performance processors and networked systems.

MINICOMPUTER: A computer midway in size and processing power between a MICROCOMPUTER and a MAINFRAME COMPUTER.

MIPS (MILLIONS OF INSTRUCTIONS PER SECOND): A measure of the speed at which a CPU operates. (*See also INSTRUCTION.*)

MIRRORING: A method of storage in which data from one disk is duplicated on another disk so that both drives contain the same information, thus providing data redundancy. A popular term for RAID-1.

MISSION CRITICAL: Any computer process that cannot fail during normal business hours; some computer processes (e.g., telephone systems) must run all day long and require 100 percent uptime.

MISSION-CRITICAL DATA: Data or information considered to be so important that its loss would cause grave difficulty to all or part of a business. For example: customer account information at a bank, or patient information at a hospital.

MNEMONIC: A shortened code for a longer term.

MODIFIED FREQUENCY MODULATION (MFM): A method of recording digital data, using a particular CODE to get the flux reversal times from the data pattern. MFM recording is self-clocking because the CODE guarantees timing information for the playback process. The controller is thus able to synchronize directly from the data. This method has a maximum of one bit of data with each flux reversal. (*See NRZ, RLL*).

MTBF: *See MEAN TIME BETWEEN FAILURE.*

MTTR: *See MEAN TIME TO REPAIR.*

MULTIMEDIA: The combination of several media formats used for the delivery of information. Many commercial CD-ROMs use a multimedia format, combining text, photos, audio, animation, and video on a single disk.

MULTIPLATFORM: The ability of a product or network to support a variety of computer platforms (e.g., IBM, Sun, Macintosh); also referred to as cross-platform.

MULTIPLE SEGMENT CACHING: A technique enabling the division of the cache into segments so that different blocks of data can be cached simultaneously and subsequent commands will have a better probability of a cache hit

MULTIPROCESSOR: A computer containing two or more processors.

MULTITASKING: The ability of a computer system to execute more than one program or program task at a time.

MULTI-THREADED: Having multiple concurrent or pseudo-concurrent execution sequences. Used to describe processes in computer systems. Multi-threaded processes are one means by which throughput intensive applications can make maximum use of a disk array to increase I/O performance.

MULTI-USER : The ability of a computer system to execute programs for more than one user at a time.

NEAR-FIELD RECORDING (NFR): An optical disk storage technology that combines elements of hard disk and magneto-optical (MO) storage. Though still under development, the technology is expected to deliver hard disk-like performance with greater storage capacities and lower cost storage costs than current technologies.

NEAR-ONLINE STORAGE: A cross between online and offline storage, usually consisting of data stored in optical jukeboxes. Near-online storage is less expensive, more durable, and takes only slightly longer to access than online storage kept on high-speed hard disks. It is significantly faster and easier to access than offline storage.

NETWORK ATTACHED STORAGE (NAS): This is the provision of storage in a form that is readily accessible on a network. A disk array storage system that is attached directly to a network rather than to the server. NAS devices typically present a networked file system in accordance with a protocol such as NFS or CIFS/SMB. These devices are often referred to as thin servers as they have the functions as a server in a client/server relationship. A typical NAS thin storage server has a processor, an operating system or micro-kernel, and processes file I/O protocols.

NETWORKING: The ability to interconnect a number of PCs, workstations, servers, and peripherals for the purpose of sharing, sending, receiving, and managing information, files, e-mail, and other data.

NETWORK FILE SYSTEM (NFS): A file system originated by Sun Microsystems that will mount remote file systems across homogenous and heterogenous systems. NFS is a client/server application. An NFS server can export local directories for remote NFS clients to use. Typically, NFS runs over IP using UDP, but there are NFS implementations that will work using TCP as the network transport service. NFS has been accepted by the Internet Engineering Task Force (IETF) in certain areas as a standard for file services on TCP/IP networks on the Internet.

NFS: *See NETWORK FILE SYSTEM.*

NODE (or NETWORK NODE): Any device that is directly connected to the network, usually through Ethernet cable; nodes include file servers and shared peripherals.

NOISE: Extraneous electronic signals that interfere with information signals (similar to radio static or TV interference). Sources of noise in computers can be power supplies, ground loops, radio interference, cable routing, etc.

NON-RETURN TO ZERO (NRZ): A method of magnetic recording of digital data in which a flux reversal denotes a one bit, and no flux reversal a zero bit. NRZ recording requires an accompanying synchronization clock to define each cell time, unlike MFM or RLL recording.

NRZ: *See NON-RETURN TO ZERO.*

NT: *See MICROSOFT WINDOWS NT.*

OFF-LINE: Processing or peripheral operations performed while not connected to the system CPU via the system BUS. A collection of data that requires some manual intervention such as loading a disk or tape before it can be accessed. For example, floppy disk, tape, CD-ROM.

OFFLINE STORAGE: Infrequently accessed data that is stored offline in a tape archive or file cabinet. Offline storage is the least expensive and slowest storage method, consisting primarily of tape, microfiche, and paper media. Restoring offline data to an online environment must be handled manually.

ON-LINE: A collection of data, typically stored on hard disks or arrays, that is immediately accessible.

ONLINE STORAGE: The fastest and most expensive storage alternative, consisting of frequently accessed files found a computer's hard disk.

OPEN SYSTEMS NETWORK: A network comprised of equipment that conforms to industry standards of interoperability between different operating systems (e.g., Unix, Windows NT).

OPERATING SYSTEM: An operating system is a program which acts as an interface between the user of a computer and the computer hardware. The purpose of the operating system is to provide an environment in which a user may run programs. The goal of the operating system is to enable the user to conveniently use the computer's resources such as the CPU, memory, storage devices, and printers.

OPTICAL DISK: A storage medium that generally uses a laser to write and read data. (*See WORM, CD-ROM, CD-R* and *CD-RW.*)

OPTICAL STORAGE: A storage alternative to hard disks that provides random-access capability like hard disks. Compared to hard disk storage, optical storage offers higher reliability and a higher degree of removability and transportability. However, optical disk access times are two to four times slower than hard disks, due primarily to the weight of the optical head that reads and writes data. Most optical storage technologies use a read/write laser to store data: to write, the laser heats the recording surface of the media, causing a physical change that is detected during reads.

OPTICAL STORAGE TECHNOLOGY ASSOCIATION (OSTA): An international trade association founded in 1992 to promote the use of writable optical technologies and products.

OUTPUT: Processing data being transferred out of the computer system to peripherals (i.e., disk, printer, etc.). This includes responses to user commands or queries.

OVERHEAD: Overhead refers to the processing time required by the controller, host adapter, or drive prior to the execution of a command. Lower command over-head yields higher drive performance. (*See also ZERO COMMAND OVERHEAD.*) Disk overhead refers to the space required for non-data information such as servo data. Disk overhead often accounts for about ten percent of drive capacity. Lesser disk overhead yields greater disk capacity.

PRML: *See PARTIAL RESPONSE MAXIMUM LIKELIHOOD (PRML).*

PARITY: A data error checking method using an extra bit in which the total number of binary 1's (or 0's) in a byte is always odd or always even; thus, in an odd parity scheme, every byte has eight bits of data and one parity bit. If using odd parity and the number of 1 bits comprising the byte of data is not odd, the 9th or parity bit is set to 1 to create the odd parity. In this way, a byte of data can be checked for accurate transmission by simply counting the bits for an odd parity indication. If the count is ever even, an error is indicated.

PARITY DATA: A block of information mathematically created from several blocks of user data to allow recovery of user data contained on a drive that has failed in an array; used in RAID levels 3 and 5.

PARKING: Parking the disk drive heads means the recording heads are moved so that they are not over the platter's data area. Many drives have an auto-park feature where the heads are automatically parked when power to the drive is shut off. Other drives require the user to run some kind of parking software to park the heads.

PARTIAL RESPONSE MAXIMUM LIKELIHOOD (PRML): A method for detecting and sampling a signal generated from the reading of a hard disk or tape. Applied in conjunction with *MAGNETO-RESISTIVE (MR)*

HEADs, PRML enables extremely high *AREAL DENSITIES* to be achieved on magnetic media.

PARTITION: A portion of a hard drive dedicated to a particular operating system or application and accessed as a single logical volume.

PARTITIONING: Method for dividing an area on disk drive for use by more than one disk operating system or for dividing large disk drives into areas which the File Allocation Table (FAT) can deal with when in use.

PATH: The DOS term "path" has three definitions and each definition involves directories. A *PATH* may be defined as: (1) the *NAMEs* of the chain of directories leading to a file; (2) the complete file or directory *NAME;* (3) a DOS command.

PC CARD: A PC card is a small form factor memory card that can be used with handheld, subnotebook, notebook, and desktop personal computers; personal communicators; industrial controllers; and laser printers and other electronic devices. PCMCIA—Personal Computer Memory Card International Association. The association responsible for defining the PC card standard.

PCB: *See PRINTED CIRCUIT BOARD.*

PCMCIA: This is the acronym for the Personal Computer Memory Card Industry Association, a trade association responsible for the promotion of removable device interfaces for a variety of products including memory, modems, disks, etc.

PEER-TO-PEER ARCHITECTURE: A network of two or more computers using the same programs or types of programs to communicate and share data.

PERFORMANCE: A measure of the speed of a hard drive during normal operation. Factors affecting performance are seek times, transfer rate, and command overhead.

PERIPHERAL EQUIPMENT: Auxiliary memory, displays, printers, disk drives, and other equipment usually attached to computer systems' CPU by controllers and cables (they are often packaged together in a desktop computer).

PERSONAL COMPUTER INTERCONNECT (PCI): An industry-standard bus used in servers, workstations, and PCs.

PETABYTE: 1,024 terabytes.

PHASE-CHANGE TECHNOLOGY: An optical disk storage technology that uses a plastic disk and metal recording layer to store data. Heat generated by the drive's laser changes the molecular structure of the metal, transforming it from an amorphous to highly reflective crystalline state.

The changes in reflectivity are detected during reads. Used for CD-RW and DVD re-writable disks.

PLATED MEDIA: Disk platters that are covered with a hard metal alloy instead of an iron-oxide compound. Plated disks can store greater amounts of data than their oxide-coated counterparts.

PLATED THIN FILM DISKS: Magnetic disk memory media having its surface plated with a thin coating of a metallic alloy instead of being coated with oxide.

PLATFORM: A hardware standard, such as IBM, Sun, or Macintosh.

PLATTER: An actual metal (or other rigid material) disk that is mounted inside a fixed-disk drive. Many drives use more than one platter mounted on a single spindle (shaft) to provide more data storage surfaces in a small package.

PLUG AND PLAY: An auto detect method used by the system BIOS to identify and configure peripheral devices. Identification numbers, interrupts and port addresses are set when the system boots.

POLLING: A technique for allocating CPU cycles to specific peripheral devices and tasks.

PORTABILITY: The ability to move storage media from one point to another. Tapes and optical disks are highly portable since they can be easily moved from a working environment to a different location for storage.

POSITIONER: *See ACTUATOR.*

PRECOMPENSATION: A technique used with some oxide media drives to write data bits closer together on the disk in order to offset the repelling effect (bit shift) caused by magnetic recording.

PREVENTIVE MAINTENANCE: A method of doing a scheduled routine observation or exchanging a part, prior to a breakdown of a piece of equipment.

PRIMARY STORAGE: Online storage of electronic data, typically found on a computer's hard disk. This includes frequently used data, work in process, or data that is not frequently used but must be immediately available at all times.

PRINTED CIRCUIT BOARD (PCB): The circuit board with the chips attached to a drive.

PROCESSING (DATA PROCESSING): The handling, manipulating, and modifying of data by a computer in accordance with software instructions.

PROGRAM: A sequence of instructions stored in memory and executed by a processor or microprocessor. (*See also APPLICATION PROGRAMS.*)

PROPRIETARY: Privately developed and owned technology.

PROTOCOL: A set of conventions governing the format of messages to be exchanged within a communications system.

QUARTER-INCH CARTRIDGE (QIC, pronounced "Quick"): A tape media recording technology that uses a mini-cartridge for tape storage. There are many QIC standards, each defining a method for reading and writing data to tapes.

RACKMOUNT: The cabinet that houses a server/storage workstation (also referred to as a server rack); to mount equipment into a cabinet.

RADIAL: A way of connecting multiple drives to one controller. In radial operation, all output signals are active even if the drive is not selected. (*See also DAISY CHAIN.*)

RAID (Redundant Array of Inexpensive Disks): A method of combining hard disks into one logical storage unit which offers disk-fault tolerance and can operate at higher throughput levels than a single hard disk.

RAID ADVISORY BOARD (RAB): An organization of storage system manufacturers and integrators dedicated to advancing the use and awareness of RAID and associated storage technologies; started in 1992, RAB states its main goals as education, standardization, and certification.

RAM: *See RANDOM ACCESS MEMORY.*

RAM DISK: A DOS operation, where part of the computer's random access memory is used to simulate a disk drive. The RAM disk and its contents will disappear if power is lost or DOS MAIN MEMORY is restarted. RAM is far faster (microseconds *ACCESS TIME*) than disks (milliseconds), so *APPLICATION PROGRAMS* that access the disk run faster.

RANDOM ACCESS: The ability to skip randomly from track to track on a storage medium. Optical disks, magnetic hard disks, and audio CDs allow random access to data tracks. Audio tapes, by comparison, allow only sequential access (i.e., fast-forward or reverse) to locate stored data.

RANDOM ACCESS MEMORY (RAM): An integrated circuit memory chip that allows information to be stored and retrieved by a microprocessor or controller. The information can be stored or accessed in any order, and all storage locations are equally accessible. Random access memory usually refers to volatile memory where the contents are lost when power is removed. The user addressable memory of a computer is random access memory.

READ: To access a storage location and obtain previously recorded data.

READ AFTER WRITE: A mode of operation requiring that the system read each sector after data is written, checking that the data read back is the same as the data recorded. This operation lowers system speed but raises data reliability.

READ ONLY MEMORY (ROM): A chip that can be programmed once with bits of information. This chip retains this information even if the power is turned off. When this information is programmed into the ROM, it is called burning the ROM.

READ VERIFY: A data accuracy check performed by having the disk read data to the controller, which then checks for errors but does not pass the data on to the system.

READ/WRITE HEAD: *See HEAD.*

REAL-TIME: Immediate processing of input or notification of status.

RECALIBRATE: Return to Track Zero. A common disk drive function in which the heads are returned to track 0 (outermost track).

RECORD: A record is a single unit made up of logically related fields.

REDUCED INSTRUCTION SET COMPUTER (RISC): A computer processing architecture that requires fewer instructions to run applications, thus increasing processing speed.

REDUCED WRITE CURRENT: A signal input (to some older drives) which decreases the amplitude of the write current at the actual drive head. Normally this signal is specified to be used during inner track write operations to lessen the effect of adjacent bit "crowding." Most drives today provide this internally and do not require controller intervention.

RESOLUTION: In regard to magnetic recording, the bandwidth (or frequency response) of the recording heads.

RESTORE: The act of copying files or data from a backup storage device to their normal location on a computer's hard disk, often to replace files or data that were accidentally lost or deleted.

RLL: *See RUN LENGTH LIMITED.*

ROBOT: A machine that can sense and react to input, and cause changes in its surroundings with some degree of intelligence, ideally with no human supervision.

ROBOTICS: The internal components of an optical jukebox or automated tape library, usually consisting of a mechanical arm that automatically transports media inside the cabinet for use and storage.

ROM: *See READ ONLY MEMORY.*

ROTARY ACTUATOR: *See ACTUATOR.*

ROTATIONAL LATENCY: *See LATENCY, ROTATIONAL.*

ROUTER: An electronic device that connects two or more networks and routes incoming data packets to the appropriate network.

RUN LENGTH LIMITED (RLL): A method of recording digital data in which the combinations of flux reversals are coded/decoded to allow greater than one (1) bit of information per flux reversal. This compaction of information increases data capacity by approximately 50 percent.

SAN CLASS 1 SERVICE: This service level guarantees bandwidth and ordering of packets. It also returns confirmations of transmission.

SAN CLASS 2 SERVICE: This service level is connectionless and can deliver packets out-of-order. Delivery of packets is however guaranteed and confirmations are sent.

SAN CLASS 3 SERVICE: This is the lowest service level and does not guarantee either ordering or delivery.

SAN HUB: This is a simple connectivity device that allows for devices to be connected to a Fibre Channel loop by being attached to a hub port. The advantage of this is that failures of a single device on the loop can be isolated from the other ports on the loop. The aggregate bandwidth of the hub is still that of a single Fibre Channel loop however.

SCALEABLE: The ability of a product or network to accommodate growth.

SCALEABLE LINEAR RECORDING: A tape format from Tandberg Data ASA.

SCAM: SCSI Configure Auto-Magically. A form of Plug and Play developed for SCSI peripherals. SCSI ID's are set boot time.

SCATTER/GATHER: A feature which allows data to be transferred to or from multiple discontiguous areas of host computer memory with a single I/O command.

SCSI: *See SMALL COMPUTER SYSTEMS INTERFACE.*

SECTOR: A sector is a section of a track whose size is determined by formatting. When used as an address component, sector and location refer to the sequence number of the sector around the track. Typically, one sector stores one user record of data. Drives typically are formatted from 17 to 26 sectors per track. Determining how many sectors per track to use depends on the system type, the controller capabilities and the drive encoding method and interface. On Macintosh and UNIX drives, sectors are usually grouped into blocks or logical blocks that function as the smallest data unit permitted. Since these blocks are often defined as a single sector the terms block and sector are sometimes used interchangeably in this context. (Note: The usage of the term block in connection with the physical configuration of the disk is different from its meaning at the system level.)

SECTOR-SLIP: Sector-slip allows any sector with a defect to be mapped and bypassed. The next contiguous sector is given that sector address.

SEEK: The radial movement of the heads to a specified track address.

SEEK TIME: The time required to move between tracks when seeking data.

SERIAL STORAGE ARCHITECTURE (SSA): A high-speed method of connecting disk, tape, and CD-ROM drives, printers, scanners, and other devices to a computer.

SEQUENTIAL ACCESS: Writing or reading data in a sequential order, such as reading data blocks stored one after the other on magnetic tape (the opposite of random access).

SERVER: A computer that provides access to a network and its resources, runs administrative software controls, and provides services (such as file storage and retrieval) for desktop computers.

SERVO DATA: *See EMBEDDED SERVO.*

SERVO MOTOR: A motor used to position the actuator arm and read/write heads on hard disk media.

SERVO SURFACE: *See DEDICATED SERVO.*

SERVO TRACK: A prerecorded reference track on the dedicated servo surface of a closed-loop disk drive. All data track positions are compared to their corresponding servo track to determine "off-track/on-track" position. Information written on the servo surface that the electronics of the drive uses to position the heads over the correct data track. This information is written on the drive by the servo track writer.

SETTLE TIME: The interval between the arrival of the read/write head at a specific track and the lessening of the residual vibration to a level sufficient for reliable reading or writing.

SETUP: Program used by type computers to store configuration in CMOS. This program is sometimes found in the system bios and can be accessed from the keyboard. On other systems, the program is on a diskette.

SHOCK RATING: A rating, expressed in terms of the force of gravity (Gs), of how much shock a disk drive can sustain without damage.

SILICON: Semiconductor substrate material generally used to manufacture microprocessors and other integrated circuit chips.

SIMPLE NETWORK MANAGEMENT PROTOCOL (SNMP): A standard protocol that runs over an IP link to provide management of network type devices without performing continual polling.

SINGLE-ENDED: An electrical signal protocol which transmits information through changes in voltage. Single-ended SCSI uses standard TTL signal-and-ground pairs to transmit information over the SCSI bus.

SKEWING: Some low-level formatting routines may ask for a Head and/or Cylinder Skew value. The value will represent the number of sectors being skewed to compensate for head switching time of the drive and/or track-to-track seek time allowing continuous read/write operation without losing disk revolutions.

SMALL COMPUTER SYSTEM INTERFACE (SCSI): An industry standard for connecting peripherals such as printers, scanners, optical drives, and tape drives to a microprocessor. SCSI covers both hardware and software standards for allowing computers and peripherals to communicate with each other.

SMART: Self-Monitoring, Analysis, and Reporting Technology can help prevent data loss and unscheduled computer downtime. It provides advanced warning of certain types of drive failures, allowing the user of data-management software to backup the data. This technology is not supported by all system manufacturers or hard drive distributors and requires third party software.

SOFT ERROR: A bit error during playback which can be corrected by repeated attempts to read, usually caused by power fluctuations or noise spikes.

SOFT SECTOR: A convention, defined by software, of setting a variable number of sectors per track in direct relationship to the drive's FCI rating in regards to the area of media that passes beneath the head. This schema takes advantage of the fact that, in actual surface area, the outermost tracks are longer than the innermost.

SOFT SECTORED: A term describing a hard drive that determines the starting location of each sector from information stored in data fields. This method is older and results in more overhead than hard sectored techniques. (*See also HARD SECTORED.*)

SOFTWARE APPLICATION PROGRAMS: Disk operating systems and other programs (as opposed to *HARDWARE*). The instructions or programs, usually stored on floppy or hard disks, which are used to direct the operations of a computer, or other hardware.

SOFTWARE PATCH: Software modification which allows or adds functions not otherwise available using the standard software program.

SPINDLE: The drive's center shaft, on which the platters are mounted. A synchronized spindle is a shaft that allows two disks to spin simultaneously as a mirror image of each other, permitting redundant storage of data.

SPINDLE MOTOR: The spindle motor is the electro-mechanical part of the disk drive that rotates the platters.

SPUTTER: A special method of coating the disk that results in a hard, smooth surface capable of storing data at a high density.

SSA: *See SERIAL STORAGE ARCHITECTURE.*

ST-506/ST-412 INTERFACE: One of several industry standard interfaces between a hard disk and hard disk controller. In the ST-506/ST-412 interface, the "intelligence" is on the controller rather than the drive. (*See also INTERFACE STANDARD, ESDI,* and *SCSI.*)

STEP PULSE: The pulse sent from the controller to the stepper motor on the step interface signal line to initiate a step operation.

STEP TIME: The time required by the drive to step the heads from the current cylinder position to a target cylinder.

STEP: An increment or decrement of the head positioning arm to move the heads in or out, respectively, one track from their current position. In buffered mode (open loop drives), the head motion is postponed until the last of a string of step pulses has been received.

STEPPER: A type of motor that moves in discrete amounts with each electrical pulse. Steppers were originally the most common type of actuator engine, since they can be geared to advance a read/write head one track per step.

STEPPER MOTOR: The stepper motor is the electro-mechanical part of the disk drive that positions the heads by step pulse on the tracks of the disk to read and write data.

STORAGE APPLIANCE: Concept of an intelligent, network-attached, storage device.

STORAGE AREA NETWORK (SAN): A network comprising multiple hosts and storage peripherals, currently conceived as Fibre Channel/SCSI Command Set-based. However, any interconnect and any network protocol could be used, theoretically, to establish a SAN, provided that the strict latency and throughput requirements of storage are met.

STORAGE CAPACITY: Amount of data that can be stored in a memory, usually specified in kilobytes (KB) for main memory and floppy disk drives and megabytes (MB) for hard disk and tape drives. The maximum amount of data that can be stored on a given media.

STORAGE DENSITY: Usually refers to recording density (BPI, TPI, or their product, *AREAL DENSITY*).

STORAGE LOCATION: A memory location, identified by an *ADDRESS*, where information is to be read or written.

STORAGE MODULE DRIVE (SMD): Storage module drive interface. An interface, used in larger disk drives, e.g., 14" drives.

STRIPE: A contiguous region of disk space. Stripes may be as small as one sector or may be composed of many contiguous sectors.

STRIPING: A method of storage in which a unit of data is distributed and stored across several hard disks, which improves access speed but does not provide redundancy. Also called RAID-0.

SUBSTRATE: In disk technology, the material underneath the magnetic coating of a platter. Common substrates include aluminum or magnesium alloys for hard drives, glass for optical disks, and mylar for floppy disks.

SURFACE: The top or bottom side of a platter, which is coated with the magnetic material for recording data. On some hard drives, one of the surfaces on one of the platters is reserved for servo data.

SURFACE MOUNTED DEVICE (SMD): A *CHIP* in a smaller integrated surface package, without connection leads.

SUSTAINED MODE: The measured transfer rate of a given device during normal operation.

SWITCH: A network traffic monitoring device that controls the flow of traffic between multiple network nodes.

SYNCHRONOUS DATA: Data sent, usually in serial mode, with a clock pulse.

SYSTEMS INTEGRATOR: An individual or company that combines various components and programs into a functioning system, customized for a particular customer's needs.

TAPE DRIVE: A sequential access memory device whose magnetic media is tape in a cassette, reel, or continuous loop.

TARGET: A device that performs an operation requested by an initiator.

TELCO: Abbreviation for "telecommunications company."

TERABYTE: Terabyte equals 1,099,511,627,776 bytes or approximately one trillion bytes.

TERMINATION: A method of matching the transmission impedance of a electrical bus so as to eliminate signal reflections from the physical ends of the bus.

THIN FILM: A type of coating deposited on a flat surface through a photolithographic process. Thin film is used on disk platters and read/write heads.

THIN FILM HEADS: A read/write head whose read/write element is deposited using integrated circuit techniques rather than being manually fabricated by grinding ferrite and hand winding coils.

THIN SERVER: Name given to a network-attached device with an embedded micro-kernel operating system. Storage appliances are thin servers, as are many NAS devices.

THROUGHPUT: A performance measurement indicating the volume and speed of data as it flows from one point to another through a data pipeline. High throughput indicates a system architecture that can carry high volumes of data at high speeds, resulting in high system performance.

TOP COVER: Together with the base casting, creates an airtight, extremely clean environment. Any attempt to remove this top cover outside of a clean room will immediately contaminate and ruin a disk drive. Needless to say, any warranty is immediately voided if the top is removed.

TOPOLOGY: Geometric arrangement of nodes and cable links in a local area network; may be either centralized and decentralized.

TPI: *See TRACKS PER INCH.*

TRACK: A track is the circular ring traced over the disk surface by a head as the disk rotates under the heads. Also known as a channel.

TRACK ACCESS TIME: *See AVERAGE ACCESS TIME.*

TRACK DENSITY: *See TRACKS PER INCH.*

TRACK FOLLOWING SERVO: A closed-loop positioner control system that continuously corrects the position of the disk drive's heads by utilizing a reference track and a feedback loop in the head positioning system. (*See also CLOSED LOOP.*)

TRACK PITCH: Distance from centerline to centerline of adjacent tracks (TPI divided into 1.0).

TRACKS PER INCH (TPI): The number of tracks written within each inch of the disk's surfaces, used as a measure of how closely the tracks are packed on a disk surface. Also known as track density.

TRACK-TO-TRACK SEEK TIME: The time required for the read/write heads to move to an adjacent track.

TRACK WIDTH: Width of data track. Also called core width of Read/Write Head.

TRACK ZERO: Track zero is the outermost data track on a disk drive. In the ST 506 INTERFACE, the interface signal denotes that the heads are positioned at the outermost cylinder.

TRACK ZERO DETECTOR: An obsolete technology that *RECALIBRATES* by sensing when infrared beams between a *LED* and infrared sensitive photo-transistor are blocked by the track zero interrupter (TZI).

TRANSFER RATE: The rate of speed at which data travels through a bus or device, typically measured in bits, bytes, kilobytes, or megabytes per second. The rate at which the disk sends and receives data from the controller. The sustained transfer rate includes the time required for system processing, head switches, and seeks and accurately reflects the drive's true performance. The burst mode transfer rate is a much higher figure that refers only to the movement of data directly into RAM.

TRAVAN: Travan is a subset of the QIC minicartridge format. At 0.315 inches, Travan is slightly wider than standard QIC.

TUNNEL ERASE: An erase scheme where both sides of the recorded data is erased when writing data to eliminate track to track interference. This is primarily used on floppy disk drives.

TURN TIME: The constant rate of rotation of a hard disk platter, typically measured in rotations per minute (RPM). Typical disks have rotation speeds of 4,500 to 7,200 RPM, but 10,000 RPM drives are beginning to enter the market.

TURNKEY: A product or system that can be plugged in, turned on, and operated with little or no additional configuring.

ULTRA-SCSI: A variant of SCSI. Doubles the bandwidth of SCSI Fast. It provides 8-bit (SCSI Narrow) data rates of 20 Mbytes per second and 16-bit (SCSI Wide) data rates of 40 Mbytes per second. Shorter cables may be required. Formerly known as Fast-20.

UNFORMATTED CAPACITY: The total number of bytes on a disk, including the space that is required to record location, boundary definitions, and servo data. (*See also FORMATTED CAPACITY.*)

UNIX: An operating system that supports multitasking and is ideally suited to multi-user applications (such as networks).

UPGRADE PATH: Generally, with disk products, a family having multiple products with varying capacities such that the system storage capacity can increase with changing application requirements simply using a different disk drive within the product family.

VAR: Value-Added Reseller. A business that repackages and improves hardware (or software) manufactured by an original equipment manufacturer (OEM).

VCX: A tape technology from Ecrix Corporation.

VERIFICATION: A process of re-reading data just written to disk to ensure the data was written correctly.

VOICE COIL: A fast and reliable actuator motor that works like a loud-speaker, in which the force of a magnetic coil causes a proportionate movement of the head. Voice coil actuators are more durable than their stepper counterparts, since fewer parts are subject to daily stress and wear.

VOICE COIL MOTOR: An electro-magnetic positioning motor in the rigid disk drive similar to that used in audio speakers. A wire coil is placed in a stationary magnetic field. When current is passed through the coil, the resultant flux causes the coil to move. In a disk drive, the *CARRIAGE ASSEMBLY* is attached to the voice coil motor. Either a straight line (linear) or circular (rotary) design may be employed to position the heads on the disk's surface.

VOLATILE: Memory that will be erased if power is lost. Typically, *MAIN MEMORY* is volatile, while *AUXILIARY MEMORY* is non-volatile and can be used for permanent (but changeable at will) storage of programs and data.

WAN: *See WIDE AREA NETWORK.*

WEB CACHE: A Web cache fills requests from the Web server, stores the requested information locally, and sends the information to the client. The next time the web cache gets a request for the same information, it returns the locally cached data instead of searching over the Internet, thus reducing Internet traffic and response time.

WEB SITE: A location on the World Wide Web that is owned and managed by an individual, company, or organization; usually contains a home page and additional pages that include information provided by the site's owner, and may include links to other relevant sites.

WEDGE SERVO SYSTEM: A certain part of each *CYLINDER* contains servo positioning data. Gap spacing between each sector contains servo data to maintain position on that cylinder.

WEDGE SERVO: *See EMBEDDED SERVO.*

WIDE AREA NETWORK (WAN): A network that uses high-speed, long-distance communications technology (e.g., phone lines and satellites) to connect computers over long distances.

WIDE SCSI: The Wide SCSI interface provides a 16-bit wide SCSI bus, as compared to the narrow 8-bit SCSI bus. The wider 16-bit bus provides a transfer rate of 20 Mbytes per second compared to 10 Mbytes per second with Fast SCSI 8-bit interface.

WINCHESTER DISK: Former code name for an early IBM hard disk model, sometimes still used to refer to the technology and design of most traditional hard drives.

WINCHESTER DRIVE: A disk drive with a Winchester head and non-removable (fixed) disks sealed in a contaminant-free housing.

WORD: Number of bits processed in parallel (in a single operation) by a CPU. Standard word lengths are 8, 16, 32, and 64 (1, 2, 4, or 8 bytes).

WORLD WIDE WEB (WWW): A global hypertext system operating on the Internet that enables electronic communication of text, graphics, audio, and video.

WORM: *See WRITE ONCE READ MANY.*

WRITE: To access a storage location and store data on the magnetic surface.

WRITE CURRENT: The optimum HEAD write current necessary to saturate the magnetic media in a cell location.

WRITE IMMEDIATE: With host-controlled write immediate, status is returned when data is transferred to the drive buffer instead of waiting until the data is written to the media. The seek, latency, and write times are cut out of the total command completion as seen by the host.

WRITE ONCE READ MANY (WORM): An optical storage technology that burns pits into the recording layer of an optical disk, allowing the disks to be written just once but read without limit. WORM drives write directly to an optical disk from a host computer. Both the drives and disks include built-in safeguards to assure that data, once written, cannot be erased, overwritten, or altered. Tape-based WORMs have just begun to enter the market.

WRITE PROTECT: The use of various safeguards to prevent a computer system from overwriting a storage medium. Floppy disks have a sliding tab for "physical" write protect. Hard disks support "logical" write protect in software. Optical disks often use a combination of physical and logical write protect safeguards.

XOR ENGINE: Process or set of instructions that calculates data bit relationships in a *RAID* subsystem.

ZERO COMMAND OVERHEAD: To reduce command overhead to zero, processing traditionally done through software can be placed in the hardware, where it is completed almost instantaneously. Zero command overhead yields a substantial improvement in system performance.

ZERO LATENCY READ: This reduces the delay in transferring data from the drive to the initiator due to rotational latency delays. Data is read out of order from the disk and transferred to the host where the requested order is restored.

ZONING: This is the term used by some switch companies to denote the division of a SAN into sub networks that provide different levels of connectivity or addressability between specific hosts and devices on the network. In effect, routing tables are used to control access of hosts to devices. This zoning can be performed by cooperative consent of the hosts or can be enforced at the switch level. In the former case, hosts are responsible for communicating with the switch to determine if they have the right to access a device.

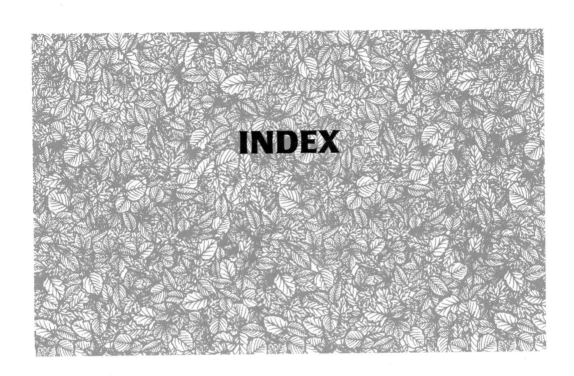

INDEX